The Democratic Revolution

About the editor

Larry Diamond is senior research fellow at the Hoover Institution and co-editor of the *Journal of Democracy*. He is also the co-editor of the multi-volume *Democracy in Developing Countries*.

FREEDOM HOUSE BOOKS

General Editor: James Finn

YEARBOOKS

Freedom in the World: Political Rights and Civil Liberties,
annuals from 1978-1991

STUDIES IN FREEDOM

Escape to Freedom: The Story of the International Rescue Committee,
Aaron Levenstein; 1983

Forty Years: A Third World Soldier at the UN,
Carlos P. Romulo (with Beth Day Romulo); 1986. *(Romulo: A Third
World Soldier at the UN,* paperback edition, 1987)

Today's American: How Free?
edited by James Finn & Leonard R. Sussman, 1986

Will of the People: Original Democracies in Non-Western Societies,
Raul S. Manglapus; 1987

PERSPECTIVES ON FREEDOM

Three Years at the East-West Divide,
Max M. Kampelman; (Introductions by Ronald Reagan and
Jimmy Carter; edited by Leonard R. Sussman); 1983

*The Democratic Mask: The Consolidation
of the Sandinista Revolution,*
Douglas W. Payne; 1985

The Heresy of Words in Cuba: Freedom of Expression & Information,
Carlos Ripoll; 1985

Human Rights & the New Realism: Strategic Thinking in a New Age,
Michael Novak; 1986

To License A Journalist?,
Inter-American Court of Human Rights; 1986.

The Catholic Church in China,
L. Ladany; 1987

Glasnost: How Open? Soviet & Eastern European Dissidents; 1987

Yugoslavia: The Failure of "Democratic" Communism; 1987

The Prague Spring: A Mixed Legacy,
edited by Jiri Pehe, 1988

Romania: A Case of "Dynastic" Communism; 1989

*The Democratic Revolution:
Struggles for Freedom and Pluralism in the Developing World*
edited by Larry Diamond, 1991

FOCUS ON ISSUES

Big Story: How the American Press and Television Reported and Interpreted the Crisis of Tet-1968 in Vietnam and Washington, Peter Braestrup; Two volumes 1977; One volume paperback abridged 1978, 1983

Afghanistan: The Great Game Revisited, edited by Rossane Klass; 1988

Nicaragua's Continuing Struggle: In Search of Democracy, Arturo J. Cruz; 1988

La Prensa: The Republic of Paper, Jaime Chamorro Cardenal; 1988

The World Council of Churches & Politics, 1975-1986, J.A. Emerson Vermaat; 1989

South Africa: Diary of Troubled Times, Nomavenda Mathiane; 1989

The Unknown War: The Miskito Nation, Nicaragua, and the United States, Bernard Nietschmann; 1989

Power, the Press and the Technology of Freedom The Coming Age of ISDN, Leonard R. Sussman; 1989

Ethiopia: The Politics of Famine; 1989

The Imperative of Freedom: A Philosophy of Journalistic Autonomy John. C. Merrill; 1990

Racing With Catastrophe: Rescuing America's Higher Education, Richard Gambino; 1990

Soviet Propaganda As A Foreign Policy Tool, Marian Leighton; 1990

Ireland Restored: The New Self-Determination Vincent J. Delacy Ryan; 1991

After the Velvet Revolution: Václav Havel and the New Leaders of Czechoslovakia Speak Out Tim D. Whipple, editor; 1991

AN OCCASIONAL PAPER

General Editor: R. Bruce McColm

Glasnost and Social & Economic Rights Valery Chalidze, Richard Schifter; 1988

Peace and Human Rights in Cambodia: Exploring From Within Kassie Neou with Al Santoli; 1990

The Democratic Revolution

Struggles for Freedom and Pluralism in the Developing World

Edited by

Larry Diamond

Perspectives on Freedom, No. 12

Freedom House

First published in 1992.

The Library of Congress Cataloging-in-Publication Data
The Democratic Revolution : Struggles for Freedom and Pluralism in the Developing World / edited by Larry Diamond.
p.   cm. — (Perspectives on freedom : no. 12)
Includes index.
1. Developing countries–Politics and government.
2. Democracy.   I. Diamond. Larry Jay.   II. Series.
D883.D453   1992   909'.09724082–dc20   91–20648 CIP
ISBN 0-932088-69-4 (cloth)   ISBN 0-932088-68-6 (paper)

Distributed by arrangement with
National Book Network
4720 Boston Way
Lanham, MD 20706

3 Henrietta Street
London WC2E 8LU England

IN MEMORY OF

DELE GIWA,

SILVIA DUZÁN,

EVELIO JAVIER,

AND THE COUNTLESS OTHERS

THROUGHOUT THE DEVELOPING WORLD

WHO HAVE GIVEN THEIR LIVES

IN THE STRUGGLE FOR DEMOCRACY.

May it be known of each of them, as it was of Evelio Javier, "...these meager words in tribute to a fallen hero who was struck down in the vigor of his youth because he dared to speak against tyranny. Where many kept a meekly silence for fear of retaliation, and still others feigned and fawned in hopes of safety and even reward, he chose to fight. He was not afraid. Money did not tempt him. Threats did not daunt him. Power did not awe him. His was a singular and all-exacting obsession: the return to freedom of his country."

—Justice Isagani Cruz, in a Philippine Supreme Court decision of 22 September 1986, awarding posthumously to Evelio Javier the legislative seat he won and was fraudulently denied in 1984.

Contents

Foreword

Carl Gershman

THE COLLECTION OF essays assembled by Larry Diamond in *The Democratic Revolution* is the first organized presentation of the stories of key participants in struggles for democracy that are now taking place throughout the developing world. The emergence during the last decade of pro-democracy movements in Latin America, Asia and Africa is part of a larger phenomenon that also involves the collapse of communism in Eastern Europe and the systemic crisis in the two Communist giants, China and the Soviet Union. While "the democratic revolution" encompasses this global phenomenon, the term has a special meaning in relation to what is still somewhat anachronistically referred to as "the Third World."

It was not so long ago that democracy was thought to be a system unsuited to countries outside the bloc of Western industrialized nations. With the collapse of many new democracies in the aftermath of decolonization, and the rise of Castroism and militarism in Latin America and state socialism in many other countries, there were few voices to challenge the notion that the options for the Third World were limited to different versions of authoritarianism, left and right. Even the human rights movement, which emerged in the 1970s in reaction to the rise of authoritarianism, did not raise the banner of democracy, since to have done so would have been seen as an attempt to impose a "Western" political system on non-Western cultures. The democratic revolution in the Third World has shown that the yearning for democracy is universal and that a democratic system can take root in countries and cultures not traditionally thought of as part of the West. While all of the writers in the present volume have had extensive contact with the United States and other Western democracies, they are authentic representatives of their own nations, and the democratic movements they speak for are entirely home-grown. Indeed, Felix Bautista is proud to claim that Filipino democracy can trace its roots to pre-Hispanic—not just pre-American—times.

Reading this volume, one must be struck by the spirit of devotion, commitment, sacrifice and struggle that permeates all the essays. Not one contributor betrays the slightest hint that democracy is something that comes easily or can be taken for granted. Some among them have been exposed to great personal danger, such as journalists María Jimena Duzán of Colombia (whose sister, also a journalist, was murdered by drug bosses); Ray Ekpu of Nigeria; Bona Malwal, now living in exile from the Sudan; Nigerian human rights activist Clement Nwankwo; and Chai-Anan Samudavanija, who was threatened with arrest following the recent coup in Thailand. All display a keen sense that democracy is not just a political system but a unifying idea that derives its power, as Monica Jimenez writes, from "the universal force" of the values it represents: "respect for humanity, truth, justice, liberty and peace."

To the American ear in the late twentieth century, this sounds almost too simplistic. We have forgotten that our own democracy was born out of the same idealism, sacrifice and vision that drive these "Third World democrats," and that its consolidation (to borrow a term now in fashion) was purchased in blood at a price that would now be considered prohibitive. We were reminded of that price, and how fragile our democracy once was, during the recent public television documentary on the Civil War. We will better understand these modern day partisans of democracy by recalling this period in our own history when, as Lincoln said at Gettysburg, "the proposition that all men are created equal" hung in the balance. What is truly remarkable about these essays, though, is not simply the spirit of sacrifice and devotion they exhibit, but the profound understanding they evince of the requirements of democracy, above all the need for an educated and alert citizenry. María Rosa de Martini, the founder of Conciencia in Argentina, describes an enormous volume of work the organization has accomplished in eight years: hundreds upon hundreds of conferences, lectures, roundtables and courses, not to mention messages about democracy conveyed through print and electronic media, all of which together have reached over 5 million people. What is most impressive about Conciencia, however, is not the quantity of activity engaged in, but the clarity, sophistication and constancy of the organization's purpose, which is to develop a democratic consciousness among the citizens of Argentina. The courses, she writes, did more than convey knowledge about democratic institutions:

In the process of educating themselves and interacting with one another, the participants discovered a new form of social respect. People learned to express ideas without feeling frightened, to value other people's opinions as well as their own, and to reach consensus on issues that mattered to them. It was a practical way of learning that democracy means more than voting. They came to understand that participation means developing mature opinions instead of unthinkingly accepting the views of the group or the state, and that democracy requires opening channels of communication between citizens and their government.

Underlying these essays is the view that democracy is not simply a political system or the process of choosing leaders through free political competition, but a way of life, a culture, a set of values based on the concept of human dignity. For Xavier Zavala, the founder of Libro Libre in Central America, it is not enough to understand democracy or believe in it intellectually: "A democrat is a person who habitually acts according to the ideas, beliefs and values of democracy." For Dette Pascual, democracy is social life informed by the *bayanihan* spirit, a traditional Filipino term suggesting communal cooperation, civic participation and social responsibility to family, neighbors and the community at large. For María Rosa de Martini, quoting Thomas Jefferson, the strength of democracy lies in "the incredible mosaic of...free associations" which are independent of state control, democratic in their internal organization, and composed of ordinary citizens—in a word, civil society.

One is tempted to call these and other activists (a large proportion of whom, it is significant to note, are women) true heroes of democracy, as A.M. Rosenthal did in a column in the *New York Times*. But they would be the first to reject such a designation, not out of modesty as much as an understanding, expressed by María Rosa de Martini, that democracy can only become institutionalized through education and informed citizen participation, not through dependence upon individual political leaders.

In that sense, though, these writers and activists are democratic heroes, precisely because their goal is not personal power but a system of self-government rooted in ordinary citizens, free institutions, lawful processes and democratic values. They have made progress toward that goal during the last decade, but they would be the first to acknowledge how formidable the challenge is that lies ahead. Lurking in these essays about democracy is an alternative vision, as María Jimena Duzán describes it, of a "nation-within-a-nation," the subsistence poor of the slum barrios whose citizens "murder in the morning to put bread on the table in the evening," and whose children are preyed upon by drug dealers who turn boys into trained assassins before they are fifteen years old.

This is not a problem limited to Colombia, or to Peru, for that matter, with its *Sendero Luminoso* (Shining Path). It is a pervasive problem that, in one form or another, afflicts all countries striving for development, modernization and integration within the world of advanced democracies. If democracy is to succeed in the developing world, it will have to find a way to bring the marginalized and dispossessed into the economic and political process. The task of addressing this challenge goes far beyond the scope of the present volume, except in the sense that nothing meaningful will be accomplished if there are not people with the determination, resourcefulness, understanding and will to provide leadership and stay the course. The writers in this volume have these qualities in abundance, yet even this will not be sufficient if they do not also have the moral and material support from the advanced democracies that they need and deserve. The present volume should help stimulate such solidarity by illuminating the struggles of some extraordinary people, whose work and moral character affirm the universality of the democratic idea.

Acknowledgements

THIS UNUSUAL VOLUME would not have been possible without the support and cooperation of a great many individuals. First and foremost, I would like to thank the eleven contributors to this volume, who undertook—in many instances under the immense ongoing pressure of the activities about which they write here—to set down on paper these accounts of their work and experiences in the struggle for democracy. Even for the journalists and editors who are accustomed to writing, it was not easy to carve out between their many recurrent deadlines and obligations the time to draft these auto-biographical accounts. For the activists, many of whose lives are oriented around doing rather than writing, the challenge was greater still. Unfortunately, a number of important accounts by activists and journalists are not represented here precisely because these people were too busily engaged in their work to accept our invitation.

Six of the accounts here—by Tony Heard, María Duzán, Felix Bautista, Dette Pascual, María Rosa de Martini and Xavier Zavala—were originally presented in September 1988 to a Hoover Institution conference on "Political Culture and Democracy in Developing Countries." That conference was funded by a grant from the United States Agency for International Development. I am particularly indebted to the Agency Coordinator for Human Rights and Democratic Initiatives, Travis Horel, who offered numerous helpful suggestions in the development of this project and whose consistent and enthusiastic support was instrumental to its success. Later stages of this project, in which additional essays were recruited and all of them revised, updated and edited, were supported by a three-year grant to the Hoover Institution from the John D. and Catherine T. MacArthur Foundation for a multidimensional program on democracy in developing countries. Throughout the production of this volume, the Hoover Institution provided a variety of additional forms of support, and I am especially grateful to its director, John Raisian, for his personal enthusiasm for this project.

The organizations headed by five contributors to this volume—de Martini, Pascual, Zavala, Jimenez de Barros and Malwal—have been supported by grants from the National Endowment for Democracy (NED), and I am deeply grateful to its president, Carl Gershman, and counselor, Marc F. Plattner, for putting me in touch with these individuals and helping me to recruit their essays. My invitation to Carl Gershman to contribute the foreword to this volume comes both in appreciation for the inspiration and tangible assistance he has given to this volume, and in recognition and admiration of the work NED has been doing to assist and facilitate the democratic revolution around the world.

Marc Plattner is also now my co-editor at the *Journal of Democracy*, and I am appreciative of his help, and that of Associate Editor Philip Costopoulos and Assistant Editors Gary Rosen and Juliet Johnson, in editing four of the essays from this volume—those by Pascual, Ekpu, Chai-Anan and Duzán—that have recently been published in slightly different form in the *Journal*.

To Juliet Johnson, I owe a much deeper and more thorough debt of gratitude. As my research assistant before joining the *Journal* in the fall of 1990, she contributed substantially to the editing and revision of the essays in this volume, and it is no exaggeration to say that this volume could not have been completed without her energetic, creative and skillful labor.

My secretary, Nicole Barnes, has borne many of the burdens of production of this manuscript with unfailing effectiveness and good cheer, and I am grateful to her, as always, for her support. I would also like to thank my research assistant, Susan Brown, for her fine work in compiling the index.

Finally, I want to thank James Finn of Freedom House for his patience, cooperation and assistance in the publication of the book. Given its long and impressive record of achievement in the global struggle for democracy, it is particularly fitting that Freedom House should publish this book.

Introduction
Civil Society and
the Struggle for Democracy

Larry Diamond

ON 19 OCTOBER 1986 Nigeria's most vigorous, fearless and important journalist, the thirty-nine-year-old crusading editor of its first
and best weekly news magazine, was blown apart by a massive
and sophisticated parcel bomb. Dele Giwa believed the mission of
the press was to serve and find the truth, wherever it might lead,
in the quest for a democratic and open society. He knew this required,
for a developing country like Nigeria, new standards of journalistic
rigor, initiative, courage and professionalism. Toward this end, he
pioneered in the development of investigative journalism in Nigeria.
When his sense of mission could no longer be squared with the
interests of the millionaire publisher whose newspaper he edited,
he struck out boldly with three like-minded colleagues to found the
weekly *Newswatch*. The extraordinary story of that magazine is described here by Giwa's co-founder and successor as editor-in-chief,
Ray Ekpu. Its searing indictments of the country's faults, repeated
exposures of corruption and abuse of power, innovative style, and
brave but professional reporting changed the face of Nigerian journalism and sustained democratic aspirations and values through a difficult period of authoritarian rule. But it also landed Giwa and his
magazine in frequent trouble with the authorities.

Shortly before his assassination, Giwa was detained by the State Security Service to answer patently preposterous charges that he was conspiring to foment a socialist revolution in the country, and to import arms for that purpose. Less than twenty-four hours before the fatal parcel was delivered to his house, the director of Military Intelligence telephoned there to ask for directions, indicating something needed to be delivered to Giwa. To this day, Giwa's murder has never been solved, and many Nigerians remain convinced that their own government was responsible.

Unfortunately, Dele Giwa was only one of many journalists who have been murdered in pursuit of the news, the truth behind the news, and the freedom to report it all without fear. In its latest annual survey of press freedom in the world, Freedom House reports that 43 journalists in 19 countries were murdered in line of service in 1990. This was down from 73 in 1989, but still alarmingly high. And this was not all. Sixteen journalists were kidnapped or "disappeared" in 1990; 145 in 45 countries were arrested or detained in connection with their work; 41 were wounded, 16 beaten, 82 assaulted, 50 threatened with death, 170 harassed, and 31 expelled. In 1990, fifty publications and radio stations were closed by governments, 12 were bombed or burned, and 30 were occupied; in addition, 37 radio programs and publications were banned. In all, Freedom House documented 834 attacks on the press in 91 countries in 1990, down from 1,164 in 1989 but still almost twice the number in 1987 or 1988. Of course, these figures underestimate both the number of press attacks and the number of individuals involved, as many cases are not reported and others may affect scores of journalists at once.[1]

Among the most disturbing aspects of these statistics is that most of these murders occur in countries that profess to be democratic. In 1990, seven took place in the Philippines, three in Peru, four each in Pakistan and Mexico, and six in Colombia (down from 20 in 1989 because of a partial but apparently only transient ceasefire).

The practice of journalism in Colombia has been under siege for several years now, as a courageous press has sought to expose and denounce the cocaine traffickers and terrorists who are ravaging the

2

rule of law in that country. In response, these powerful groups have mounted a war on press freedom in Colombia. One of the more recent casualties of that war, Silvia Margarita Duzán, was the sister of another contributor to this volume, María Jimena Duzán, who herself has been a target of the drug dealers. María Jimena's newspaper, *El Espectador*, has been a leader in exposing the identities and activities of the traffickers and demanding their extradition. For that it lost its publisher, Guillermo Cano, to narco-assassins in December 1986 and its offices to a massive bombing by the drug mafia in September 1989. Yet still it has persevered, despite the murder of numerous staff members and countless death threats to others, including María Jimena, who has frequently been forced to take refuge overseas.

Silvia Duzán was killed on 26 February 1990 along with three leaders of a nascent peasant union movement. The latter were attempting to find a peace formula for a troubled region of the country's drug-producing highlands that had been contested by leftist guerrillas and death squads financed by the drug traffickers and wealthy landowners of the region. A freelance journalist, Silvia Duzán was working at the time on a documentary for British television about the efforts of the union leaders to relieve the peasants of the region from the pressures of these two armed forces beyond the control of the state. She was one of more than forty Colombian journalists to have been killed since the war against the press began in earnest in the early 1980s.[2]

And it is not only journalists who are at risk. Wherever people struggle for democracy, for human rights and social justice, for openness and accountability in government, they threaten powerful interests, and are liable to be arrested, intimidated, tortured, murdered or "disappeared." The files of Amnesty International and the various regional branches of Human Rights Watch are stuffed full of horrendous accounts of both great and ordinary people who have been murdered or viciously attacked in this cause.

Evelio B. Javier was simply one such person. He was shot dead on 11 February 1986 defending the sanctity of the ballots cast four days previously in the presidential "snap election" Ferdinand Marcos called and then tried to rig in order to restore his shattered legitimacy. Elected governor of Antique province at age twenty-eight (the youngest in Philippine history), Javier had crusaded against political corruption while launching popular and innovative development projects and adroitly managing to maintain a democratic style of provincial governance during the first eight years of Marcos' martial law rule (1972-1980). At the time of his assassination, he was provincial chairman of the opposition alliance led by Corazon Aquino, and his political talent, courage and vision were leading many to speak of him as a leader of the potential greatness of President Magsaysay or Benigno Aquino. He was watching over ballot boxes in the town plaza of San Jose, Antique, when gunmen attacked, pumping twenty-four bullets into him.

Although his assassins have never been brought to justice, Evelio Javier's murder was one of the battlecries in the massive popular protest that brought down the Marcos dictatorship two weeks later. Moreover, the principles of his life and the manner of his untimely death inspired a group of prominent Filipinos to form a foundation, named after him, to advance his dream of developing a new breed of public official committed to serving the public honestly. The Evelio B. Javier Foundation—whose former executive director, Dette Pascual, is another contributor to this volume—now works to train local political leaders, especially mayoral candidates and incumbent municipal and city mayors, in the ethics and skills of democratic governance. It also lobbies for greater local government resources and autonomy and trains young people for future leadership positions in local government. Like another organization about which Dette Pascual writes in this volume, the Women's Movement for the Nurturance of Democracy (KABATID), and countless others in the Philippines and throughout the developing world, it is on the front lines of the long, slow, arduous and subtle struggle to develop a democratic citizenry and value system capable of sustaining democratic government and making it work to improve people's lives.

4

Martyrs and heroes of democracy

This book is dedicated to Dele Giwa, Silvia Duzán and Evelio Javier, and this introductory essay is begun in their memory, not because they were unique among the many martyrs to the cause of democracy worldwide, but because the democratic revolution—like all great struggles for change in human history—has its martyrs, and they deserve to be recognized and remembered for the sacrifices they made. I have chosen these three people because of the special meaning they have to three of the contributors to this book, and to the struggles about which they write. In addition, Dele Giwa had a special meaning to me as a personal friend and inspiration, someone who stood out from the greed and cynicism destroying his country. He offered it some hope for a democratic future precisely because, to quote Justice Isagani Cruz in his tribute to Evelio Javier, "He was not afraid. Money did not tempt him. Threats did not daunt him. Power did not awe him. His was a singular and all-exacting obsession: the return to freedom of his country."

Democracy does not generally come these days via the kind of bloody revolution that brought it forth in the United States, but the changes that give it birth often amount to a revolution, and rarely are they made without a great many people risking their comfort, security, wealth, livelihoods and—too often—their lives. I have introduced this volume in this way not only to pay tribute but to make this important substantive point. Democracy is not achieved simply by the hidden process of socioeconomic development bringing a country to a point where it has the necessary "prerequisites" for it. It is not delivered by the grace of some sociological *deus ex machina*. And neither is it simply the result of the divisions, strategies, tactics, negotiations and settlements of contending elites. Political scientists who conceive of democratic transitions simply in this way miss an important element. That element is struggle, personal risk-taking, mobilization and sustained, imaginative organization on the part of a large number of citizens. Some of them may be "elites" in the sense that they have privileged social status and wealth, if not access to power. And in challenging a corrupt and autocratic

5

status quo, they who are expected to be a part of it take the greatest risks. In doing so, they often lose, if not their lives, their jobs and perhaps their personal freedom.

Several of the contributors to this volume have suffered for the risks they have taken to advance the cause of freedom. Anthony Heard lost his editorship. Bona Malwal was imprisoned for a year, lost his newspaper and, more than once, was in danger of losing his life. Clement Nwankwo was arrested by state security agents, and then suffered a serious attempt on his life. María Duzán has lived for most of a decade under continuing threat of assassination by the cocaine traffickers. They and their fellow contributors to this volume have made many other sacrifices, of their time, money and energy. They are represented here not only because their stories are important, even extraordinary, but because their lives are exemplary; they are not just democratic citizens, they have devoted their lives to the cause of democratic citizenship.

But the democratic revolution is not the work of lone heroes. It is the cumulative achievement of tens and hundreds of thousands, sometimes millions of citizens who become actively involved in civic movements and independent media. It has been to the cause of promoting and informing such civic participation that all of the contributors to this volume, in one way or another, have been dedicated. In this sense, their work has been self-effacing; for democracy, perhaps alone among the forms of government, cannot triumph on the basis of heroic leadership and action. It requires an educated and active mass base, alert to the dangers of hero-worship, conscious of the perpetual need to replenish the ranks of political leaders, and poised to return to the ranks of ordinary citizens any who would abuse or aggrandize their political power or fame. This is the type of democratic citizenry all of the journalists and activists in this volume have been struggling to create.

How civil society contributes to democracy

Although some of our contributors have served briefly in political office, one thing that distinguishes them all is their lack of interest in acquiring political power for themselves. They have chosen as their arena of action not politics and the state but civil society, that complex realm of community life that lies between the individual family on the one hand and the arenas of the state and the electoral struggle for state control on the other. Stepan has defined "civil society" as

> that arena where manifold social movements (such as neighborhood associations, women's groups, religious groupings, and intellectual currents) and civic organizations from all classes (such as lawyers, journalists, trade unions and entrepreneurs) attempt to constitute themselves in an ensemble of arrangements so that they can express themselves and advance their interests.[3]

In such a civil society, autonomous mass media and cultural life constitute another important dimension of interest and expression. Such movements, organizations and institutions may address themselves to powerholders and express their preferences in the contest for state power, but they do not seek to control it directly. "Political society," by contrast, is the arena in which political actors and institutions—in a democracy, parties, factions, politicians, alliances, electoral campaign and voter turnout organizations, etc.—contest for control of the state, in all its administrative, bureaucratic, legal, legislative and coercive dimensions, at all levels of its authority.

The struggle for democracy must have as one of its primary goals the establishment of a viable and democratic political society, of democratic political parties and campaign machineries that contend for power through regular, free, fair and peaceful elections.[4] This much is obvious to the casual observer. But democracy also requires the construction of a vibrant, vigorous and pluralistic civil society. Without such a civil society, democracy cannot become developed and secure.

A strong civil society can contribute to democracy in many ways. Perhaps most fundamentally, it represents a reservoir of resources—political, economic, cultural and moral—to check and balance the power of the state. A strong array of independent associations and media provides "the basis for the limitation of state power, hence for the control of the state by society, and hence for democratic political institutions as the most effective means of exercising that control."[5] If the state controls the mass media, there is no way of exposing its abuses and corruption. Even if the independent media are simply weak and professionally underdeveloped, rather than legally barred or harassed, democracy will suffer. Likewise, it is the presence of a vast array of noisily assertive and creatively resourceful interest groups that keeps the state from being captured by any one interest and forces the state to be accountable to its citizens and responsive to their claims and concerns.

In the latter respect, it is not only the strength of civil society that matters but also its diversity, its pluralism. When a wide range of interests are organized, they provide an important basis (both beyond political parties and working through them) for democratic competition. Functional groups—business and producer organizations, trade unions, professional associations, peasant leagues, student associations—are able to press their various interests; issue-oriented movements—for environmental protection, women's and minority rights, community development, civil liberties—theirs; and ethnic, cultural and religious organizations theirs as well. Not all groups will have equal resources or access to power proportionate to their numbers, but the presence of conflicting interests, pressures and pulls will tend to keep the state in a democratic system from becoming the captive of any one group or interest, and will compel some accommodation of divergent interests. Moreover, it is precisely the freedom to organize, and to mobilize the political power implicit in their numbers, that gives poor and disadvantaged groups in a democracy the capacity to improve their lot—more gradually, perhaps, than under the banner of a socialist revolution, but in the long run more enduringly and humanely as well.

Third, a rich associational life supplements the role of political parties in stimulating political participation, increasing the political efficacy and skill of democratic citizens, and promoting an appreciation of the obligations as well as rights of democratic citizenship.

Alexis de Tocqueville, in his early observations on democracy in America, was perhaps the first to note the symbiotic, mutually reinforcing relationship between participation in civil society and participation in political life:

Civil associations, therefore, facilitate political association; but, on the other hand, political association singularly strengthens and improves associations for civil purposes....Political life makes the love and practice of association more general....[6]

Construing "political associations" to include, more broadly, the kinds of civic associations represented in this volume, de Tocqueville observed that people are often reluctant at first to come together in "civil partnerships" (read business firms or economic interest groups) because they risk financial resources in the process.

They are less reluctant, however, to join political associations, which appear to them to be without danger because they risk no money in them. But they cannot belong to these associations for any length of time without finding out how order is maintained among a large number of [people] and by what contrivance they are made to advance, harmoniously and methodically, to the same object....Political associations may therefore be considered as large free schools, where all the members of the community go to learn the general theory of association....

In their political associations the Americans, of all conditions, minds, and ages, daily acquire a general taste for association and grow accustomed to the use of it. There they meet together in large numbers, they converse, they listen to one another, and they are mutually stimulated to all sorts of undertakings. They afterwards transfer to civil life the notions they have thus acquired and make them subservient to a thousand purposes.[7]

Some of the democratic civic associations represented in this volume, and many similar efforts of other groups, large and small, throughout the developing world, draw quite purposefully on

Tocqueville's image of the association as a "large free school" where members of the community go to learn the general art of association. The Argentine women's group, *Conciencia*, which has spread to fourteen other countries in the past few years, has sought not only to educate citizens about the specific elements of the constitutional and electoral systems, but to develop more general and subtle features of democratic participation and association: the need for tolerance and respect for the views of others, the dynamics of reaching consensus within a group, the means by which people can cooperate to solve the problems of their communities. Conciencia has developed a program to enter the schools and develop these arts of association in young people, and another to facilitate community improvement efforts by neighborhood and district groups. Recently it has taken on as one of its major missions the nurturing and training of associational leaders all over the country, so that, in the words of Maria Rosa de Martini, "they can become the 'backbone' of a democratic society." KABATID in the Philippines and Participa in Chile are also engaged in programs that seek to enlarge and energize independent organizational life in those countries.

There is much of the Tocquevillian spirit in what these groups are doing. It is not just in their conscious efforts to promote the skills of active citizenship and organizational involvement, and not just in the fact that once such civic organizations take root successfully they "tend amazingly to multiply," to quote Tocqueville again. Their further contribution lies in a fourth function, appreciated by Tocqueville but often overlooked in an age when social scientists still worry that societies with too many strong interest groups and movements demanding too much can become "ungovernable." "Freedom of association," Tocqueville mused, may, "after having agitated society for some time,... strengthen the state in the end."[8] By giving people a deeper stake in the social order, a society rich in participation and organization may give stability to the state. By bringing people together in endless combinations for a great diversity of purposes, a rich associational life may not only multiply demands on the state, it may also multiply the capacities of groups to improve their own welfare, independent of the state, especially at the local level.

A fifth function of a democratic civil society is recruiting and training new political leaders. Typically, again, this emerges as an unplanned byproduct of whatever else associations may be seeking. As individuals emerge to leadership positions within civic and interest groups, social movements, and community efforts of various kinds, they may gain recognition as possible new leaders in the political arena as well. Where leadership recruitment within the established political parties and networks has become narrow, unrepresentative or stagnant, the introduction of leaders from other sectors of society can be a particularly important function for democracy.

Most of this is on-the-job training, learning by doing. A citizen who discovers how to organize her neighbors or co-workers effectively, how to mediate their conflicts and produce consensus, how to manage their associational finances responsibly, also learns, often unwittingly, skills and insights necessary for effective and responsive management of affairs of state. Less formally, through leadership in pursuit of collective interests, or on behalf of democratic consolidation—or through the public articulation of a clear and compelling alternative vision of politics and policy—new personalities emerge in the public realm who may be recruited for political office.

Here, too, some democratic civic groups are playing this role very consciously and effectively. I have already noted Conciencia's leadership training courses, which have been attended by activists in voluntary organizations, community groups and trade unions, as well as by local politicians. A prime purpose of the Evelio B. Javier Foundation in the Philippines, as Dette Pascual explains in her essay, is to train able and honest political leaders at the local and provincial levels, both elected public officials and candidates from all parties.

There is a sixth democratic function of civil society that often precedes all of these in temporal terms: to resist the domination of an authoritarian regime and hasten its exit from power. The distinguishing feature of totalitarian rule is that it eliminates civil society, subjecting all forms of expression and organization to control by the state, and by the mobilizational party that runs the state. In such regimes, the emergence from the underground of the first faint glimmers of unofficial expression and independent organization represents the first real crack in the armor of totalitarian domination. The movement of a regime from totalitarianism to "merely" authoritarian rule closely corresponds to this emergence of a civil society independent of the state. The movements for democracy in Eastern Europe, the USSR and China—and now, on the periphery of the surviving Communist world, in countries like Vietnam and Cuba—all had their seeds in and have drawn their primary energy from the growth of autonomous organizational, cultural and intellectual life.[9] As Vilém Precan observes, the first step in transforming Eastern Europe from totalitarian rule toward democracy was "the cultivation of citizenship, the implementation of the principle of life in the truth, and the rise of independent culture and samizdat." As this "moral revolution" took hold, autonomous organization spread (first and most importantly demanding respect for human rights) and Communist domination eroded and fell, until "civil society enter[ed] the political arena as a self-assured and independent force."[10]

Where the transition is from authoritarian rule and civil society survives in a battered and fearful state, its emergence from fear into public action marks a turning point in the struggle for democracy. To be sure, one reason for the emergence or persistence of authoritarian rule is that powerful elements of society, typically landowners, bankers, industrialists, etc. accept or actually collaborate with it. When these groups turn against the regime, a crucial element of its support falls away and its demise is usually near. But long before that happens (and an important reason why it happens), authoritarian domination is eroded by what O'Donnell and Schmitter call "the resurrection of civil society." We would only modify this description to note that in some developing countries large elements of civil society are only newly emerging. This phenomenon involves a veritable explosion of civic consciousness and activity:

the sudden appearance of books and magazines on themes long

suppressed by censorship; the conversion of older institutions, such as trade unions, professional associations, and universities, from agents of governmental control into instruments for the expression of interests, ideals, and rage against the regime; the emergence of grass-roots organizations articulating demands long repressed or ignored by authoritarian rule; the expression of ethical concerns by religious and spiritual groups previously noted for their prudent accommodation to the authorities....[11]

Many of the contributors to this volume have been on the cutting edge of this outpouring of civic activity that has undermined authoritarian rule. Monica Jimenez de Barros played a leading role in organizing the Crusade for Citizen Participation that mobilized Chileans to register and vote in the December 1988 plebiscite, which defeated General Pinochet's bid to extend his dictatorship with the cover of popular support. Dette Pascual was a leader in NAMFREL, the National Movement for Free Elections, which frustrated Ferdinand Marcos's effort to steal the 1986 presidential election victory of Cory Aquino. Felix Bautista edited *Veritas*, the one publication that dared to expose the lies and abuses of the Marcos regime and to call for its ouster through elections. Through their courageous writing and editing, Ray Ekpu in Nigeria, Bona Malwal in Sudan, and Anthony Heard in South Africa pushed out the boundaries of what was possible in opposing authoritarian rule. So did the Civil Liberties Organisation, and its co-founder, Clement Nwankwo, in bringing to national and international attention the human rights abuses of an avowedly liberal military regime in Nigeria. Xavier Zavala's *Libro Libre*, published from exile in Costa Rica, helped sustain democratic ideas and values in Nicaragua until the people were finally given the chance to vote the Sandinistas out of power.

Many groups that have been instrumental in struggles such as these are, unfortunately, not represented in this volume, and indeed are too numerous to mention. We should not lose sight of the important role that has been played by religious institutions. The Catholic church, for example, sponsored and helped to shield from harassment the voter mobilization in Chile, the weekly *Veritas* in the Philippines (and ultimately the "Miracle at Edsa" there that brought the downfall of Marcos), as well as many other democratic and human rights movements throughout Latin America. Nor should we forget that lawyers have been active, often at great risk, in resisting authoritarian rule through their bar associations (as in Nigeria and Brazil) and human rights groups they have helped form. Recently lawyers have been on the front lines of the struggle against the increasingly repressive rule of President Daniel arap Moi in Kenya, and two of the leaders in that struggle, Gibson Kamau Kuria and Gitobu Imanyara, have found themselves respectively in exile and in and out of detention, with Imanyara's crusading *Nairobi Law Journal* officially banned.[12] Leaders of trade unions, such as Frederick Chiluba of the Zambia Congress of Trade Unions, and of student and intellectual associations have also taken the lead in mobilizing mass pressure for democracy in China, Burma, Bangladesh, and recently across the African continent, from Algeria to South Africa.

Through their exemplary actions and statements, but more so through their quiet daily work, such people have mobilized effective popular resistance to authoritarian rule and quickened the transition to democracy. Some of them, such as Dette Pascual and Monica Jimenez de Barros, subsequently helped to establish new organizations that strengthen and consolidate democracy after the transition. Others, such as María Rosa de Martini and her colleagues in Conciencia, and Chai-Anan Samudavanija in his civic education work in Thailand, took the task of deepening and consolidating emergent democracy as their organizational starting point. Others still, such as Clement Nwankwo in his human rights work, and Xavier Zavala in his efforts to promote democratic values and ideas, continue to adapt their work when the political context changes from an authoritarian to a democratic regime.

These types of organizations, by their very nature and purposes, contribute to democracy in many ways, both through their explicit objectives of democracy promotion and through the democratic procedures of discussion and popular involvement they employ internally toward that end. It should be emphasized, however, that

14

not any and every organization contributes to democratization simply because it may be autonomous. There remain in many struggling democracies, such as El Salvador, Peru, and the Philippines, a good many organizations in civil society, both on the right and the left, that have as their goal not democracy but some version of its opposite, and whose methods of internal governance are authoritarian, if not rigidly Leninist. Whatever their explicit interests or goals, independent associations will contribute to democracy if in their own affairs they govern themselves with democratic procedures and respect and promote democratic norms of participation, tolerance, cooperation, accountability, openness and trust. Any association can become "a large free school" for democracy if it inculcates these norms. But a civil society that systematically trounces them is not an ally of democracy, no matter how autonomous and vigorously organized it may be.

The organizational imperative

The troubles of many new and emerging democracies in the world demonstrate that it is one thing to install a democracy, and another, sometimes more difficult, task to maintain it, to consolidate and breathe vitality and meaning into it. Democracy often arrives amidst a kind of revolutionary wave of popular mobilization, what O'Donnell and Schmitter call a "popular upsurge," in which diverse elements of civil society come together in a massive common front that identifies itself as "the people" and mobilizes huge numbers of them into the streets. Such mobilization may be episodic and controlled, spurring on negotiations for a democratic transition, or it may be massive, sudden, desperate and decisive, as in the "miraculous" outpouring of "people power" to stop Marcos's tanks at Edsa, or the huge demonstrations that brought down one East European Communist regime after another in the final stunning months of 1989, until the last Stalinist, Ceaucescu himself, came crashing down to a fatal collapse. But as Schmitter and O'Donnell rightly observe, in either case, such mobilization cannot last.[13] Sooner or later the question must be faced, what comes after the deluge?

15

Whether or not it achieves its immediate aim of pushing out the authoritarian regime, the popular upsurge eventually leaves in its wake "many dashed hopes and frustrated actors."[14] Expectations deliriously raised cannot be quickly met. The challenge shifts to making democracy work, politically and economically. Old conflicts resurface and new ones emerge among diverse groups in civil society that had united in their commitment to democracy but may share little else in common. Not all interests and expectations can be satisfied, and probably none can be met completely. Policies must be crafted and interest conflicts played out and reconciled while new political institutions are still being forged and tested. It is a delicate and difficult time, a period of many large and a thousand small challenges of politics and policy, and very few of them compare in excitement and moral clarity with the crusade to rid the country of despotism. Typically, this is the period when democracies founder— in the early years when institutions are inchoate and norms fragile.

In such circumstances, how can the moral energy and commitment of the democratic revolution be sustained? One crucial answer, our contributors tell us, is organization. Obviously, new and effective parties must organize to provide the citizenry with clear policy alternatives and effective capacities to mobilize support for them. But effective parties are not enough. Civil society must organize, too, and now in new and different ways: not for the short-term emergency of mobilizing against dictatorship, but for the longer, more multi-dimensional, less thrilling struggle to make democracy work.

This task is a slow and complex one. It requires, in part, training and empowering the politicians, elected officials, and legislative staffs who must make democratic institutions work effectively. This type of work, in which the Institute of Public Policy Studies in Thailand and the Evelio B. Javier Foundation in the Philippines are actively engaged, has a defined but still very large constituency, since if democracy is to work it must work not only at the top but at the grassroots, in local and provincial governments. And effective leadership training requires intensive work with small groups of individuals over extended periods.

Mass civic education also involves meticulous attention to individual citizens and to many aspects of democratic citizenship. People must come to learn not only the value of democracy but the *ways* of democracy: the importance of voting and being informed; the need to temper partisanship with respect for opposing parties and viewpoints; the means through which grievances and needs can be brought before elected officials, both directly and through the mass media; the techniques by which communities can organize themselves to achieve common ends; and the details of how their own electoral system, legislature, bureaucracy, local government and legal system work.

All of this can be conveyed by instruction, by seminars and lectures, but instruction alone is not enough. As Conciencia so often emphasizes, it must also be internalized through repeated practice. Citizens learn by doing, by groping together for solutions in extensive workshops, by meeting frequently to discuss issues and hear the views of others, by teaching these principles to others, by repeatedly listening to civilized and substantive debates of the issues, by keeping actively informed, by creating new organizations of their own. One reason why the task of educating and training democratic citizens is so slow and difficult is that learning by doing requires intensive work with small groups: ten, twenty, thirty people at a time; housewives in a living room, students in a classroom, workers on a shop floor, strangers around a discussion table. Large numbers of trainers and facilitators must themselves be trained. Effective dynamics of small groups must be developed, refined and replicated many times over.

This work is time-consuming and resource-intensive, most especially in human resources. It must also become increasingly specialized. If the civic organization is to survive and succeed, it must undertake effectively a growing range of tasks. Some staff, even a great many, must become skilled at lecturing and training citizens. Others may become more skilled at facilitating interactive workshops. Others at working with the schools. Others at raising money, at recruiting and motivating new members, at designing brochures, at developing campaigns through the mass media, at working with

17

businessmen and trade unions, and at networking with like organizations and foundations in the regional and international communities. And some people must evince skill in managing all of this growing and increasingly differentiated organization.

The story of Conciencia, in Argentina and throughout Latin America, of KABATID in the Philippines, Participa in Chile, and many other such groups throughout the developing world is one of dynamic organization: working, expanding, specializing, consolidating, expanding further into new regions and groups, adapting to respond to new issues and problems. Decentralization of authority and flexibility are crucial in this undertaking, as Monica Jimenez de Barros observes in her reflections on the Crusade for Citizen Participation in Chile:

Flexibility, promoted at all levels of our organization, enhanced our ability to work on multiple campaigns simultaneously. Flexibility made it possible to maintain unity in purpose yet diversity in action within our communal groups. We reached compromises between autonomy of action for territorial groups, which facilitated creativity, and unity in objectives and goals.

These qualities of dynamism, adaptability, openness and ingenuity have much to do with the success of the civic organizations represented in this volume. So does the clarity and depth of their unifying moral commitment to democracy as a value and way of life. But most of all, their success derives from their willingness to undertake, and to recruit a great many others to undertake, the hard, unglamorous, painstaking organizing that builds an enduring civic foundation for democracy.

The power of words

It could be considered quite strange that so many journalists and writers in so many countries are subjected to so much pressure, repression and intimidation. After all, one might say, paraphrasing Napoleon's cavalier dismissal of the Pope, how many troops has the press?

On occasions, the press can mobilize people into the streets in anger, but that is hardly its primary function. A free press is dangerous first and foremost because it denies the state, or privileged social groups, control over "the facts," "the truth," the way that citizens perceive reality. Real tyranny can only survive by a combination of force and fraud. When fraud is exposed, when the lies and untruths that disguise its abuses and fantasize or inflate its achievements are revealed, all that is left is force, and force alone is not normally enough to sustain a regime for long. For a dictatorship, then, the truth is a dangerous thing, for it unravels the entire web of deceit on which whatever tenuous legitimacy it may have is based.

Words, and in our times the visual images of photo journalism and television news and documentary, are indeed powerful. The first mission of the press in a democratic society, or a society struggling to become democratic, is to report the facts. This is not easy to accept in a situation of massive injustice and polarized divisions, as in South Africa or Colombia, where caring journalists are inclined to want to take sides and to use the press as a weapon of opinion and mobilization. As Heard notes in his essay, and Duzán in a different way in hers, there is a place for such "advocacy journalism" in the struggle for democracy. But unless the journalistic profession in general devotes itself first to honest, full, and truthful reporting of the facts, it will sacrifice the credibility it needs to become an effective counter to and check upon the state, and citizens will lose the one best hope for the information they need to exercise their rights intelligently and effectively.

Of course, facts are open to interpretation, are often empty without a context of understanding, and are never fully "out there" to be seen with the naked or lazy eye. These challenges point to the additional functions the press must perform in the struggle to get and keep and deepen democracy. A democratic press must probe for the facts, sometimes taking risks to dig them out when they are threatening to powerful forces. It is precisely the risk-taking, investigative reporting of *Newswatch* that has made it an important and notably democratic innovation in Nigerian journalism. It was this seeking out of dangerous facts and alternative views that landed Anthony Heard's newspaper, *The Cape Times*, and others, such as the *Rand Daily Mail*, in constant trouble with the South African authorities during the 1980s, and those of Bona Malwal and Felix Bautista in their countries and times as well. Such constant harassment and repression subject the editors to a very subtle form of torture: the daily or weekly anguish of determining what can be printed, how things can be stated, how far one can go, without risking permanent closure. The contributors to this volume have all faced this dilemma. It is perhaps most difficult in a semi-authoritarian context where the boundaries are unclear, and a serious-minded editor must balance the need to press out and test those boundaries with the need to keep the publication alive. In contrast to the underground or alternative press, which can rage against dictatorship and injustice, this dilemma of the more established democratic press is one where the moral imperatives conflict and blur.

A democratic press must not only report, it must also interpret and, with clear demarcation, offer opinions. These challenges again tax the nerves and imaginations of embattled democratic editors. Sometimes they must find a way to denounce, but not too blatantly, to clarify, but also to leave their readers to draw certain conclusions on their own. Sometimes they must reach for a special, more symbolic, even poetic language of opposition and resistance. Part of the achievement of *Newswatch* has been its skill in treading this fine line in recent years as it has sought to stay in print without being banned once again by the military regime. A serious magazine whose opinions become too elliptical and revelations too muted and selective risks being criticized for having been "tamed" by the regime, but the decision on how much and how often to risk closure and imprisonment is one that few outsiders could claim to have the moral right to judge.

This points to the need for journalists and editors to practice their profession with discretion, balance, restraint and responsibility. As one of Nigeria's leading editors, Stanley Macebuh, declared in a lecture to his colleagues some years ago, "Journalism is not the proper profession for bloated egos." Journalists in developing countries must sometimes be willing to take risks to uncover and analyze the news. But they must not, by reckless commentary and sensational language, generate risks gratuitously because of some "deliberate desire to be noticed by the authorities"—what Macebuh calls the "martyrdom syndrome."

> In our circumstances, every journalist is entitled to assume that he will, in all probability and at some point in his career, be pulled in by the authorities. There is nothing spectacular or dramatic about it. But we have no obligation to permit ourselves to be pulled in merely so we can become famous, or simply on account of our own stupidity. When a reporter goes to jail, and his peers judge him to be innocent of any guilt which they recognize, then he is a great man indeed. But when even his peers cannot pronounce him innocent, then his ordeal is not only pointless, but can in fact be detrimental to the interests of the profession of journalism.[15]

There is another challenge, too. Effective interpretation of developments, or "news analysis"; aggressive investigative reporting that exposes hidden truths but only responsibly, when the facts can be proven and documented; and even regular, informed, and versatile commentary on a range of issues—all of these require resources. Specialized staff are needed for such functions; a single major investigative or interpretative story may require the full-time work of several journalists for several weeks. And those journalists must be trained in the more advanced tools of such work. If it is interpretation they are doing, they may benefit from advanced education in the particular field, be it economics, diplomacy or criminology. Few newspapers and magazines in developing countries have the money to maintain the large, specialized staff and research library and materials to perform these functions well. Few journalists have the advanced training needed to interpret comprehensibly and authoritatively complex policy questions for a general readership. Moreover, democratically committed media in developing countries are often the least well funded precisely because their challenge to established interests may limit potential advertising revenue.

The global struggle to develop and institutionalize democracy in the coming decade must involve the mass media. The skill levels and resources of democratically committed journalists, editors and writers, and of their publications, need to be improved. So does the capacity of the journalistic profession overall to monitor and educate itself, to maintain high standards of integrity and responsibility, and to defend journalists and publications legally against attacks. Investments also need to be made in opening up the radio and TV airwaves to a free and full flow of information and an array of viewpoints. Anthony Heard proposes in this volume a Free Expression Foundation to perform these types of functions in South Africa. In South Africa there is, outside the state, the money to fund such an important independent effort, if the white business community will recognize its own long-term interest in free, pluralistic and effective mass media. However, in many developing countries, private resources are hardly available on the necessary scale and, to the extent they exist, are heavily concentrated among groups little inclined to favor, much less to invest in promoting, free expression. A major question underlying all of these democratic initiatives is always, where is the money to come from?

Supporting the democratic struggle

Increasingly, the democratic revolution is an international one. As the world becomes a global village, linked by jet travel, booming trade, satellite television, fax machines, and CNN, countries are more and more densely, profoundly and complexly affected by one another. Ideas, techniques and principles; people, goods and services; all of these are spilling across borders at rates that seem to increase exponentially. It was Marx and his followers who forged the idea of international revolution; Lenin and his disciples who constructed an international Communist movement for that purpose. But it is the disciples of Thomas Paine and Thomas Jefferson, of Susan B. Anthony and Martin Luther King, of Madison, Bolívar, Montesquieu,

Locke, Voltaire and Gandhi, who are making revolution today internationally—and nonviolently.

From the time of the American revolution, democrats in the United States have appreciated that the fate of freedom in one country was bound up, ultimately, with its development in the rest of the world. Now there is an opportunity, unprecedented in world history, to foster that development simultaneously in dozens of different countries. Contrary to many assumptions, democrats in the developing world are not poor in ideas and insights into how to structure democracy. Certainly, their experiments can be enriched by the experiences of established and stable democracies like those in Europe, Japan and North America. Nor are Third World democrats poor in energy, commitment and ingenuity. They are lacking in one primary element: resources. Money. Skills. Technology. This is what we in the West have most to offer, and how we can make the greatest difference to the worldwide struggle for democracy.

The creation of the National Endowment for Democracy in 1983 marked a turning point in the United States experience. This was the first time that an agency, albeit a nongovernmental one, had been officially established for the sole and explicit purpose of promoting democracy and strengthening freedom and pluralism in other countries. But as Xavier Zavala notes in concluding his essay, that effort began with little in the way of resources, and although the annual Congressional allocation to NED has been increased from $16 to $25 million in the current fiscal year, with the prospect of further future growth, it remains tiny by any calculation of U.S. capacity. Other, official, U.S. agencies—in particular the U.S. Information Service and AID—are also engaged in democracy promotion, and spend perhaps $100 million or more each year on activities that serve this goal. Recently, AID has listed support for the evolution of stable democratic regimes as one of its six principal goals in offering development assistance. But resource commitments remain well below what this country is capable of, and for the sensitive work of assisting democratic groups in civil society that are challenging both a nondemocratic state and privileged elements outside it, support

23

from official arms of the U.S. government may not be politically feasible or desirable.

In the United States and throughout the wealthy and industrialized democracies, we need to increase the financial and technical assistance we offer to these many brave and clever efforts springing up from the grassroots of developing societies to democratize—in a fundamental and enduring way—their politics, institutions and ways of life. Specialists on any of these emerging or aspiring democracies know that there are many incipient or struggling associations and publications in these civil societies that die stillborn or limp along with limited impact because of a lack of resources. Even with some of the enterprises represented in this volume, there is much more work that could be done to build democracy if the resources were there. Ultimately, such efforts need to become self-sustaining, but that is partly dependent on the economic development of these countries. In many of them, it has been their very political tyranny and instability that has constituted the largest obstacle to their economic development.

The resource needs of media and organizations like the ones in this book are not great by international standards. Often thirty, fifty or a hundred thousand dollars can make the difference between success and failure for a new or innovating think tank, magazine, human rights group, trade union, small enterprise association and so on. Like amounts can enable such groups, once established, to take on new functions and programs. Larger amounts are needed to help finance the crucial work of developing effective political parties and legal and administrative structures.

It is not only to sympathetic governments that democratic forces in the developing world look for assistance. Important forms of support—moral, informational, financial and technical—come from civil societies in the established democracies, from voluntary organizations funded by private individuals and groups. I have mentioned leading human rights groups like Amnesty International and Human Rights Watch. A lesser known but crucial group in the struggle worldwide for press freedom is the New York-based Committee to Protect Journalists, which closely tracks abuses against journalists and news organizations in more than 100 countries; documents them in its bimonthly *Update* and its systematic annual *Attacks on the Press;* publicizes abuses in the news media; and sends protests to offending governments and fact-finding delegations to countries with patterns of press abuse. María Jimena Duzán is only one of many beleaguered journalists around the world who have been helped by CPJ and in turn have collaborated closely with it.

The Committee to Protect Journalists is only one example of the growing number of nonprofit, nonpartisan voluntary organizations that are playing a role in the struggle for democracy and freedom worldwide. International in their networks and concerns, and sometimes in their memberships and funding, they represent the early signs of development of a globally based civil society rooted in democratic principles. This emerging *global* infrastructure, beyond control by any government, will be an important foundation on which to build in the coming decade. Indeed, if a democratic Karl Marx were writing today a manifesto for the global revolution already underway, he or she would undoubtedly proclaim, "Democrats of the world, unite!"

Notes

1. Leonard R. Sussman, "The Press 1990: Contrary Trends," *Freedom Review,* Vol. 22, no. 1. p. 58.

2. In addition to María Duzán's account in this chapter, the murder of Silvia Duzán is also reported in *CPJ Update,* no. 38, May 1990, p. 8, of the Committee to Protect Journalists.

3. Alfred Stepan, *Rethinking Military Politics: Brazil and the Southern Cone* (Princeton: Princeton University Press, 1988), pp. 3-4. The distinction between state and civil society dates back to Hegel, and in recent treatments "civil society" has often been conceived of as the entire "non-state (market-regulated, privately controlled or voluntarily organized) realm" (John Keane, ed., *Civil Society*

and the State: New European Perspectives, New York: Verso, 1988), p. 1. Important for our purposes, here, however is the emphasis not only on "non-state" but on "voluntarily organized."

4. I define democracy as a system of government with three essential features: extensive competition for state power through regular, free and fair elections; highly inclusive access to rights of political participation, such that no adult social group is excluded; and civil and political liberties—freedom of speech, the press, association and the rule of law—sufficient to ensure that political competition and participation are meaningful and authentic.

5. Samuel P. Huntington, "Will More Countries Become Democratic?" *Political Science Quarterly 99,* no. 2 (Summer 1984), p. 204.

6. Alexis de Tocqueville, *Democracy in America, Volume 2* (New York: Vintage Books, 1945 (1840), p. 123.

7. Ibid, pp. 124, 125.

8. Ibid., p. 126.

9. See for example, Jacek Kuron, "Overcoming Totalitarianism," and Vilém Precan, "The Democratic Revolution," *Journal of Democracy,* Vol. 1, no. 1 (Winter 1990), pp. 72-74 and 79-85; Christine M. Sadowski, "Autonomous Groups as Agents of Change in Communist and Post-Communist Eastern Europe," report prepared for the National Council for Soviet and European Research; S. Frederick Starr, "Soviet Union: A Civil Society," *Foreign Policy,* no. 70 (Spring 1988), pp. 26-41; Gail Lapidus, "State and Society: Toward the Emergence of Civic Society in the Soviet Union," in Seweryn Bialer, ed., *Politics, Society, and Nationality: Inside Gorbachev's Russia* (Boulder, CO: Westview Press, 1989, pp. 21-47); Thomas Gold, " The Resurgence of Civil Society in China," *Journal of Democracy,* Vol. 1, no. 1 (Winter 1990), pp. 18-31; Andrew Nathan, "Is China Ready for Democracy?" *Journal of Democracy,* Vol. 1 no. 2 (Spring 1990), pp. 50-61; Vo Van Ai, "Reform Runs Aground in Vietnam," *Journal of Democracy,* Vol. 1, no. 3 (Summer 1990), pp. 81-91; Carlos Alberto Montaner, "Castro's Last Stand," *Journal of Democracy,* Vol. 1, no. 3, pp. 71-80; and Susan Kaufman Purcell, "Cuba's Cloudy Future," *Foreign Affairs,* Vol. 69, no. 3, pp. 113-130.

10. Precan, "The Democratic Revolution," p. 80.

11. Guillermo O'Donell and Philippe C. Schmitter, *Transitions from Authoritarian Rule: Tentative Conclusions about Uncertain Democracies* (Baltimore: Johns Hopkins University Press, 1986).

12. Todd Shields, "Kenya: Lawyers vs. the Law," and Gitobu Imanyara, "Africa through Blinker," *Africa Report*, Vol. 35, no. 4 (September/October 1990), pp. 13-18; *CPJ Update*, no. 40 (November 1990), pp. 1-2, 24.

13. O'Donnell and Schmitter, *Transitions from Authoritarian Rule*, pp. 53-56.

14. Ibid, p. 56.

15. Stanley Macebuh, "The Responsibilities of the Press," in Dokun Bojuwade, ed., *Journalism and Society* (Ibadan: Evans Brothers, 1987) (Nigerian Institute of Journalism Guest Lecture Series, Vol. 1, No. 1), p. 71.

Civil Participation in the Argentine Democratic Process

María Rosa S. de Martini

> There are those who believe that the control of government by the representatives of the majority makes any other limitation of the State's powers unnecessary. Democracy, thus understood, is undoubtedly an error: we agree with those who maintain that a form of government wherein the majority can decide that any matters they wish are public and subject to their control, is abominable. Hence the importance of movements such as Conciencia, which jolt women into defending democracy and its freedoms.
> —Ms. Esther Silva de Ghersi, president of *Conciencia Peru*, at the second Latin American meeting of *Conciencia*, 7 November 1988.

THE RECOVERY OF democracy for Argentina was not only a success but a challenge as well. A democratic form of government is like a child: it must be bred, educated, cared for and strengthened.

Defending democracy means defending not just an institution but a system. Since 1983, the Argentine Republic has been democratic. Through its own efforts it recovered a system most of its inhabitants had forgotten, some had never known, and others even disbelieved in.

However, my purpose here is not to theorize about democracy.

On the contrary, I want to tell the story of a civic experience, perhaps a miracle for us. In August 1982, after the call to general elections, twenty women decided they needed to relearn long-forgotten civic education and convey it to as many citizens as possible. They were women and decided to address women—51 percent of our country's voters—because women transmit culture generation after generation and can raise awareness in the citizenry, both within the family and throughout the country as a whole.

While we were searching for a name for our organization the word *conciencia*, which means awareness, consciousness, kept sounding in our ears. Thus Conciencia was born to transform a passive citizenry accustomed to authoritarian governments into a mature one, educated in democratic principles and values through the teachings of our history and national constitution. But we also wanted to instill self-confidence in the people and unleash their creative energies so that individuals, knowing their rights, would know also their civic obligations and the advantages of democratic *participation*. We believed democracy in Argentina would never become strong if the conscience of a responsible citizenry was not awakened.

Conciencia's actions are based on these few premises:

• Democracy is valuable and it must be consolidated and maintained.

• People will not defend what they don't value, or value what is unknown to them.

• Women play a particularly important role in transmitting values.

• Education about democracy is crucial for conveying democratic values.

• Civic education is a responsibility shared by the whole society. Nongovernmental organizations must play a role in this educational process.

Because Conciencia is a nongovernmental, nonpartisan organization, we have been able to reach a diverse audience and attain credibility in a society that has a strong desire to make democracy work. Eight years have gone by, and we consider the task to which we have committed ourselves to be partially fulfilled. We have come very far, but there remain many projects for the future. Education for democracy must be ongoing if we are to preserve the system we fought so hard to establish. As I explained in my address to the second Latin American meeting of Conciencia, our present circumstances show that fresh chapters in the history of Latin America are being written. Generating a democratic culture by stirring the beliefs, values, ideals and deep sentiments of our people must always be our top priority.

Participation: democracy's strengthening axis

In well organized and democratic societies, intermediate organizations play essential roles in the formation and development of a country's political, social and economic life. These groups, because of their autonomy and specialization, act as permanent consultants for the rulers and as an expression of the people's needs. Their survival depends on citizen participation.

In the developing countries, it is all too common for people to use such organizations without knowing the real benefits they can obtain from them. That is why, even though people believe that autonomous groups are essential for achieving social and political goals, they do not appreciate the need for individual commitment towards those common goals. The role of Conciencia is fundamental in this sense, as its purpose is to demonstrate the importance of citizen participation in a free and democratic society.

What are the best methods to resolve new problems and achieve collective goals, both political and social? How can the citizenry be actively incorporated into civic and political life? Conciencia is continuously seeking answers to these queries.

Education through interactive workshops

Our initial efforts were directed towards our Basic Course on Citizen Participation. It attempted to explain how Argentina's democratic system works and what role the average citizen could play in a democratic government.

The course began with a discussion of the historical background of the constitution and the reasoning behind the balance-of-power structure in our government. We explained the many ways that citizens can participate in government and political life. We stressed that it is a citizen's right to be informed about public affairs, and that if they make an effort to become involved, through both official and unofficial channels, they can make significant contributions to society. But we also warned that citizens and public servants alike must temper their actions with the principles of objectivity, fairness, tolerance and patriotism.

The second part of the course explained the citizen's relations with the three branches of government, and we gave the participants special brochures that had been prepared for every topic. As we always move from theory to practice whenever possible, classes on the legislature were given at the Congress or at the provincial legislatures, where we provided information on the development of legislative activity: how legislative drafts emerge, how legislative committees work, how to pass a law, how to present a bill, and how to interview deputies and senators. We taught the participants how to keep abreast of legislative activity and how to lobby the legislature so it would effectively respond to their concerns. The course emphasized the power of organized citizens to influence this branch of government.

We then analyzed the structure of the Argentine judiciary, and explained some of the fundamental principles of the criminal justice system such as the statute of limitations, parole and commutation of sentences. We informed the participants that if they were ever to be arrested and could not afford a lawyer, they had the right to request free legal counsel appointed by the court.

An overview of the executive branch's organization covered the role of the bureaucracy, the different types of taxation, and the functions and powers of the president.

Then we spoke about the Town Hall, a base for citizen participation in government. We talked about the services that citizens had a right to expect from municipal organizations and explained how to ask for an audience with their municipal council. We also discussed the use of community councils and petitions.

But we wanted to go beyond these passive teaching methods. How could we do so from the very beginning? We found that civic workshops were the answer, small groups directed by coordinators who related the daily discussion topics to current events in Argentina.

Our programs had to be organized at different hours, because our premises were too small to accommodate all those interested in hearing the distinguished professors who lectured on the Constitution's origins, its rights and guarantees, the balance of the state's powers, federalism and local government.

The course, given in many different parts of the country, dealt only with the basic aspects of our institutional life, because people knew very little about these issues. In fact, the best-selling book in Argentina in 1983 was the text of the National constitution.

These courses accomplished much more than merely conveying knowledge about our democratic institutions. In the process of educating themselves and one another, the participants discovered a new form of social respect. People learned to express ideas without feeling frightened, to value other people's opinions as well as their own, and to reach consensus on issues that mattered to them. It was a practical way of learning that democracy means more than voting. They came to understand that participation means developing mature opinions instead of unthinkingly accepting the views of the group or the state, and that democracy requires opening channels of communication between citizens and their government.

Expanding our education

Could the courses reach all levels and groups of the population? Needless to say, they could not. Therefore we had to devise a new strategy to approach the women who did not come to us due to distance, work or habit. We decided to go to their homes and use the direct-sales method. Could ideas be sold door-to-door?

There were many skeptics. However, we tried and succeeded. We organized meetings of six to eight people, arranged with a housewife who offered them her living room or kitchen and perhaps a cup of coffee. In two consecutive meetings we explained basic knowledge about the constitution and the township and about Conciencia's role in spreading this information throughout the country. Even some of the men in the families listened to us with interest!

Another housewife who agreed to bring her friends together was designated from that group, and the process continued and multiplied until it reached a vast number of women. Many of those women joined Conciencia as volunteers, and others also helped to spread our message. We continue to progress with this original method of informal education, which we have improved by elaborating the information provided and trying to stir up in the groups a desire for civic participation.

Service to the community

Women could not be the sole targets of our efforts, however, so we decided to deal with important national issues in roundtable discussions and to organize open debates with the candidates. The panelists in these debates always hold different political ideas, so that the audience can draw its own conclusions on the subject under discussion.

Then, immediately before elections, we arrange lectures to explain the voting system and we hand out brochures. The first brochure, entitled, "How do you elect your candidates?" covers the importance of voting, what the current election will determine, how to analyze the platforms and abilities of political parties and candidates, and why each citizen must attempt to cast an informed vote. The second, "Direct and Indirect Election," explains the electoral college system used to choose the president and vice-president. During the 1989 presidential campaign, 2 million brochures were distributed in railway and subway stations, airports, universities, supermarkets and streets all over the country.

At the end of 1989, the Legislature of the Province of Buenos Aires issued a law to reform the Provincial constitution and called for a popular referendum to approve or disapprove the reforms. The importance of the issue had not reached the street and the media, so Conciencia decided to stimulate public discussion. We published the

34

first comparative study of the constitution and the proposed reform and distributed it among well-known journalists of every media organization. We then sold it to political parties, associations, schools and people in general. Roundtables were organized throughout the province. Testimonies that demonstrated the widespread public ignorance about the referendum were videotaped and broadcast on cable TV. Talks explaining the reforms were given by our volunteers, and local radio and television stations broadcast our information and analysis.

Schools' program

Something was still missing from our activities—we needed to get in touch with the youngsters. The Schools' Program was created for them.

When Conciencia was born, we promised ourselves that never again in Argentina would an eighteen-year-old have to wonder about what a ballot is or what are the advantages of living in a democracy. How could this be done without making them feel that we were trying to impose our ideas on them? How could they themselves discover the benefits of participation in order to strengthen democracy.

We decided to start working in secondary schools, with the hope of including other educational levels in the future. Administrators and teachers had to be convinced of the value of our project, because we needed two school hours for our lectures. But they were persuaded, and now the way is eased for us by our record of success.

The Schools' Project tries to show young people the importance of participation in society as a right that we must exercise and incorporate in our way of life. In our workshops we put two questions to the group: (1) What is the ideal society?, and (2) How would they cooperate in order to create this society?

The teenagers suggest many proposals, analyzing the present circumstances with critical minds. Most of them admit that they long for a society without discrimination, with equal opportunities and rights for all, fair salaries, job opportunities, and honest and capable public officials. They feel the need to strengthen the values of freedom, justice, and respect. Concepts such as supporting the family, aiding the handicapped, the need for green spaces, the protection of air and water, the struggle against hunger, and rejection of the military service seem to be recurring concerns.

They have a more difficult time with the second question, because it is much easier to express desires than to develop solutions. However, their suggestions include educating people about addictions and diseases, raising money for charities, creating development and tourism plans, working for the country's welfare, studying, cooperating with the housework, and modifying the teaching system.

After each exercise, a proposal is prepared and the workshops determine how to put the ideas and proposals into practice. In about 90 percent of the cases, the prevailing opinion is that through education and individual participation in society, the goals can be attained. They then analyze the fundamental roles of both volunteers and voluntary associations in undertaking these tasks and learn about the feeling of personal achievement that grows in people who serve others. Once the session is over, we hand out a brochure that encourages them to join community organizations and to cooperate through work with their families, school, and society. It then explains how they can begin community projects through their own initiative by defining problems, setting goals, and forming their own organizations to deal with these problems.

Through evaluations we confirmed that 70 percent of the participants felt that they were needed by the community, and that these exercises encouraged them to become volunteers. In two years we visited seventy schools, and the 3,300 pupils who became interested in the project demonstrate the success of our program.

Local communities
In small towns or quarters of large cities neighbors started asking Conciencia for advice on how to solve community problems. As a result, support and technical assistance to neighborhood and district groups were included in our programs. Conciencia offers them information and training, and then the newly formed district associations start taking care of a park or a street. These groups learn how to work with municipal authorities and achieve outstanding

success in areas such as cleanliness, order and safety. In 1989 Conciencia signed an agreement with the municipal government of Buenos Aires to provide training to "Friends of the Park" groups.

Reaction to the crisis

In 1989, when our chaotic socioeconomic situation exploded into hyperinflation, Conciencia decided to attack the crisis with energy. Our first step was to organize a communication campaign to help people find the best ways to overcome the crisis. It included distribution of half a million brochures, talks followed by workshops searching for solutions to local problems, advertisements for TV and radio, a script for TV ("How to work with groups"), roundtables, and even cartoons. Every chapter of Conciencia received a special kit with materials and instructions for its use.

We then organized a fund-raising campaign through the media, which provided aid to fourteen coordinated assistance organizations in order to help relieve the food emergency in poverty-stricken areas. A total of 3,570,000 persons, mainly children, were fed through this program.

Economic education

The economic crisis in which Argentina finds itself is indicative of a new challenge confronting the nation: to maintain political freedom while fostering internationally competitive economic development. This cannot be done if people do not understand the language of economics and how economic forces work. To fill a real gap in our education Conciencia now offers courses on Basic Economics. As a result of a cooperation agreement we signed with the Ministry of Education in February 1990, the inclusion of Economics in the secondary school curricula is being studied.

Symposia and seminars...on civic education

Is it worthwhile to educate the base of society without getting the leaders of different sectors to understand the importance of developing a civic conscience?

This question motivated us to try a new experiment in October of 1985: to gather together high-level representatives of decision-making groups—educators, politicians, reporters, unionists, and businessmen—for a symposium under the theme, "Civic Education in Different Areas of National Society." Our purpose was to identify more effective means for civic group formation and citizen participation. We asked the participants to discuss four questions. First, based on their experience, how could better mechanisms for civic education and participation be generated so as to consolidate the democratic system? Second, what did they see as the main obstacles to implementing their suggestions? Third, how, through the means they suggested, could greater participation be produced? And fourth, what concrete actions would they take in their own sectors to improve civic education and participation? Each group was then given a series of more specific questions to address that reflected their specific interests and problems.

The political parties' sector admitted that the population lacked civic education and that their own organizations lacked the preparation and experience to provide it. They believed that democratic participation could only be attained through education, and that it was important for democracy to become institutionalized in this manner so that its survival would not become dependent on individual political leaders.

The business sector concluded that although they had an organization that could cope with their role in the country's political system, they lacked the training to manage their relationships with the Republic's institutions efficiently and to contribute to the civic education of their members. They mentioned specifically the absence of suitable channels for communication between the legislature and business concerns, in contrast to the extensive interaction their businesses had with labor organizations. They also recommended that more businessmen take part in politics and use their leadership abilities for the common good.

The mass media sector called for giving priority to the search for adequate ways to address the nation through simple, interesting civic programs to which citizens could relate, and that these programs could be made more credible through the use of popular moderators. They suggested encouraging the establishment of cultural television channels that would exist independently of the tyranny of ratings, and they highlighted the need for self-criticism in the media. They stressed that the print media should act as a primary opinion former and that the media in general should play a major role in civic education.

The position of the union representatives was conditioned by many years of union inactivity in Argentina. Many of the trade unions were in the process of revising their statutes, thus enabling their affiliates to exercise coherent democracy within their own institutions and to be aware of their civic rights and obligations. They emphasized the importance both of participating in government and rebuilding their dismantled trade-union structures. However, they believed it was impossible to expect people to exhibit civic and participatory behavior if they were unable to read and write. Therefore, they stressed the fundamental importance of starting literacy campaigns.

The educational sector, which has the greatest opportunity to shape citizen values, focused on the proper methods for achieving deep changes in attitudes, employing every aspect of the teaching process. The obstacles to change in education they enumerated included the rigidity of the system, inadequate teacher training, fear of participation, and a lack of funds. They suggested that teacher training be completely reevaluated, and that the educational system be closely integrated with the community as a whole.

This symposium was highly productive and innovative. It was refreshing to hear leaders from so many sectors openly criticizing their own inability to lead their followers into democratic participation processes. After a short time, we noticed different attitudes within these groups. Various sectors began to work together more effectively and with a better understanding of their common goals.

...on the constitutional reform

After the success of our first symposium we decided to arrange another session. This time we gathered leaders of different sectors in the same workshop to discuss the project to reform the nation's constitution. Legislators from four political parties expressed their views, which ranged from the belief that the legislature, not the constitution, needed reforming to a statement that the constitution had to be reformed soon so that it would reflect the views of all of the people. Afterwards the different groups coordinated by Conciencia exchanged ideas on the need for reform, and identified areas where consensus towards a change could be reached. Some of the participants stated it was the first time they had taken part in such work, sharing a table with people from different sectors.

"People and mass media"
In 1988 and 1989, Conciencia, with the Fundación Roberto Noble sponsored by the newspaper *Clarin*, organized a forum called "People and Mass Media." It took place in the Federal Capital and five other cities, with results so satisfying that Conciencia repeated it the next year in every province and in Buenos Aires.

This forum began with the presentation of findings obtained by an investigation of "Freedom of the Press and Public Opinion," with the aid of visual projections and panels. (The investigation was done by a prominent firm at the request of the Noble Foundation). After the verbal and graphic presentation, the participants formed groups, individually answered a questionnaire, and attended several workshops on "Freedom of the Press," "Readers vs. the News," and the "Objective and Subjective Press." Finally, each group examined a previous government decision involving the media and reached its own conclusions about its issue.

New endeavors
In November 1989, hoping to expand on the success of our seminars, we held a Seminar on Effective Negotiations in Tucuman for young educators, politicians, unionists and businessmen. Its goal was to provide knowledge of and active training in the arts of participation,

cooperation, and negotiation in order to foster better relations between future political, labor and business leaders.

Recently, in conjunction with several other groups, Conciencia created PROAC (Program for Civic Action) to train and educate leaders in civics and politics. So far it has organized three seminars in different provinces on "The Municipality: An Interaction Project." Through negotiation and management techniques, leaders from different sectors of the community are expected to formulate an action plan to deal with a specific community problem. Leaders develop the plans within the following six months, and we provide monthly follow-ups and evaluations.

Education in the participation process

Our Symposium on Civic Education clearly identified the failure of our educational system in teaching about civic and political issues in Argentina. People agreed on the values on which education should be based: freedom, justice, equality, solidarity, and responsibility. The trouble was that these principles were not acted upon. The reason was not only the many previous interruptions of democracy, but also an outdated approach to general education.

Our Educational Programs Committee conducted a survey of Latin American countries (summarized in Appendices 1 and 2) and carried out research to design plans aimed at improving civic education within our democratic and pluralistic society.

Pedagogic congress

In 1984, the Argentine Congress passed an Act calling people to a large Educational Assembly, the Pedagogic Congress, whose aim would be to study educational problems and look for solutions. The resulting proposals would aid the legislature in preparing a future education law for Argentina. The call went out to students, parents, parents' associations, unionists, teachers, scholars of education, political parties, and social organizations to join this historic conference.

Conciencia saw an important mission for itself in this endeavor.

We first organized a wide campaign to stimulate the citizens throughout the country to respond to the call. Through lectures and brochures we explained the meaning of the Congress and the issues proposed for discussion.

Conciencia presented four proposals to the Pedagogic Congress. One summarized the problems of our present educational system and suggested solutions; another outlined methods to create responsible and participative citizens; the third supported the organization of parents', teachers' and pupils' associations; and the fourth presented a plan for permanent, informal civic-political education.

In accordance with our proposal to join together the schools and communities, we organized meetings under the theme, "Education is Shared Responsibility." They were attended by school principals, teachers, pupils and parents from both public and private schools. In the workshops, the obstacles to dialogue between school and community were identified and solutions were designed.

Intermediate associations

As Jefferson said: "The great strength of our democratic society is the incredible mosaic of our free associations, not the central government authority." These associations are essential to democracy because they are autonomous of state control, democratic in their internal organizations, and composed of ordinary citizens. In countries such as ours that have been so unstable and authoritarian, it is important to nurture and train the leaders of these associations so that they can become the "backbone" of a democratic society.

Understanding acutely the importance of strengthening intermediate associations in Argentina, we have designed training courses for their leaders and teach them all over the country. They have been attended by members of different voluntary organizations, local politicians, unionists, and police members.

Our objectives are to train these leaders in the practice of civic education and to pass on techniques for efficient development of community activities. We explain basic organizational principles such as attentiveness to members' needs, work and motivation, leadership, planning, communication, and conducting meetings. For those who wish to go further, Conciencia teaches a course for managers, which covers organizational development and group dynamics, civic political education, fund raising and treasurership, press and communication, and motivation and recruitment.

In February 1990 we offered a version of this leadership training course to a group of rural teachers, who are the natural leaders of small communities. This program was carried out with the "Argentine Rural Missions," an NGO that supports schools in rural areas. In less than seven months, fully 70 percent of the teachers we trained had organized community projects.

The dynamics of Conciencia: motivation, recruitment and training

Due to the variety of challenges we face, we need an ever-growing number of volunteers who believe in our mission. Our experience shows that the best recruiting system is a personal appeal in meetings where we give motivational speeches. In the beginning we had a massive recruitment program, as there was a real need for training to prepare for the 1983 elections. After some years of successful achievements, we felt that certain societal patterns were changing and that we were failing to understand fully the nature of these changes. Through special research carried out with a private polling firm, we studied new strategies to reach more people with issues that really concern them. This led us to initiate our Friends of Parks and Municipalities programs, as we learned that people were primarily interested in solving immediate and local problems.

Like any voluntary association, our success depends not only on recruitment but also effective training of volunteer workers. We decided to hire consultants to design internal training projects for our volunteers according to the tasks they performed. Each of the members who receives training becomes in turn an instructor. Groups of instructors are periodically trained and then work in the adults' training program in different chapters of our organization.

In addition, as nothing can be done without financial support, we plan our fundraising strategies carefully. Membership contributions, special donors, fundraising events, and economic support from foundations and private enterprises provide for specific projects. Grants from international organizations that share our goals, such as the National Endowment for Democracy, also help significantly to cover our expenditures.

Expanding our organization

At the national level, as we saw our programs attracting more and more people, we expanded into several quarters of Buenos Aires, its surrounding areas, and various cities in the provinces. At present Conciencia is working in sixteen provinces of the Argentine Republic with a total of thirty permanent chapters. They hold regional and provincial meetings, through which we can evaluate the experiences of many sectors of the nation. In addition, these groups develop Conciencia's national programs, which are determined by the delegates at the annual national meeting. These groups work on issues related to the specific needs of each community.

After demonstrating that an organization like Conciencia could make a difference in Argentina, we contacted other Latin American countries and promoted the creation of similar organizations. We shared our experiences with them and proposed to develop joint programs to increase citizen participation in the democratic process. Chile, Brazil, Uruguay, Paraguay, Peru, Ecuador, Colombia, Mexico, Costa Rica, Bolivia, Honduras, El Salvador, and the Dominican Republic are at present part of the Latin American cooperation network of Conciencia.

Thanks to this geographic expansion, in October of 1987 we were able to carry out the First Latin American Meeting on the "Role of the Woman in the Consolidation of Democracy." Its aims were: to exchange ideas with people from fifteen countries in the region in order to support and consolidate democratic values and institutions on the continent; to motivate and train women so that they could take an active part in this consolidation; and to explore common goals and strategies for the strengthening of our democratic systems. We reached agreement on the importance of the rule of law, freedom, justice, and respect for human dignity, and reasserted the leading role of women in promoting and consolidating democracy.

The participants asked Conciencia to create a committee "for the promotion and consolidation of democratic systems in America's countries." This Promotion Committee has since been acting as a "clearinghouse" for information from member countries.

Regional meetings took place in Guatemala, Colombia, and Paraguay before both the second Latin American meeting in Buenos Aires in November 1988 and the third meeting in Santo Domingo in October 1989. The goals of these multinational meetings were to:

• identify common problems in our educational systems;

• design common strategies for formal, informal, and mass civic education;

• design strategies to foster the organizational development of the participating groups;

• design a Latin American organizational model; and

• exchange concrete experiences.

For example, the regional meeting in Guatemala (for Mexico, Central America, and the Caribbean) identified several aspects of the area's educational systems that could be improved. Their report notes that there are too few civic and political education programs, that many teachers are inappropriately political, that women are encouraged to begin to work too soon, that politicians themselves have not had sufficient exposure to civic education, and that, in general, citizens lack interest in obtaining civic education. They suggested strategies for combatting this ignorance and apathy that went beyond our original method of disseminating information through pamphlets and forums. To reach many sectors of the society, they suggested ideas such as beginning a civic education "program in the streets" for children and combining lessons in civic education with training in handicrafts.

This meeting also included a workshop on "The Regional Project on the Civic and Political Training of Women," initiated by the

Guatemalan branch. It addressed the varied roles women play, and their potential for civic leadership in politics, family, society, and education. The workshop stressed the need to develop women leaders with a good understanding of civic rights and responsibilities in a democratic society. To this end, the participants believed that both formal and informal education should be altered to include more civics topics, communications skills, and moral values. They felt that this would strengthen community and family ties and help people gain a greater appreciation for a democratic form of government. The workshop thus elected to devise a broad action plan addressing priorities, design recruitment strategies, increase member participation, reach out to the media, obtain more international cooperation, encourage greater fundraising efforts, and improve volunteer training in all branches of Conciencia. It is interesting to note that with the opening up of democratic politics in Paraguay, the Paraguayan "Women for Democracy" were able to fully apply what they had learned through our work; some even successfully entered into politics.

The mass media

How could our educational message reach the population all the way from the grass roots to the top leadership? How could we gain credibility? How could we use those true "accelerating agents" of education such as the mass media?

We knew we had to use the mass media properly in order to broaden our work and make it more effective. From the very beginning we sought professional advice. We improved our relationship with the media until the most important publications in the country gave extensive coverage to our activities. In 1988 Conciencia was able to introduce a weekly quiz show on the highest-rated television program in the country. We also created popular micro-programs for the provincial broadcasting stations that employed question and answer games on civic issues. This ongoing promotion on national and provincial television and radio programs combined our organizational and educational messages and gave Conciencia extensive publicity. The growth of Conciencia would have been impossible without this communication strategy.

In addition, we began our own newsletter. Since 1983, "Conciencia en Accion" has been informing our members of our schedule of activities and new issues facing our organization, and has stimulated the recruitment of new members. Then, because the chapters in the provinces are far from the central premises in Buenos Aires, we felt it was necessary to publish another newsletter, "Conciencia Informa." It provides monthly details of the activities of all our various committees and chapters.

Another newsletter, "Carta Latinoamerica," resulted from the contacts we made during the First Latin American meeting of Civic Associations. It is an information bulletin that summarizes the activities of Latin American groups.

Toward the consolidation of our democratic system

During our first eight years of existence, our activities have encompassed 560 conferences attended by 45,000 persons, 480 lectures on national issues with an audience of 25,000, 320 roundtables in which 34,000 persons took part, 180 courses which included 15,000 persons, 2,800 direct approaches to homes, 21 interprovincial and 6 national meetings, and 3 Latin American meetings.

We have printed over two and a half million brochures on different civic and political subjects. Fifteen Latin American countries, through various nongovernmental organizations, exchanged educational programs and information or received technical assistance through Conciencia. Five hundred of our leaders received managerial training and twenty of them joined political parties and were nominated for elective office.

Considering all of our activities, we estimate that our message reached directly over five million people—about a quarter of Argentina's entire population.

History shows that in Argentina we are accustomed to the "don't get involved" attitude, to never-ending complaints without positive actions. However, the members of Conciencia believe participation is a right that citizens must exercise if democracy is to mature and endure as a system.

"Become Aware, the Country Needs You" has been our motto during these years of work. We have tried to make people understand that *democracy does not end in a vote* and that people must know both the rules of their democratic state and their responsibilities as democratic citizens. It is comforting to watch the evolution our citizenry has undergone in the last few years. We believe part of it is a result of our efforts.

We know that the trend towards participation generated by the democratic restoration in 1983 is now tapering off due to the absence of an economic recovery. However, our economic problems must not interfere with the citizens' feelings towards the participatory process. New motivating stimuli must be created so that individuals will take an active part in strengthening our democratic system.

Argentina is making up for wasted time. After almost fifty years of political instability, democracy in Argentina faces a formidable challenge. In spite of the difficult times we are going through, recovery is still possible through the consolidation of democratic institutions, the preservation of peace, the active support of the citizenry for the democratic system, and the rediscovery of our sense of justice.

Our challenge is not only to be aware of the crisis, but to be aware of the solutions. For Conciencia, that challenge started a long-time ago.

Appendix 1

Formal Civic Education

Does the school curriculum include civic education?

Country	Pre-school	Primary	Secondary	College
Costa Rica	--	--	YES	YES
Ecuador	YES	YES	YES	YES
Colombia 1	YES	YES	YES	YES
Honduras	YES	YES	--	--
El Salvador	YES	YES	--	--
Dominican Rep.	YES	YES	YES	YES
Colombia 2	YES	YES	YES	YES
Uruguay	--	YES	YES	--
Mexico	--	YES	YES	--
Peru	--	YES	YES	--
Brazil	YES	YES	--	--
Chile	--	--	YES	--
Argentina	YES	YES	YES	--
Totals	8/13	11/13	10/13	5/13

Is attendance at Civic Education class obligatory?

Country	Pre-school	Primary	Secondary	College
Costa Rica	--	--	YES	--
Ecuador	--	YES	YES	--
Colombia 1	YES	YES	YES	--
Honduras	YES	YES	--	--

Country	Pre-school	Primary	Secondary	College
El Salvador	YES	YES	--	--
Dominican Rep.	YES	YES	YES	YES
Colombia 2	YES	YES	YES	YES
Uruguay	--	YES	YES	--
Mexico	--	YES	YES	YES
Peru	--	YES	YES	--
Brazil	YES	YES	--	--
Chile	--	--	--	YES
Argentina	YES	YES	YES	--
Totals	7/13	11/13	9/13	4/13

Appendix 2

Informal Civic Education

Do organizations offer informal civic education? If so what kind of oganizations are they and to whom are their programs directed?

Country	Organization	Government	Programs addressed to
Costa Rica	YES	--	Adults. Women.
Ecuador	YES	YES	General public
Colombia 1	YES	YES	Children, youth, adults, women.
Honduras	--	YES	Youth.
El Salvador	YES	--	Youth, adults, women.
Dominican Rep.	YES	--	Adults, women.
Colombia 2	YES	YES	
Uruguay	YES	--	Youth, adults, women.
Mexico	YES	--	General public.
Peru	YES	--	Adults, women.
Brazil	YES	--	Children (4 to 6 years old).
Argentina	YES	YES	Children, youth, adults, women.
Totals	12/13	5/13	

I. Do teachers have enough encouragement and help from the school?

II. From the educational system?

III. Do students participate in the community?

Country	Quest. I	Quest. II	Pre-School	Quest. III Primary School	Quest. III Secondary School	College
Costa Rica	--	--	--		YES	YES
Ecuador	Limited	--	--	YES	YES	--
Colombia 1	YES	YES	--	--	YES	YES
Honduras		YES	YES	YES	YES	--
El Salvador	--	--	--		YES	--
Dominican Rep.	--	--	--		--	--
Colombia 2	Partly	Partly	--	--	--	YES
Uruguay		--	--	--	--	--
Mexico		--	--	--	--	--
Peru		--	--	--	--	--
Brazil	YES	YES	--	YES	--	--
Chile		--	--	--	--	YES
Argentina		--	--	--	YES	YES
Totals	4/13	4/13	1/13	4/13	6/13	6/13

Building a Democratic Culture in the Philippines

Dette Pascual

FIVE YEARS AGO, the Philippines regained its freedom after a blood-less revolution. Men, women and youth—using their frail bodies as shields—stood between two opposing armies and brought about a peaceful change of government. The chant during this demonstration of "people power" was, "Tama na! Sobra na! Palitan na!" ("Enough is enough! We want a change!")

Today we realize that loving freedom and regaining it are not enough. Maintaining democracy also requires responsibility. We must be responsible for what we love and what we fought for. Just as Filipinos organized themselves to bring down the Marcos dictator-ship, so today they are joining together in citizen groups dedicated to preserving and strengthening our nation's democracy.

Under the dictatorship, there were basically only two kinds of interest groups: pro-Marcos or anti-Marcos. You were considered eith-er a loyal follower or a subversive rebel. Today, however, the Philip-pines teems with nongovernmental organizations pursuing a wide range of concerns, including economic development, human rights, land reform, and environmental protection. Such is the pluralism of democracy.

I have been actively involved in three citizen groups in the Philippines: the National Citizens' Movement for Free Elections

(NAMFREL), the Evelio B. Javier Foundation (EBJF), and the Women's Movement for the Nurturance of Democracy (KABATID, or "Kilusan ng Kababaihan na Tumataguyod sa Demokrasya" in Tagalog). These three organizations will be the focus of this chapter not only because I am most familiar with them, but because I see in them a natural progression, with one building upon the accomplishments of the other. Tracing this progression can help to illuminate the vital role played by civic groups both in the transition from authoritarian rule and in the consolidation of democracy.

NAMFREL

NAMFREL was born during the crisis that followed the assassination of opposition leader Benigno Aquino on 21 August 1983 as government soldiers led him off the plane that had brought him home from exile. Cries of "Justice for Ninoy!" and "Marcos resign!" rang in the streets of Manila. The grief and anger provoked by his murder quickly led to widespread public defiance of Marcos' authority for the first time since the declaration of martial law in 1972. More than 2 million people joined Aquino's funeral cortege. This unprecedented turnout was surpassed only by the 4 million who came three years later to hear his widow, Corazon Aquino, speak out against the fraud committed by President Marcos in the 1986 election.

NAMFREL began on a September evening in 1983, when a group of twenty concerned citizens led by Jose Concepcion, Jr. gathered in the home of Mariano Quesada to discuss the acute political tensions in the Philippines following Aquino's murder. The discussions that night among a mixed group of professionals, businessmen, housewives, church leaders and students led us to three conclusions about our country's political future. First, Marcos would never voluntarily resign, for to give up the protection of Malacanang Palace would be tantamount to suicide. Second, the regime's use of violence against continuing street protests would eventually drive a frustrated people to opt for its own violent means of forcing a change of government. Finally, the resort to violence would force Filipinos to choose between living under an increasingly repressive regime or fleeing to the hills to join the leftist insurgency of the New People's Army.

From the outset, NAMFREL's goal was to restore popular faith in the electoral process, despite the clamor in the streets for a more violent approach. We decided at this first meeting to press for an early presidential election that would channel popular energy toward a democratic method of changing the nation's leadership. A fair election would inspire confidence in the electoral process as a peaceful method of change. José Concepcion warned, however, that if the election turned out to be a travesty, then the Philippines was likely to become engulfed in political violence—and there would be no possibility of turning back.

That same evening, we resolved to establish a citizen's movement advocating free and fair elections as the only peaceful means for change. This movement's principal task would be to protect the integrity of the polls to ensure that the true will of the people would be honored.

Impact: The birth of "People Power"

It is said that for a movement to succeed, it must resonate in the minds and hearts of the people. It is like a gong. Once struck, the gong resonates, reverberates, and quivers, because of what occurs within it. The idea of NAMFREL resonated and moved within us. It was something that the Filipino people could identify with. It called for patience. It sought to educate the people about their rights as citizens to choose their own government. It respected the Filipino preference for resolving conflict in nonconfrontational ways. It called for hope that the Marcos regime would be willing to face the test of a popular election. Above all, it called for faith that the Filipino people would be willing to risk their lives peacefully defending the cause of free and fair elections.

The citizens answered the call. In the short period between NAMFREL's founding and the May 1984 parliamentary elections, 200,000 Filipinos volunteered for training as pollwatchers. Thanks to NAMFREL's efforts to counter electoral fraud, opposition forces won 30 percent of the seats, an unprecedented showing during the Marcos years. When less than two years later Marcos called a "snap election" for the presidency in an effort to regain international legitimacy for his rule, NAMFREL was able to field half a million volunteers throughout the Philippines. The concept of peaceful change through the democratic process of elections had galvanized the nation.

Those who watched the 1986 Philippines presidential elections on American television may remember those scenes of young seminarians, teachers, uniformed students, and housewives linking hands and protecting ballot boxes. One of the most stirring descriptions I have read of that episode was written by Tom Ashbrook of the *Boston Globe*, datelined Manila, 10 February 1986:

It is clear that something extraordinary is happening in the Philippines. Something rare in Asia. Something rare in the world.

In a country haunted by the specters of fear and rifle butts and bribes, democracy is trying to break loose...and the people flared—with hope and yearning. They knew. They knew the stories—of rifle butts that broke bones but not spirits on election day; of poor farmers who banded together, defying thugs and M-16s, to walk their ballots miles to town; of the nuns who sat on ballot boxes until armed men shoved them to the floor; of people whose ballots were dumped into the sewer and of how they fished them out again by flashlight in the dark; of the poll watcher shot to death for defending slips of paper marked with dreams.

NAMFREL was the forerunner of the "people power" revolution that ushered in Corazon Aquino's presidency. Through NAMFREL's vigilance, the whole nation and the world were made aware of the election fraud committed by Marcos and his supporters. NAMFREL's vote tallies made it clear that Corazon Aquino had won the presidential election despite the dictator's false claims that he was the people's choice. Although there were attempts to distort or suppress the news of Aquino's victory, they were foiled by the courageous efforts of the "alternative press" and by the fact that so many Filipinos had been witnesses to what occurred at the polling places. Yes, this time the people knew.

The democratic vision and sense of community engendered by NAMFREL gave rise to a potent force—people power. So when the call came over Radio Veritas in the bleakest hours of that February dawn in 1986, the people were ready. In a way, NAMFREL served as a practice run for the even greater risk of facing up to an army of soldiers and tanks to bring down the dictatorship.

The Evelio B. Javier Foundation

After an initial period of euphoria following Marcos' flight and the victory of the February Revolution, Filipinos turned to the task of rebuilding the nation. During sixteen years of dictatorship, they had been largely deprived of the right to select their own leaders. An authoritarian system in which all power comes from only one man does not provide the conditions required for the emergence of independent political leadership. It produces, with few exceptions, self-serving politicians and sycophants.

Thus the task of rebuilding the nation required not just an emphasis on democratic values, but the selection of effective public officials at all levels of government. A democracy must have fair elections, but it is equally important that there be good candidates to choose from. While NAMFREL fulfilled the role of promoting clean elections, the Evelio B. Javier Foundation's efforts to encourage good leadership represented the next logical step for the newly restored Philippine democracy.

Evelio Javier, a former governor of Antique province and a martyr of the Philippine democratic movement, asked two questions: "Why is politics dirty? Why are politicians corrupt, abusive, and obsessed with holding on to power forever?" He answered his own questions as follows: "Because the citizens, the good and the decent, have chosen to stay away from politics. They have abandoned the affairs of the state to the rapacity of the corrupt and abusive." [1] Javier lived by his convictions and devoted himself wholeheartedly to political opposition to the Marcos regime, running for the Philippine parliament in 1984. Despite being cheated out of that election by a Marcos-backed candidate, he persevered in the political struggle and actively campaigned for Corazon Aquino in the 1986 presidential election.

Javier's life was cut short just a few weeks before his country regained its freedom. He was chased and gunned down by six masked men as helpless townspeople looked on. His murderers have never been identified or brought to justice.

Evelio Javier's martyrdom opened people's eyes not only to what he died for, but even more importantly, to what he lived for. Throughout his political career Javier was a model of probity. His record was unblemished by corruption. He stood for the ideal of public service, and held that anyone "elected to public office must transform it into a genuine public trust by serving the people's interests before his own." [2]

The mission of EBJF

The Evelio B. Javier Foundation carries on the spirit of Evelio Javier's life. Its mission is to strengthen grassroots democracy through educational projects designed to train able and honest political leaders. The EBJF focuses particularly on local officials, believing that they play a critical role in encouraging ordinary citizens to participate in the democratic process.

The first phase of the EBJF program sought to promote the values of true public service and to teach the technical and administrative aspects of municipal government. Before the January 1988 local elections, the EBJF offered seminars to candidates for governor, mayor, and other local offices. This nonpartisan program was open to all political candidates, regardless of party affiliation. Despite limited resources, the EBJF conducted thirty-five seminars in thirteen regions of the country. Nine different political parties were represented at these seminars, which trained 418 candidates for public office.

The second phase of the EBJF program continues to promote the ideal of selfless public service by offering elected officials the opportunity to learn new leadership skills. EBJF's local executive leadership seminars focusing on "service in governance" are available to governors, mayors, and to officials of *barangays* (the basic unit of government in the Philippines).

The Foundation's emphasis on moral values and public accountability fit in well with the Aquino administration's call for "transparency" in government service. In 1988, the Department of Local Government invited the Foundation to give two workshops on values and "transparency" to all the newly elected governors and city mayors. EBJF is now presenting its seminars to the mayors of the smaller municipalities, their councillors, and the barangay captains. As there are 1,408 municipalities and 42,000 barangays with 294,000 barangay officials, the task is enormous. Fortunately, the Department of Local Government has recognized the importance of the Foundation's mission. A local government academy is in the planning stages, and EBJF has been invited to help train its staff. We hope that through a collaborative effort between the government and nongovernmental sectors, we will eventually reach officials of all the municipalities and barangays. This effort promises to improve the quality of grassroots leadership, and thereby enhance the people's satisfaction with their government.

KABATID

Whereas the EBJF focuses its efforts on candidates for office and elected officials, the Women's Movement for the Nurturance of Democracy concentrates on what ordinary citizens can do to affect their government. A nonpartisan women's civic education movement, KABATID is dedicated to enhancing people's understanding of the opportunities and responsibilities that come with citizenship in a democratic society.

The women who have joined KABATID, many of them veterans of NAMFREL, recognized the need for new forms of citizen action to help consolidate our country's newly restored democracy. Like other developing countries, the Philippines has its growing pains. An armed leftist insurgency continues to pose a threat to the countryside, and rightist forces have made several attempts to seize power through a coup d'etat. Thus it is not enough simply to have put democratic institutional structures in place. Like a child growing up in a dangerous environment, Philippine democracy must be cherished and nurtured—a task for which Filipino women are particularly well-suited.

The origins of KABATID, like those of NAMFREL, can be traced back to the outrage of Filipinos at the assassination of Benigno Aquino. A few weeks after Aquino's murder, Marcos appointed his chief justice of the Supreme Court, Enrique Fernando, to head the official investigation. The public saw Justice Fernando as a Marcos tool and concerned citizens were apprehensive that the investigation would be a whitewash. Students from Ateneo University started picketing Fernando's house, while the alternative press published several pointed commentaries on the situation.

We were three women who sat drinking coffee while discussing the death of Aquino. We were in shock—shaken out of our complacency. We wanted to demand justice for Ninoy. As we talked, we realized that Fernando must be forced to listen to the feelings of the people. We wrote a letter to Chief Justice Fernando reminding him of his duty as a public official to serve his country and the interests of justice. "Our countrymen expect you to have the vision and the courage to do what is just—whatever the personal cost to yourself," the letter said. We signed it, "Chita Almario, mother of eight; Sony Sison, mother of eight; Dette Pascual, mother of seven." Perhaps frightened by our own audacity, we sought to hide behind our motherhood. But those were uncertain times, with Marcos at the height of his dictatorial powers. Our letters to Fernando continued— praising him for what we thought were just actions and suggesting alternatives when we felt he was wrong—until his resignation and replacement. We did not start a women's movement right away, but the idea was conceived at that time.

KABATID in society

Since its formal establishment in 1988, KABATID has grown to provide a wide variety of services. KABATID serves as a "school of democracy" for its members, exposing them to free discussions and teaching them the respect for accommodation and procedural rules that are intrinsic to democratic politics. Our members in turn pass this learning on to the larger community through their activities in KABATID.

We focus our attention on both everyday citizens and government officials. Our public programs include informative forums on various issues, seminars on leadership and democratic values, a speaker's bureau for women leaders, lobbying efforts, letter writing campaigns, and KABATID's monthly newsletter. Our newsletter is the core of our communications system. In it we discuss the activities of KABATID chapters, publish information on government activities, provide a forum for discussing issues both through opinions columns and letters, and profile active women who have made a difference in our society.

With an eye towards accountability in governance, we actively monitor government performance in Congress, the Cabinet, and other government agencies. Then, we not only point out to our officials the areas in which we believe they need improvement, but we also give praise where it is due. In the words of John Culver, "We should...properly reward those who meet the test and not just criticize the ones who fall short. If we constantly disparage our politicians, politics will not be viewed as a worthwhile endeavor by our young people, and our elected officials will live down to our expectations."

We have a "flowers and thorns" system. Each month we reward certain politicians with "flowers" for excellence in service to the nation, and give others "thorns" for questionable actions. For instance, Miriam Defensor Santiago, the Commissioner on Immigration, received "flowers" from KABATID. She was cited for her courage in publicly identifying crooked syndicates despite threats to her life. On the other hand, we presented "thorns" to House leaders for their plan to transfer their offices to more luxurious quarters. Their attempted relocation, estimated by critics to cost approximately 4.3 billion pesos,[3] was met with howls of protest which caused them to reevaluate the project. Vice-President Salvador Laurel also received "thorns" in December of 1989 for his statement in the midst of the coup attempt that he would be willing to serve in a military government. Although he attempted to equivocate later, the plain fact is that he, a sitting vice-president, did not condemn the men who wanted to topple the government he professed to serve.

In addition, we keep in touch with our officials through a guardian angel system in which individual members adopt a government leader and continuously correspond with them. While all communication must be signed, it does not always have to be in the form of a letter. One member sends her children's drawings to add a personal touch, and others send newspaper clippings, poems, or prayers. This approach enables the official to receive continuous feedback on his performance while encouraging our members to keep themselves informed about current affairs. We have found this program to be very successful in encouraging constructive dialogues between the government and its citizens. Our KABATID-Panay coordinator, Tita Hontiveros, related an incident that occurred when she went to a public meeting about a proposed bill chaired by Senator Jovito Salonga. Salonga noticed her KABATID identification tag and exclaimed, "KABATID! Even here there's KABATID!" Tita said, "Of course. Why, sir, are you receiving letters from KABATID?" Salonga replied, "Yes, that's why I'm in a state of anxiety." Another public official we correspond with, Department of Transportation and Communications Secretary Rainerio Reyes, was our guest for lunch in September of 1989. There he told us that:

> I am very pleased with your confidence in me... It inspires me to know that we share the same tasks of nation building and developing front-line leadership where government service is rendered in a most transparent and honest way. May we continue to work together for the development of an effective democracy in our nation.

Through positive reinforcement and a focus on quality performance, KABATID has helped to develop leaders with a heightened sense of values. Our leaders must realize that their power comes from the people, and not from a nebulous political machine. While we are only a few women, with no formal political power, we must never underestimate the force of persistent and thoughtful attention to the leaders and issues in our society.

We continually evaluate ourselves as well, through our regional conferences and seminars. For example, in August of 1988 KABATID-Cebu held a conference which combined concrete, public activities with group discussions in which members recommitted themselves to KABATID's goals. On the second evening of the conference members were interviewed on the radio, and the group arranged to hold a public forum immediately after the conference on "Women and the Constitution." The optimistic spirit engendered by the conference infused everyone with new resolve. One woman stated afterwards that, "I feel happy, aware, and excited to do whatever I can, now that I can already see the direction to take if I want to be a catalyst of change." Another said that "I feel whole again, since my traumatic experience of losing a beloved husband to the Communist ideology...making me believe, at least, that democracy does wonders for women."

We had a similar experience at our leaders' conference in November of 1989. As we discussed our activities and goals from the past year, we discovered that we were indeed living the KABATID vision. Our Cordillera group had focused on monitoring appropriation and use of government funds, and was able to identify non-existent roads and daycare centers. These errors were pointed out to the government and the public, and our members then organized a group of concerned citizens to make spot inspections of future government projects. In Surigao, members coordinated a leadership training seminar for 250 women government officials. The Antique group was working to replace the biased judge in Evelio Javier's murder case, which had been dragging on for three years. The Visayas group agitated for a referendum that would allow citizens to vote on the fate of the U.S. bases. Manila members concentrated on pending bills in Congress, sent out a survey on the bases, and were also able to focus on the cancellation of a beauty pageant in Quezon City. And so on. We had been working on problems at all levels of government and society that affected many different groups in the Philippines. We discussed ways to expand and improve our programs, and left the meeting feeling empowered and determined. We KABATID women learned again that everyone has a right to dream, and that together we can be a strong force to turn our dreams into reality.

KABATID today

After experiencing the distrust and fear of the Marcos years, people in the Philippines have become wary of being manipulated by the government. For this reason, citizen groups rather than the government itself will continue to be more effective in encouraging discussion of popular attitudes towards government and democracy. The nonpartisan stance of groups such as KABATID makes them useful pulse-takers and consensus builders on national issues.

KABATID's first public activity stemmed from strong citizen demands for responsibility in public service and fairness in elections. We initiated a public forum for candidates in a hotly contested local election, which enabled the candidates to sit down together and discuss issues rather than exchange derogatory personal comments. This exchange raised the electoral contest to a higher level.

Since then, KABATID has been invited to organize and participate in many activities on the national level. Members are occasionally guests on the radio talk show "Magtanong sa Pangulo" (Ask the president), and KABATID attended the Dialogue Series on the Senate Committee on Local Autonomy, which asked citizen groups to react to proposals by local officials to move towards greater decentralization of the nation's political power structure.

The Mindano Peace Commission asked KABATID to facilitate the workshop for the Mindano Regional Consultative Commission (RCC), held on 4-8 April 1988. The RCC's mission is to organize the first autonomous region in the Philippines, which those familiar with Philippine history will recognize as quite significant. The Muslims of Mindano have long felt exploited and neglected by the national government, and extremists continue to harass the citizens of that area. The creation of an RCC will help to change these people's attitude towards the government, and is the first step towards stability and peace in the region. We followed this up by, more recently, holding two forums in October and November of 1989 to discuss the Organic Act. The Organic Act spelled out the specific conditions the government had arrived at for autonomy in Muslim Mindanao, and the people were to vote YES or NO on the act in a plebiscite. Both the Muslim and the Christian women who attended agreed on the importance of a balanced, rational evaluation of the government's plans to create this autonomous region in order to make a decision responsive to the needs of the people. At the October forum, we asked Press Undersecretary G. Noel Tolentino to clarify the issues surrounding the plebiscite. Our members discussed all sides of the issue at both forums, and while there was much disagreement, in the end everyone had a much better understanding of the implications that a YES or a NO vote would have. The participants will thus be able to make an informed vote either way, which was KABATID's primary goal.

KABATID is still in the process of strengthening its organizational base and building its communications network, both of which are vital to a group in an island nation. There is a danger of spreading ourselves too thin as demands mount for our involvement in national affairs. However, issues such as education and the retention of the United States bases cannot wait. Amidst conflicting rhetoric from the extreme left and right, the people must be presented with balanced pictures so that they will be able to examine questions objectively.

Since its formal establishment in February 1988, KABATID has provided Filipino citizens with a voice to call for higher quality in public service. As the KABATID slogan states, "We get the government we demand and deserve." Our programs benefit both our own members and the citizenry at large. The women who join KABATID are able to develop their leadership skills, obtain constant support and assistance from a network of politically active women, and find a productive outlet for their desire to improve their communities and strengthen Filipino democracy. The country, in turn, profits from what has been a largely untapped resource in the "machismo society" of the Philippines. KABATID channels people power toward a reinforcement of grassroots democracy, rather than seeking to harness it to the self-serving ambitions of individual politicians or political parties.

I think Paz Fernandez, a member of KABATID-Cebu, said it best:

> The KABATID seminar was a turning point in my life when it dawned on me that we all can do something to effect a change, not only for one's self, but also for the country, no matter how small and insignificant it may be...
>
> It's so easy to get discouraged and depressed if we look around us...yet amid this darkness hovering over us, a glimmer of hope kindles and that's the KABATID spirit. A flicker of light can be seen. And this light is us—the peace-loving Filipinos. By joining our hands and working for peace, surely we can make a chain strong enough to bind this war enveloping us. No war is ever over until the human beings involved have ended the wars in their hearts.

Overall impact of citizen groups

What role did citizen groups play in the transition from dictatorship to democracy in the Philippines? How are these groups evolving to become part of the democratic culture of the country? What will be the continuing impact and role of citizen groups in the growth and development of a democratic culture? To arrive at a comprehensive view of the impact of citizen groups in general, I shall discuss the contributions of NAMFREL, EBJF, and KABATID in the context of the democratic culture.

Influence on the conduct of future elections

During the wide mobilization and effective organizational efforts of NAMFREL, people learned to monitor elections. Therefore, during the local elections in January 1988, people asked the NAMFREL

Secretariat whether they should mobilize again. The NAMFREL Secretariat itself decided not to poll watch actively in local elections, but it encouraged local chapters to do so if they wished.

In many areas of the country, concerned citizens closely observed the polling places to watch for any unusual incidents. NAMFREL volunteers reported on the conduct of the elections and asked questions of government officials on "Radio ng Bayan" (National Radio), and invited members of the Government Commission on Elections to lecture in public forums. In some hot spots where political fighting was intense, civic groups trained students and boy scouts in pollwatching. "Makialam!" (make it your responsibility to know) has been our watchword.

Political consciousness-raising

People now respond more quickly to calls for civic involvement. For example, when the newly restored government of President Corazon Aquino wanted the people to participate in the drafting of a new constitution, citizen interest and civic groups were tapped to help disseminate information on the potential provisions of the constitution.

As part of the team assembled by the Bishop's and Businessmen's Conference (a joint group of church and private business leaders formed in 1971), my friend Cynthia Dominguez and I went to Agusan (a remote province in the Southern Philippines) only to discover that no one had been told we were coming. We decided to attempt to hold a public forum anyway. As luck would have it, as we wandered through town we chanced upon a man fixing a tire who was wearing a NAMFREL T-shirt. On the strength of that T-shirt, Cynthia and I introduced ourselves. The man turned out to be a priest, Father Cesar Gotelo, and after the tire was fixed he enthusiastically escorted us from house to house to invite people to the meeting.

We were strangers at 9:30 in the morning, yet only three hours later a group of citizens—professionals, jeepney drivers, market vendors, NAMFREL volunteers, local officials, and women from the Legion of Mary, to name only a few—were gathered to discuss position papers on the new constitution. They called it a "snap meeting," but it had an important effect, as average citizens were enabled to express their views on the different provisions of the proposed constitution, particularly the issue of autonomy for Mindanao. This kind of quick response to the participatory process is a legacy of citizen movements. In marked contrast to previous years, it is now easier to get people together to meet, discuss ideas, and express opinions on political issues. The democratic practice of consensus building has become more familiar to us.

This is further illustrated in an editorial from the *Philippine Star* on 8 July 1988:

> The failure of last month's transport strike to mobilize the bulk of Metro Manila's public utility drivers highlighted a major shift in citizens' attitudes—from preference to use the parliament of the streets and radical solutions to availment of the institutionalized grievance mechanisms...
>
> Correspondingly, the bulk of the citizenry has shown signs of opting for peaceful and less adversarial postures in calling attention to problems and complaints and in articulating their positions on vital issues. This is because the citizenry knows that our democratic processes have been restored to handle grievances. Responsiveness by the government leadership and the silent but determined efforts by the private sector to help solve some of our country's endemic problems, whether structural or improvised, have helped undercut the lure of vitriolic language.

National recognition

The impact that citizen groups have made in the Philippines is reflected in two articles of the new constitution:

> *Article XIII; Section 15*: The State shall respect the role of independent people's organizations to enable the people to pursue and protect, within the democratic framework, their legitimate and collective interests and aspirations through peaceful and lawful means. [4]

Article XIII; Section 16: The right of the people and their organizations to effective and reasonable participation at all levels of social, political, and economic decision making shall not be abridged. The State shall by law facilitate the establishment of adequate consultative mechanisms.

The new constitution also includes a further step, in *Article VI; Section 5, Paragraph 2*:

For three consecutive terms after the ratification of this Constitution, one half of the seats allocated to party list representatives shall be filled, as provided by law, by selection or election from the labor, peasant, urban poor, indigenous cultural communities, women, youth, and such other sectors as may be provided by law, except the religious sector.

By providing support structures for government agencies, the people have already become a working part of government projects. They are represented on the "People's Economic Council"[5] of the Department of Trade and Industry, the "Peace and Order Council" of the Department of Local Government, and "Haribon," an environmental concern group working with the Department of Natural Resources, among others. But this is only the beginning of the long process of ensuring people power in government. As Congressman Florencio Abad observed in 1988, in sponsoring a measure to encourage the participation of citizens' organizations in government:

It is extremely urgent that we institutionalize people's power in the government, especially at the national level. In this way, we are able to harness positively and creatively the time and talent of our people. We are also able to share in political decision making and ensure that our policies and programs are in accord with the aspirations of our people.

The sooner we are able to institutionalize these avenues for participation, the stronger our government will be, and the better we will be able to resist any destabilizing efforts that seek to destroy the democratic processes which we have fought so long and hard for.[6]

Difficulties faced by citizen groups

An account of citizen groups will not be complete unless we also look at the problems they must contend with. As in any cataclysmic situation, where events happen so fast, there was not time to learn fully from the EDSA Revolution. Everyone who was a part of that experience—citizen groups, religious groups, the military, Marcos loyalists, leftists, etc.—has a story to tell. Now the government must devise quick responses to questions and needs that have accumulated over the past twenty years. How fast can we assimilate and reconcile?

Conservative congressmen called the measure to encourage the participation of citizens' organizations in government "Communistic" and feared that it would create "a government outside of the Aquino government."[7] One went so far as to label it the "handiwork of Lenin." They argued that there is no need for such representatives since the congressmen already speak on behalf of the people. The late Representative Elfren Sarte said that a proliferation of party-oriented lawmakers would only result in a "seriously fragmented lawmaking body," since these congressmen would always be at loggerheads with the rest over major issues.

Acting on these fears, the House suspended the appointments of four sector representatives who had already been sworn into office by President Aquino and it proposed to delete from the constitution the provisions allowing citizen groups to participate actively in government affairs. Since one of the sector appointees was a woman, many women's groups took up this issue. KABATID published letters and our officers were interviewed on the radio. We stressed that it was more than simply a women's issue—the issue was the importance of a faithful interpretation of the constitution.

Congressman Florencio Abad pointed out that the representatives' fears were largely unfounded and emphasized that the House would gain more credibility if it allowed people access to the political and economic mainstream. He accused the legislators of jealously guarding their turf and resisting changes that could improve and further democratize the existing political order.

The *Bayanihan* spirit

Citizen groups in the Philippines have begun to draw back the veil of mistrust and fear that had separated citizens from their government ever since the beginning of the Marcos era. In so doing, they have revived the ancient Filipino spirit of community—the *bayanihan* spirit. The literal translation of bayanihan, "people-carrying-a-house," describes a tradition of communal cooperation. In rural areas, where most houses are constructed of lightweight material like bamboo, a family that wants to move its residence to another locale may give a party for its friends and neighbors. At the end of the party, all those who have joined in the festivities pick up the family's house and carry it to the new site.

Today, the term "bayanihan" refers to any endeavor calling for the participation of the community. It means having a special responsibility to family, neighbors, and the community at large. Bayanihan signifies an indigenous appreciation of democracy that has been a Filipino tradition since the earliest Malay settlers arrived on Philippine shores.

Sixteen years of repression under the Marcos dictatorship have tested and proven the strength of the bayanihan spirit and the depth of our attachment to democracy. Despite having endured economic hardship, injustice, and bitter political strife, the Filipino people never gave up the hope that one day they would again be able to choose the kind of government they wanted. Now we must prove that we can work together to maintain a peaceful and democratic nation.

During the election campaign between Marcos and Cory Aquino, U.S. Assistant Secretary of State Paul Wolfowitz commented that the new president would need "the support of a people who believe in their democratic institutions, and thus themselves, if they are to address successfully the pressing national agenda. They will need skill, determination and courage." People power triumphed in 1986, and we must continue to nurture it today. The efforts of citizen organizations offer evidence that the skill, determination, and courage are still there. In the strength of these virtues lies the foundation of an enduring democratic Philippines. Mabuhay!

Notes

1. Speach delivered by Evelio Javier before the Rotary Club of Intramuros at the Manila Hotel, 29 March 1985. Javier had also been secretary-general of the Liberal Party.

2. Javier, Rotary Club, March 1985.

3. "Yap Debunks Mitra Claim that Congress Transfer Will Be Free," *Daily Globe*, 8 July 1988, p. 6. To date, no further action has been taken on the project due to budgetary constraints.

4. People's organizations are defined as associations of citizens with demonstrated capacity to promote the public interest and with identifiable leadership, membership and structure.

5. The People's Economic Council is a community-based organization mobilizing various resources in the community to define economic problems affecting the poor, potential entrepreneurs and other business groups.

6. Abad's measure is, at this writing, moving forward toward passage in revised form.

7. "Comment," *Manila Chronicle*, 28 May 1988, p. 4

Mobilizing for Democracy in Chile: The Crusade for Citizen Participation and Beyond

Monica Jimenez de Barros

IN MARCH 1988, when the Crusade for Citizen Participation was initiated, Chile had been ruled by an authoritarian military regime for fifteen years. From September of 1973 until 11 March 1981 all political power was concentrated in the hands of the military, who ruled without a proper legal system and under extra-constitutional states of emergency. At that time there came into effect a new constitution, written by the military junta and approved on 11 September 1980 in a suspicious plebiscite without appropriate electoral procedures or widespread dissemination of electoral information to the public. This constitution's transitional arrangements sanctioned the leadership of the authoritarian military regime until March of 1990 if it lost a popular plebiscite, and until 1997 if it won. It retained a powerful executive while creating a weak congress, and gave the Chief of the Armed Forces veto power over public policy.

The military regime placed executive power in the hands of the commander-in-chief of the army, General Augusto Pinochet Ugarte. A junta composed of four generals (the commanders-in-chief of the navy and the air force, the director general of the "Carabineros," and a general of the army, chosen by the executive) controlled the judicial and legislative powers.

This curious power distribution demonstrated the absence of a state of law in Chile. In addition, two writs of exception to the constitution had been in effect for over fifteen years—the State of Emergency and the Perturbation of the Interior Peace of the State. Both exceptions permitted the chief executive to ignore or limit the exercise of human rights such as the rights of assembly, free speech, organization, and unionization, as well as to arrest people without charge for five days, to prohibit entry into Chile, to expel anyone considered a danger to the state, and to impose internal exile for "security reasons." None of these measures, if taken in conformity with transitional article No. 24 of the constitution, could be appealed in the Tribunal of Justice.

I must also highlight the repression of the media—radio, newspapers, and especially television. The heavy-handed management of many means of communication, such as National Television, so strongly biased news reporting in favor of the government that it significantly contributed to the disoriented and misinformed population. The government continually harassed the dwindling number of journalists in the independent press by filing complaints against them in military tribunals, accusing them of offenses against the military. Such actions took advantage of the junta's laws restricting freedom of the press.

By March 1988, despite the impending plebiscite and potential elections, there were only five legally registered political parties. Of these five parties, three were supporters of the government. Seven other parties were going through the process of registration, including the principal parties of the opposition. Much of this reluctance was due to the military's continuous, fifteen-year disinformation campaign aimed at delegitimizing political parties, provoking much of the population to view the sudden appearance of political parties with distrust and fear.

The poorest groups in society (peasants and marginalized urban groups) were cowed in the face of the police and military authorities, who frequently used massive repression against these sectors. Another important part of the population, with a higher level of political sophistication, was imprisoned by their profound skepticism about the possibility of a clean plebiscite with minimal democratic guarantees while a military authoritarian government was in power. "History," they said, "shows that dictatorships only hold plebiscites in order to win them, utilizing all sorts of pressures in order to reach this objective." On the other hand, even groups that supported the government were worried. They wondered if confrontational situations like those from the time of Salvador Allende's government (which General Pinochet overthrew in 1973) would recur, or if institutional disorder might lead to a retrogression of Chile's economic development.

There was only one institution with a high level of credibility in Chile—the Catholic church. Its bishops, in their episcopal conferences, made frequent calls for understanding and nonviolence. In August 1987, the church's declaration "In Service of Peace" proclaimed the conditions under which they believed the plebiscite would have moral legitimacy. These conditions included widespread registration and participation, peaceful elections, and fair conduct by the government. However, few expected these conditions to prevail.

This was the sociopolitical atmosphere of March 1988. It was characterized by profound fear in vast sectors of the population, and by skepticism and disbelief that a plebiscite with even minimal democratic guarantees could be held given the widespread social frustration, demobilization, and deepset "immobility" of Chile. At this time the Crusade for Citizen Participation came into the public spotlight.

The mission of the crusade

I am a married woman with five children and a social worker with a Master's degree from The Catholic University of America. I have devoted my life to my family, to the University, and to the Catholic Church. My parents, their family, and the guides and scouts youth groups of Chile instilled in me a belief in social activism and an interest in politics, while my own family has given me great support and continual stimulation in my commitment to public service.

75

From my profession as a social worker and from the Catholic University (where I am at this time a full professor and a member of the Superior Council), I received my dedication and ability to educate formally and informally, and I teach both college students and working-class groups. From the Catholic church I received clear moral values and principles. I presided over the Justice and Peace Committee of the National Episcopate for more than ten years, and I was a member of the Pontifical Committee on Justice and Peace for five years.

Through these commitments I became acquainted with the violations of human rights in Chile, Latin America, and around the world. I came to understand the urgent necessity of working for peace, truth, and justice—those values that underpin a democratic system based on the dignity of the human being, the ideals of freedom and equality, the principle of promoting, respecting and defending human rights, and popular sovereignty expressed through free and competitive elections.

Because I was involved in family, university, and church activities, I was invited, along with thirteen other people, to found the Committee for Free Elections (CEL). CEL entered Chilean political life in March of 1988, committed to work in Chile for free elections for the presidency and congress. At that time, a law for popular and regulated voting had not been approved yet, nor had a precise date for the plebiscite been established. In this way the government managed to maintain political uncertainty by increasing the skepticism of both politicians and citizens.

The voter registration law had been in effect since February 1987, but only four-and-a-half million citizens had registered out of a potential voting population of over eight million. It was necessary, consequently, to register—before the announcement of the plebiscite— at least two million more in order to reach a total of 6 million, the figure established by the opposition politicians as enough to legitimize the plebiscite.

The fourteen members of CEL began to crisscross Chile. We knew that we needed to generate a big motivational campaign in order to register voters and educate them about their political rights. We hoped that our activities would foster ties among an atomized people, freeing them from fear in a way that would allow them to participate nonviolently in the new political processes.

I was chosen by the group to design our program of socio-political change. I accepted the idea with difficulty and almost with fear, since I felt this task to be beyond my capacities. While constructing the plan, I sought aid from people who had had similar experiences, in Chile as well as in Argentina and the United States. The Interamerican Institute of Human Rights (IIDH) and The Interamerican Center for Electoral Advice and Promotion (CAPEL), with headquarters in San José, Costa Rica were especially helpful. In the United States I was inspired by the League of Women Voters, as well as by other university, church, and union programs devoted to promoting citizen participation. These people guide me and still provide me with new ideas.

The Crusade for Citizen Participation (the public name for the civil education campaign) represents the collective work of many Chilean men and women, of our friends in North and South America, and of cooperating agencies. Its story intertwines with my personal life, as my family has continually inspired me to work from a nonpartisan perspective for the education of all citizens.

I do not want to attribute to myself the merits of the Crusade; on the contrary, the true beauty of the campaign was that it included hundreds of people who at that time did not have other ways to participate in the advancement of Chilean democracy. Today, on the other hand, Chile is different. Chileans with political aspirations can work with a freely elected president, 47 senators, and 120 members of the Lower House of the National Congress.

What needed to be done in our country was not at all clear when we began the Crusade. If we decided to accept the plebiscite as a democratic, free decision, it could mean endorsing an act of public opinion that did not reach minimal guarantees of democratic legitimacy and, therefore, would endorse the persistence of the authoritarian regime until 1997. There were political parties that,

77

even at that moment, were asking people to abstain from voter registration. Yet we opted to run this risk and face the democratic challenge.

Our mission would be expressed publicly and, therefore, had to be clearly neutral. We could not support either the YES or the NO option (which meant, respectively, to support or not support the regime's candidate).

Under these conditions, we believed our campaign for "voter education" should have the following objectives:

• To ensure that all Chileans older than eighteen registered to vote.

• To motivate the people so that registered Chileans actually voted, and to ensure that they could do so conscientiously and with sufficient information.

• To urge civilian control of the plebiscite in order to guarantee its fairness and transparency.

In order to formulate rapidly an educational program for voters, we needed to find an already existing institution with legal status to help us. There was no time to create our own organization; for this reason, it seemed sensible to us to accept the collaboration of CIVITAS, the social foundation of the church, which agreed to shelter the Crusade for Citizen Participation.

We also presented the Crusade's program to IIDH and to its specialized arm, CAPEL, which assumed the responsibility of supervising our program. This organization gave us a series of technical, administrative, and methodological suggestions that perfected our program and made its execution possible in those difficult times. The Crusade, in turn, allowed IIDH and CAPEL to broaden their experience and technical capacity for sponsoring similar programs and projects in other Latin American countries.

Our executive organizational structure included the Directorate of the Program, the Executive Committee, the Executive Directorate and the Representative and Supervisor from CAPEL. We then created three departments beneath the executive level in order to implement territorial activities: the Department of Operations, the Department of Communications and Public Relations, and the Department of Administration and Finance.

In order to cover the entire nation, given the unique geographic features of Chile, the Department of Operations created a base of regional supervisors who organized groups of volunteers from the different "comunas" of the country (the "comuna" is the smallest geographic unit in which the Crusade worked, since this unit corresponded to the lowest level of political-administrative division). We worked officially in 105 "comunas" of the country, most of which had more than 45,000 voters each.

One of the first tasks that the Crusade undertook was to recruit communal coordinators who would be trained in three-day seminars. Our initial goal was to recruit 315 Level I volunteers. We trained more than 600 people in these seminars, and to our surprise and pleasure 500 became active volunteers.

We taught these seminars with the idea of "coaching coaches." We gave the prospective volunteers intensive information on democracy and the plebiscite while also training them in interactive teaching methodologies so that, in turn, these newly trained people could teach others. In this way it was feasible to reach a large proportion of the voting-age population in a short period of time. Our seminars were fundamentally participatory, using group activities for reflection, discussion, and decision-making, which allowed people's creativity to unfold. The participants in our initial three-day seminars lived together during that time, which created cohesion between the volunteers. During the seminars there were not only formal learning activities (discussions and group work) but also symbolic events at night such as the ceremony of compromise, bonfires and cultural presentations. All of these were designed to generate a group mystique, to produce integration and cohesion, and to increase the participants' confidence in order to enable them to undertake their mission.

This contingent of volunteers, selected from throughout the country, came to constitute the backbone of the Crusade's work. They promised to advocate peace, participation and tolerance, and committed themselves to political non-partisanship and community service.

Educating and inspiring these first volunteers was not easy. We needed to teach them in detail what the "Crusade" was and what it aspired to be. Many politically partisan people were not ready to do objective, neutral work and preferred, for good reasons, to work in favor of either the YES or NO option. This is the principal reason why not all of the people who attended the seminars took on the commitment of working for the Crusade.

Also, there was a great deal of fear. To recognize publicly the legitimacy of both options at stake was frowned upon by the government, whose propaganda and pressure in support of the YES option was suffocating long before the junta nominated General Pinochet as its candidate.

The first group of volunteers began the imperative task of creating groups in their respective "comunas" by recruiting and training Level II volunteers. Two or three communal coordinators would carry out seminars in their respective "comunas," employing the training that they received in the Level I seminars, so that by the time that our third and fourth first-level seminars were in progress, the communal coordinators trained in the first two seminars were already running their own Level II seminars.

These Level II seminars were only a day long, but their content was similar to the Level I seminars. They each ended with a solemn promise by the new Crusaders to perform non-partisan volunteer work to promote the civic education of Chileans. We organized 517 Level II seminars, at which 7,352 people (surpassing our initial goal of 7,200) committed themselves to the Crusade. This contingent of volunteers, together with the communal coordinators, formed 150 "communal groups."

Creating and mobilizing these communal groups was not an easy task; we had to overcome many diverse obstacles. In some "comunas" we could count on the support of the Church; in others, the local authorities exerted pressure on us, attempting to impede our work by denying us permits for meetings, detaining volunteers, and making threats. Nevertheless, these and other difficulties simply enriched our learning experiences. As the communal groups were forced to focus on solving their problems while serving their communities, they became more cohesive and thus worked more efficiently. In the end, the communal groups were not only active in their own "comunas," as we had originally planned, but were also able to help "comunas" without other communal groups or where the communal groups were not particularly strong. Because of this we managed ultimately to work in 211 "comunas."

As the communal groups began working with the citizenry, a surge of demand arose for more specialized advice on the legal aspects of the plebiscite. In response to this, we founded a group of 60 legal counselors (advanced or terminal law students), who were integrated into the Crusade as volunteers and worked in Santiago, Concepción and Valparaíso.

But the principal educational problem we had to face was the need to disseminate rapidly civic education while at the same time preserving its quality. The subjects that Chileans needed to learn— which had not been a part of our everyday lives for fifteen years— included the nature of a rule of law, the fundamentals of democracy and human rights (especially civil and political rights), and the characteristics of democratic elections. These were foreign subjects, especially to those less than thirty years old. This plebiscite would be the first opportunity for 40 percent of the population to cast a ballot.

Our mass educational strategy was the responsibility of our pedagogical division (a subsidiary of our Department of Operations). The pedagogical division's principal functions were to produce written materials (such as booklets and flyers) and to supervise seminars. They produced numerous publications, the first and most important of which was the *Volunteer's Notebook*, a thirty-three-page handbook that contained basic information about voter registration, political regimes, and the legal and political ramifications of the plebiscite, of which we published 220,000 copies. We then produced a 165-page book, *Civic Fundamentals for My Vote*, by the constitutionalist Humberto Nogueira Alcal. It included all of the legal and electoral information necessary to understand the plebiscite and its significance, and was written especially for the Crusade. The 15,000 copies of this work served as a significant reference aid for our volunteers.

We prepared and printed several thousand booklets designed for the civic education of both volunteers and regular citizens. The topics they covered included the Crusade for Citizen Participation; the volunteers of the Crusade; serving peace: conditions for the plebiscite; contemporary political regimes; the legal and political options in the plebiscite; our organization in the comunas; planning action in the comunas; planning residential canvassing; and registering for elections.

In addition to these materials, we printed millions of flyers for mass distribution, which called for voter registration, informed people about the options of the plebiscite and its significance, and asked for peaceful behavior on the day of the plebiscite.

We knew, though, that in order to reach several million people and to gain widespread credibility, volunteers and pamphlets were not enough. The Crusade had to be covered in the mass media. With this goal in mind the Communications Department created a strategy that would, through the media, promote voter registration, agitate for civilian control of the plebiscite, and encourage people to become well-informed and conscientious citizens.

We solicited bids from different public relations agencies. The agency we eventually chose proposed a communication strategy centered on television, with radio only secondary. We bought several time slots, especially in September, in order to present information related to the voting itself. Nevertheless, many television stations set very high advertising prices, and others, such as the state's channel, would not accept the Crusade's advertising at all. The channel of The Catholic University censored a part of our first, animated advertising spot which encouraged potential voters to register.

This obliged us to redesign our strategy, giving higher priority to radio. We publicized our activities through sixty AM and FM stations that covered the entire nation. We also broadcast a periodic five-minute mini-program entitled "United from North to South" on the two most important national networks, "Chilena" and "Cooperativa." These mini-programs enabled us to communicate en masse with members of the Crusade while also announcing our activities to the general public. At the same time, these paid public announcements opened the door to broadcasts about the Crusade at the initiative of the stations themselves.

The Crusade did not ignore the press, either. We ran advertisements about the plebiscite in several papers and eventually became a part of the news itself, gaining more coverage little by little. Of course, not all of the news was positive. In fact, especially in the beginning, the Crusade received strong criticism from the official press (*El Mercurio* and *La Nación*), directed against our first flyers. These reports intended to present the Crusade as a partisan of the "No" option. This disinformation campaign was orchestrated by a government agency, the National Direction of Social Communication (DINACOS). Nevertheless, we overcame this initial difficulty and managed step by step to earn a place in the national news.

The other specific problem the Crusade had to confront—one that illustrates the hostility certain political sectors felt towards us—was the appearance of thousands and thousands of booklets distributed anonymously in Valparaíso, Talca and Concepción. These apocryphal booklets copied the style of our flyers, but advocated the YES option, that is, yes to retaining Pinochet in power. We had to organize conferences in order to denounce these forgeries.

Action in the community

While our communal groups were being formed, we initiated different kinds of communal and territorial activities. All of them aimed to stimulate voter registration, to provide information about the plebiscite, and to call for active participation in the election.

The "hand-to-hand" was a personal distribution of flyers about voter registration and the plebiscite by volunteers through home visits and in public areas such as supermarkets and churches. Through this program, we contacted thousands of citizens. We also carried out simulated voting in all of the "comunas," with thousands of citizens participating. People practiced voting with facsimiles of the ballot and became acquainted with the procedures that would be followed on the day of the plebiscite. In addition, we held video presentations, forums, and cultural activities in those "comunas" where the volunteers were better organized and had more extensive facilities.

To demonstrate to the citizenry that constructive political dialogue was possible, we held forums with various political leaders. People learned to discuss ideas without violence and, at the same time, to enlighten others about issues in dispute. We held them in universities, with unions, and in poor suburban areas, especially in the sixty days prior to the plebiscite on 5 October.

However, these methods often did not reach younger people (eighteen to thirty), the segment of the population most reluctant to participate in the electoral process. So, we organized a series of concerts with well-known national artists and required the spectators to be registered to vote. We announced these concerts and their requirement on the radio well in advance, using prestigious, nationally recognized disk jockeys. During the concerts we asked our audiences to vote conscientiously and to become informed about the plebiscite, and tried to clear up some of their fears and skepticism. We held these concerts in seventeen cities nationwide, and 60,000 young people attended.

In June and July of 1988, as the date of the plebiscite began to draw near, a climate of growing tension and violence was developing. This was understandable, given the confrontational character that the injunction to vote YES or NO represented. The Crusade thus initiated a campaign for peace with the motto "Let's work in peace, for peace," in conjunction with the pleas of the Catholic Church.

During this campaign, our communal groups organized a variety of activities. Its culmination was an ambitious project—hugging Santiago in a massive Human Chain for Peace. We also undertook this project in six other important Chilean cities. On the 25 September, with a wide audience and the support of the press and celebrities, thousands of Chileans took to the streets to demonstrate publicly their longing for peace. In Santiago alone one hundred thousand people wrapped themselves around a 68 km long circular highway, united in a gesture without precedent in our country.

Through this campaign for peace, the Crusade helped to create a peaceful environment for carrying out the plebiscite and to promote public behavior epitomizing the values of peace and democracy. Amazingly, the abstention rate in the plebiscite was only 2.4 percent, the smallest in Chilean history. The Crusade's impact was recognized by political leaders of different parties and, in a more private way, even by the agents of Pinochet's government. Politicians, citizens, the press and religious leaders all pointed out the important and vital role that the Crusade played in Chile's successful plebiscite of 5 October 1988.

Our route to success

An element that helps to explain our success lies in the universal force of the values that the Crusade promotes: respect for humanity, truth, justice, liberty and peace. In short, we wanted to restore the Chilean dignity that had been trampled upon during fifteen years of authoritarian governments.

These same values are explicit in our advertising and educational materials, in our volunteers' testimony, in our campaigns, and in our interviews. Gradually, we have introduced them into the press and into group and institutional conversations. Step by step these values have been disseminated, and they have displaced the widespread feelings of skepticism and fear. Our work of presenting and promoting these values has deepened dedication to them on the part of the citizenry. This helps to explain why, on the day of the plebiscite, Chileans displayed exemplary democratic behavior.

These democratic values allowed for the appearance of another element that also explains the success of the Crusade: unity in diversity. The geographic conditions of the "comunas" in which the Crusade worked were extremely varied. The socioeconomic status and ideological and religious beliefs of our volunteer coordinators were diverse, too, and the people we addressed came from all walks of life. Surmounting the potential problems of this great heterogeneity, Chileans grew together through their common adherence and active dedication to these values.

Flexibility, promoted at all levels of our organization, enhanced our ability to work on multiple campaigns simultaneously. Flexibility made it possible to maintain unity in purpose yet diversity in action within our communal groups. We reached compromises between autonomy of action for territorial groups, which facilitated creativity, and unity in objectives and goals. Indeed, given the need we discovered to adapt our activities to the unique demands of each "comuna," flexibility was a necessary virtue. It compelled us to initiate a variety of new and original activities, such as mock voting, public forums, legal counselling, special events such as the concerts, and strongly symbolic cultural events such as the chain of peace.

For the entire group that worked in the Crusade, it was an unforgettable and very rich human experience. The essence of that experience is reflected in the motto of PARTICIPA, the institution of which I am the executive director and which continues to educate for democracy: Democracy is Everybody's Responsibility. Everyone—men and women, civilians and soldiers, partisans or not—must assume responsibility for the democratic future of Chile. This means embracing in full the politics of alliances, agreements, negotiations, and dialogue.

PARTICIPA

The plebiscite of 5 October 1988, in which the Chilean people rejected General Pinochet's bid for an additional eight-year presidential term, was a turning point for Chile. At this time, Participa emerged as an outgrowth of the Crusade for Citizen Participation. I established Participa in 1989 as a grassroots organization devoted to the discussion of political issues in Chile and the promotion of civic participation at all levels of Chilean politics. We have undertaken five major programs since our inception with ideas drawn from our experience in the Crusade. These include voter education, training pollwatchers, press seminars encouraging nonpartisan reporting, candidate debates at several levels, and seminars on family and democracy at the Catholic University of Chile. We received financial help from both the U.S. Agency for International Development and the National Endowment for Democracy to start these programs.

The first meeting we organized focused on women and democracy. Over 300 women attended the debate, sitting in mixed groups of ten around thirty tables, each with its own moderator from the Institute Carlos Casanueva. These women were candidates, wives of candidates, government, media, and opposition workers, and Participa volunteers. In the first part of the meeting we played a game called "Knowing Chilean Women," and in the second we held a panel discussion with several women candidates. These presentations and the subsequent question-and-answer periods were transmitted by "Radio Gigante."

Following this successful program, Participa organized nine debates for senatorial candidates. Each one was coordinated by our volunteers, primarily young people involved in the political process for the first time who subsequently became a dedicated group aiding us in future Participa activities. Over forty candidates took part in the debates, representing the entire spectrum of political parties. The audiences, totalling more than 7,000 people, were the largest debate audiences in Santiago; including radio coverage, we estimate that over half a million people heard some portion of these debates. Both the candidates and the audiences evaluated the debates favorably, stating that they were well organized and that the candidates had all been able to express their opinions thoroughly.

Then, in September 1989, we ran a seminar at the San Joaquin campus of the Catholic University of Chile on "Citizens, the Family, and Their Role in a Democracy" attended by approximately eighty people. We discussed public health care, housing, employment and social security. The seminar received television and news coverage and reflected a wide range of perspectives on each theme, ensuring extensive debate. We successfully accomplished our goals of organizing discussion groups representing different political perspectives, examining the social and political roles of the family, promoting the University School of Social Work, and gaining experience in running seminars.

Participa has been able to directly influence the open discussion of ideas during the presidential, senatorial, and deputy campaigns, and our impact on Chilean society has been extensive. Building upon the foundation of the Crusade for Citizen Participation, we have developed a volunteer network of over 900 people in all of Chile's major regions while a core of fifteen coordinators based in Santiago travels throughout Chile to instruct and inspire the volunteers. The activities of both Participa and the Crusade have become models for other autonomous groups interested in becoming involved in the political process, because we draw our strength from our ideas and our organizational ability to put these ideas to work effectively.

The challenge ahead

Chile's free elections were a step along the road to democracy. The next few years will be very important for our future. During this period we must expand and consolidate the democratic base of our society. This is the grand goal of the transition, in the face of Latin American upheaval and a new world in which there have been profound technical, communication, economic and ecological changes and the traditional ideological responses do not fit anymore. It is necessary to renew our politics, and for this we need to develop an open, tolerant citizenry ready for dialogue and understanding with others. This will be a difficult road for Chile, but I have faith that our people will recognize the value of a democratic, pluralistic society. Now that we have gained a toehold, we must never slip again.

Translated by Marzena Grzegorczyk and Dane Johnson

Fostering Democratic Culture in Central America: The Experience of Libro Libre

Xavier Zavala Cuadra

CENTRAL AMERICA IS a region of political contradictions. Costa Rica, Latin America's oldest democracy, was until recently surrounded by the totalitarian dictatorship of the Sandinistas to the north and the narco-military dictatorship of General Noriega to the south.

The Panamanian people had chosen new authorities in internationally supervised elections, but General Noriega annulled these elections. The Organization of American States tried to solve the problem but was thoroughly inoperative. U.S. forces invaded Panama and removed the dictator. Those who had been elected in the previous elections were sworn in. But what comes next is the rebuilding of a nation. New laws have to be passed, the old army and police forces have to be cleaned up and reorganized, new institutions have to be created. As Vice President Ricardo Arias said recently, it is a government *for the transition* toward democracy.

In Nicaragua the people voted the Sandinistas out, but since, in the mind of the Sandinistas, elections do not give or take away legitimacy, they are doing their best to stay in power through an ambiguous and equivocal accord with the new government. The true and full transfer of power has not yet taken place. Perhaps it will. I am referring mainly to the subjective aspect of the transfer of power: the clear internal recognition that somebody else has been invested by the people with the power to govern.

In Guatemala, El Salvador, and Honduras truly elected presidents have been replaced at the end of their constitutional periods by also truly elected presidents. However, these three countries still suffer from Marxist-Leninist guerrillas who kill people, wreck the economy, and simultaneously attend endless rounds of talks with government representatives in different capitals of the world, where they present themselves as enlightened and peace-loving citizens. These guerrillas knew they would never attain power in their nations through electoral processes and therefore they resorted to violence. Having failed to obtain a military victory, they now explore the path of internationally publicized negotiations where their unspoken weighty argument is their capacity to continue to destabilize their countries: If the whole government is no longer a feasible objective, a slice of it could be a beginning. But guerrillas are not the only problem. Old political flaws keep reappearing. For example, in Guatemala and El Salvador, Christian Democratic political parties won the elections in the mid-1980s because they presented themselves to the electorate as a promising new breed of politicians, but the electorate soon became disenchanted again by widespread allegations of corruption, human rights violations attributed mainly to the military, and the absence of practical solutions to economic ills. The Christian Democrats lost the following elections.

In summary, with the exception of Costa Rica, in Central America we have tentative democracies with a feeble and flawed traditional democratic culture. I analyze that traditional political culture later in this essay, but first I should highlight the siege it has endured over the past years. The collapse of the Communist ideology in Eastern Europe and the Soviet Union will likely weaken and even halt this offensive in the future, but it is too soon to forget about it. Furthermore, the Marxist-Leninist's persistent effort to change the political culture of a region could be an example for democrats who disregard the world of ideas, beliefs, and values.

The Marxist-Leninist cultural offensive

Most people know of the Marxist-Leninist guerilla movements in

Central America, but they may not know that guerrilla warfare is only one of many political tactics used by Marxist-Leninist forces. They resorted to armed force only after the ground had been prepared through changes in the political values of many young students and a good number of other citizens. This cultural manipulation long preceded armed attacks and was therefore the most ominous social tool that the pro-Communist forces used against democracy.

This does not mean that violence against democracy in Central America should be disregarded. Armed challenges continue to exist and must be faced with realism and courage. However, these armed Marxist-Leninist groups camouflage themselves in democratic vocabulary and rely on a powerful propaganda network in the United States, Europe and Latin America to polish their image, justify their existence, and promote their cause.

The subtle cultural subversion of democracy represents a greater danger than the armed threat precisely because it tends to pass ignored or underestimated. The long-term damage it might do often does not seem to merit our attention now—the theory of present value is as relevant in politics as in economics, and a Marxist textbook draws less attention than a march in the streets or a terrorist bombing. And ironically, by taking advantage of the democratic principle of freedom of thought, the cultural subversion of democracy is rendered perfectly acceptable. Throughout Central America, this silent attack has seeded anti-democratic, pro-Communist ideas and values.

This strategy aimed to gradually mold a new system of beliefs and values in Central America. For example, they teach that not everyone has an equal right to influence and direct the country's politics; citizens should follow an enlightened vanguard of new men. To believe that the future depends on free choice is antiquated bourgeois thought; rational, scientific minds seek and accept the destiny of history. Capitalism exploits the people's work and wealth; an economy in the hands of the state brings justice and equality. The ills of the Third World and of Central America result from North American imperialism; to try to resolve them without destroying that empire is naive. The United States is evil; socialism will solve our problems.

This war, which does not make noise and does not make the news, has been waged primarily in educational institutions such as universities, teacher-training schools, and journalism schools. Thus, the chosen targets have been future professionals, future school teachers, and future public opinion shapers.

Let me expand a bit on the case of the universities. Thirty years ago, all Central American universities were national and autonomous, run with public funds transferred obligatorily by the governments but free from government interference in administrative and academic matters. In practice this meant that the administration and faculty were guaranteed administrative and academic freedom as well as financial security. The Communists, taking advantage of this situation, planned and implemented a powerful attack against democracy. The plan was facilitated by the introduction of General Studies Programs in all universities at the end of the 1950s.

The General Studies Programs were supposedly established to provide the university student with a complete, balanced humanist education. The idea was that it did not make sense for a young law student to be prepared only for the legal profession, or for an engineering student to study only engineering. Two years of humanities became obligatory for all new students before they could begin their professional studies.

However, carefully placed professors were prepared to deviate the program from humanism to indoctrination. The new required courses in philosophy, history, culture, and social studies became powerful instruments which turned young university students against democracy and towards the Soviet model of government. For example, there was in democratic Costa Rica a national university that officially established as a specific objective of some General Studies courses that the student should "become conscious of economic and cultural dependency...and endorse the Cuban revolution as an option for the overcoming of underdevelopment and dependency."

Important weapons in this war of ideas and values have been

the textbooks and assigned reading materials presented to the students. Publishing houses have been set up to supply the necessary books. The types of texts on sale at the bookstore of the National University of Panama were revealing—in April 1987 more than 80 percent of the titles in the political science section were released by pro-Soviet publishing houses; in history, more than 50 percent; in economics, 39 percent.

In short, pro-Communist forces in Central America planned the takeover of our educational centers many years ago. As a result, for at least thirty years a good percentage of our youth have passed unaware through a battleground against democracy where the bullets were ideas and values, and the weapons were professors, educational programs, and books.

One of the first things the Sandinistas did when they took power in Nicaragua was to abolish the autonomy of the universities: what was supposed to protect higher education from undue government interference became obsolete when the government was the enlightened vanguard of the people. But as soon as they were defeated in the February 1990 elections, the Sandinistas reinstated the autonomy of universities so that they could reintrench themselves there.

A flawed traditional democratic culture

This carefully planned, long-term cultural assault is not the only problem democracy faces in the realm of political culture in Central America. With the exception of Costa Rica, men and women who favor democracy and even fight for it have within themselves anti-democratic attitudes inherited from our own traditional political culture.

Before examining these counterproductive elements, it is important to stress that our traditional political culture is basically pro-democratic. Since the days of independence, Central Americans have believed that democracy is the most desirable form of government. Although we have not enjoyed prolonged democratic experiences, we have constantly striven to achieve democracy.

Our attempts were, obviously, insufficient as they usually resulted in new dictatorships and civil wars, but the fact that we have kept on trying means that the ideal of democracy is somehow solidly grounded in the political culture of Central Americans. Our sad history of failure has not dissuaded us from democracy. I like to insist on this because, during the years of Sandinista dictatorship in Nicaragua, Nicaraguans heard many visiting observers from Europe and the United States cynically questioning our demands for democracy "now" when, according to them, we never cared for it in the past. Indeed, the defeat of the Sandinistas at the ballot box in February 1990 was a stunning demonstration of our underlying belief in the value of a democratic system.

However, if by political culture we mean a people's predominant beliefs, attitudes, values, ideals, sentiments and evaluations about the political system of their country and the role of the self in that system, I find a clear inconsistency in the political culture of Central America. When I reflect on our ideas about politics, on what we write and say about politics, and on our political behavior, I am struck by what at first seemed to me an inexplicable contradiction— we think that democracy is a good way to be governed, but not a good way to govern. How is that possible?

Our political culture contains a veiled double standard. We use one standard to evaluate the system in general, but another to evaluate the role of the self in that system; one to judge the performance of others and another to judge the performance of the self. This cultural ambivalence explains the paradox—we believe in democracy, but we are not democrats.

The intellectual acceptance of democracy does not make one a democrat. A democrat is a person who habitually acts according to the ideas, beliefs, and values of democracy. Except for the Costa Ricans, Central Americans have not possessed, nor cultivated, the active virtues of democracy. It is one thing to recognize intellectually that peaceful social life rests upon compromises, but it is another to be ready and willing to give in. Our history shows that we are not tolerant; we are not willing to compromise, nor to accept defeat. Our history shows that we have tried to build democratic institutions as if a working democracy could rest on structure, but a working democracy is fundamentally a way of behaving, a way of life. Our democratic institutions resemble convents with all the specifications of convents, with cloisters and cells, but filled with "monks" who do not behave according to the virtues of poverty, chastity, and obedience. That "convent" is not a true convent. True monks make a true convent. True democrats make a true democracy.

When the Nicaraguan "contras" became famous and the in-fighting among their leadership was exposed in the media, perhaps with the purpose of presenting them as insincere in their claim to fight for democracy, what was being exposed was just another case of intellectual acceptance of democracy combined with undemocratic behavior. It often happens in democratic political parties, in democratic trade-unions, and in all sorts of democratic organizations in Central America.

A second anti-democratic tendency in our traditional political culture is our conception of an omnipotent state. To be more precise, those who govern tend to regard the powers of the state as limitless. The great nineteenth century Argentine jurist and writer, Juan Bautista Alberdi, best described this characteristic of our political culture:

...one of the deepest roots of our modern tyrannies in South America is the Greco-Roman notion of patriotism and the Nation....The Nation, as the Greeks and Romans understood it, was...an institution of a religious and holy origin and character, equivalent to what is today the Church....Its power was omnipotent and limitless with respect to the individuals who formed it....The Nation, thus understood, was and had to be the negation of individual freedom....The individual man owed himself completely to the Nation; he owed it his soul, his person, his will, his fortune, his life, his family, his honor. To hold back from the Nation any of these things was to betray it, was an act of impiety. According to these ideas, patriotism was not only reconcilable with the most absolute despotism, but also one and the same with it.[1]

For Alberdi, Christianity represented a great revolution in this political culture, with its notion of the dignity and autonomy of each human being. But in spite of it, the Greco-Roman concept of state omnipotence has filtered down through the ages. During the monarchies, "the omnipotence of the kings took the place of the omnipotence of the Nation."[2] When the Latin American republics declared their independence from the King of Spain, the republics freed themselves from foreign control but the individuals who belonged to these republics continued to define themselves as dependents of the state, thereby subordinating themselves to those who personified the powers and interests of the state.

Alberdi observed, however, that the United States inherited a different political culture from the Anglo Saxon countries, where "the sacred freedom of the individual limited the freedom of the nation, where man's rights held equal weight with the nation's rights, and, if the State was freed from the foreigner, individuals were no less so from the State."[3]

Jose Ortega y Gasset, the great Spanish philosopher of this century, agrees with Alberdi and adds that the Germanic feudal lords were the ones who taught Europe that individual freedom takes precedence over law and state, lamenting that Spain received very little of this influence. The ancient democracies of Athens and Rome taught us that the collectivity of citizens should exercise public power, but the Germanic feudal lords asked what the limits of public power should be. The answer, Europe learned, is that whether power is exercised by an autocrat or by the people, it cannot be absolute because the individual has rights which supersede those of the state. This transcendental lesson did not permeate Spain nor, consequently, reach us in Latin America.

These are, in my understanding, the principal characteristics of the Central American political culture. Our firmly rooted belief that democracy is the most desirable form of government is undeniably a powerful positive force, but it is encumbered and restrained by the hidden double standard which allows permissive self-evaluation and explains the lack of democratic virtues in everyday behavior, as well as by our tendency to conceive of the state as omnipotent, a temptation experienced by almost all those among us who hold political power.

Interest groups and the promotion of democracy

When a region's political culture has these characteristics, civic groups are needed to reinforce what is positive and check what is negative. If we do not encourage those in power to recognize the limitations of that power, it is unlikely that they will take the initiative to inform citizens that state power should have limits and that they should exercise and demand their individual rights. A variety of organizations promoting democratic culture, particularly if they are private, allow for a multiplicity of ideas, interpretations, and dialogues which facilitate the development of pluralistic thinking.

Unfortunately, however, in underdeveloped countries interest groups dedicated to promoting democratic culture are like the Andean condor or the Central American quetzal—hard to find. On almost any street corner in Central America, there are people interested in buying or selling, planting or harvesting, and even politicians trying to win support. However, you do not often come across people interested in promoting culture. I do not think this is the case in developed nations. It certainly is not in the United States, where the country's moral-cultural dimension is dynamic, effervescent, and has its own varied and innovative institutions. But a Central American who realizes that improving people's culture is to his personal benefit is an unusual phenomenon, and an understanding of the importance of political culture in general is practically non-existent.

Central America differs from the developed countries in another respect as well. I said that in the latter the activities and institutions of the nation's moral-cultural dimension are strong and varied. They also enjoy a certain amount of respect. This is not the case in our region. In Central America there is little understanding between the political and economic sectors and the moral-cultural sector.

This means that private civic organizations dedicated to fostering democratic culture in Central America will be working, if not against the stream, then certainly by its wayside. For example, one can obtain financial support to improve a country's economic infrastructure, but it becomes more difficult to finance cultural development, and it is almost impossible to obtain funding for the development of political culture.

The struggle of Libro Libre

Libro Libre is a private civic organization contributing to the promotion of democratic culture in Central America primarily by publishing and distributing books and organizing seminars and lectures. It grew out of the conviction that democracy cannot survive and mature unless citizens understand both the value of democracy and the responsibilities that democracy entails. As a Central American, I applied this belief to my region, where our political culture suffers from internal handicaps and external threats. I conceived of Libro Libre as an organization entirely dedicated to civic education in democracy.

Libro Libre is a non-profit organization because we have learned that political culture projects such as ours can only survive through grants. The recipients of our products and services do not value them because they do not believe they are necessary and, consequently, are not willing to pay for them. The minute importance ascribed to democratic education in aspiring democracies is the clearest sign that it is needed. If Libro Libre could be a regular profit-making business through promoting democratic culture in Central America, half the battle would already have been won.

Libro Libre has gone through several metamorphoses. It started as a journal in Nicaragua, *Revista del Pensamiento Centroamericano*. First published in 1960, it devotes itself primarily to Central American culture, economics, politics, history and art. It encourages Central Americans to write about themselves and their culture and also opens their horizons to foreign opinions. The *Revista*, for the reasons just mentioned, could not finance itself. Therefore its cost was assumed by a profit-making business, an advertising agency. The agency provided the magazine with office facilities, secretaries and designers, and paid its printing bills. Our motivations for publishing this magazine inevitably led to thoughts of expansion, of promoting research, publishing books, building libraries, and organizing lectures and conferences. These plans were beyond the abilities of my small advertising agency, so we set up a nonprofit organization in anticipation of future projects that would require outside grants—the Center for Cultural Research and Activities.

We schemed and planned, but very little could actually be done; a booklet here, a pamphlet there, a few painting exhibits, an occasional lecture—nothing of substance except the journal, which continued to be subsidized by the advertising agency. But we strongly wanted to publish books. It seemed so natural to have a publishing house grow around a journal, as a forest can grow around a tree. We tried a scheme combining funds from writers with funds from the Center, in which both individual writers and the Center would buy shares of a profit-oriented publishing house, Writers United, Inc., but the plan fell through.

After the Sandinistas took over the government of Nicaragua, Central America entered into a new period where democracy was threatened as it had never been before, and where the future of Central America depended upon how well we defended freedom and democracy. The publishing house became more urgent than ever and thus we made a bolder effort to establish it. I went to Costa Rica several times to take the necessary legal steps to found the Asociacion Libro Libre. I chose Costa Rica rather than Nicaragua in order to avoid Sandinista censorship and frustrating shortages of paper, ink, and plates, and also to have at hand the intellectual and cultural resources of that democratic nation. For funding, we had planned to knock on the doors of democratic governments and U.S. private foundations. After several trips to the United States in search of funds, I learned, to my surprise, that neither governmental nor private sources had been established to finance programs like Libro Libre. The United States had institutions to promote economic and social development abroad but nothing for political development.

When the National Endowment for Democracy was later created by the United States Congress, we received a grant from the labor institute[4] connected to the Endowment. The U.S. Congress at last had recognized the importance of an institution to promote democracy, but the recognition was fearful and timid—the National Endowment for Democracy was not adequately funded.

By the end of 1990 Libro Libre had published one hundred and ten titles; five of them in a second edition and one in a third. In a series we call *Classics of Democracy*, we have presented the political and ethical writings of De Tocqueville, Montesquieu, Kant, Jefferson, Lincoln, Thomas Paine, Adam Smith, Lord Acton, Ortega y Gasset; we also published in that series a selection of the Federalists Papers. In another series named *Democracy Today*, we publish political books addressed to more contemporary issues. Other series are concerned with history, anthropology, economics, religion, literature, etc.

We distribute our books in Central America including Panama. Sales have risen every year. In 1985 we sold 7,941 copies; by 1990, our sales had more than doubled, to 19,566. Our retail prices are below unit cost in order to make our books available to a larger segment of the population. It would help to have a small office in each Central American country in order to promote and better place our books in countries other than Costa Rica, as we had planned, but we have not been able to get the funds to open them.

To prepare future book publishing projects, we studied the textbook situation in Central American universities. We wanted to know what books were used in order to pinpoint the areas with an urgent need for democratic textbooks. The study also tried to locate respected, democratically oriented professors in those universities who might be willing to be future textbook authors. Unfortunately, we have not been able to continue with this project because we lacked sufficient funds.

In 1986 Libro Libre took over the journal I used to publish in Managua, the *Revista*. The strangling of the private economy by the Sandinistas forced me to close down the advertising agency. More or less at the same time, the security police seized an entire issue of the *Revista* while it was still at the printers and ordered that all future issues be submitted to the government for censorship. Libro Libre has since kept the pace, publishing four issues a year.

But books and magazines do not occupy all our time, as there are other things we must do in order to contribute effectively to the democratic culture of Central America. We have, for example, organized two large seminars for Central American intellectuals and politicians. One focused on international responsibilities towards finding solutions to the Central American crisis. The other conference examined the contributions of the American continent to democracy. In addition, Libro Libre has promoted the creation of the Group for Freedom and Democracy in Central America. Composed of two respected citizens from each Central American nation, the Group has met several times, examined the progress of freedom and democracy in the area and recommended actions.

We have also put together a small library and archive on the Central American crisis, the Communist threat, and the efforts to defend freedom and democracy. This library is open to all those who want to use it.

There remain many difficulties to overcome. Some of our problems come from the economy of the region: for example, central banks must approve the use of dollars for imports, but there are priorities for the small amount of available dollars in each country, and books are not high on the list. On top of this, the persistent devaluation of the colon (Costa Rican currency) increases our paper and printing costs, and our efforts to reduce these costs have been overcome by inflation.

Other problems have been closely tied to our region's political tribulations. For example, a person in charge of distributing our books in Panama left that country as a result of political unrest during the rule of General Noriega. Our books were not allowed to enter Nicaragua while the Sandinistas ruled—even courtesy copies sent to Cardinal Obando y Bravo were returned to our office with a postal stamp saying "address unknown." We had to devise different ways to introduce them.

Another set of difficulties and limitations results from our cultural quirks. One of them is a ridiculous provincialism; Costa Rican writers are well known within Costa Rica but not outside of Costa Rica, and the same can be said about writers in each Central American country. *Revista del Pensamiento Centroamericano* is the only democratic international journal in the area. This provincialism limits the market for some of our books and does not allow us to take advantage of economies of scale. We are also limited by poor reading habits all over Central America, with similar results.

And finally, again, we are limited by the lack of disposable funds. The German Konrad Adenauer Foundation has more funds available just for Latin America (and in practice only for Christian Democratic political projects), than the U.S. National Endowment for Democracy has for the whole world and for the whole spectrum of democratic thought. Private foundations are less interested in international projects, particularly if they deal with political culture. What this means is that things that should be done are not done, and there are many worthwhile services we have been unable to perform.

A general overview, however, is unquestionably encouraging. Bookstores changed first: pro-Communist books were no longer the only ones carried. Then, a subtle shift of mental fashions began to take place: intellectuals, writers, professors, students, became less reserved and cautious, and more affirmative in their reasoning in favor of freedom and democracy; they began to realize they did not have to talk leftist to be in vogue. The results of elections in Guatemala, El Salvador and Honduras plainly revealed the leanings and persuasions of the popular majorities in spite of the discourses, intimidations and threats from the guerrilla camp. Later came the news of prodigious changes in Eastern Europe and in the Soviet Union itself. Finally, came the Nicaraguans' repudiation of the Sandinistas in an electoral process that had been tailored to provide the Sandinistas with a title of legitimacy.

There are setbacks, but the new wind keeps blowing. People talk about the need to educate for democracy. Very little is being done in that direction but the talk is a step forward. An evolutionary democratic revolution is taking place in the area. I like to imagine that Libro Libre is contributing to it with its mere presence, with its books and journals, with its book shows, seminars and panel discussions.

If we look ahead, our main challenge will be to build on all fronts: new attitudes, new habits of conduct, new institutions.

Notes

1. Juan Bautista Alberdi, *La Omnipotencia del Estado* (Guatemala: Centro de Estudios Economico-Sociales, 1986), pp. 1-2.

2. Ibid., p. 2.

3. Ibid., p. 4.

4. The labor institute grant was approved thanks to the efforts of William Doherty, Director of the American Institute for Free Labor Development, who also had volunteered, some time earlier, a ten thousand dollar donation from his Institute to get us started. Enthusiastic from the beginning about our project, Dr. William Douglas, who was at that time teaching political science at Georgetown University and at AIFLD, and later was a member of the group that studied the feasibility and structure of the NED, devoted much time and effort to introduce Libro Libre to as many people and foundations as possible.

The Civil Liberties Organization and the Struggle for Human Rights and Democracy in Nigeria

Clement Nwanko

> The cell is a smelling house. There is a corridor about four feet six inches across and some 24 feet long that separates the two rows of cages...In that 24 feet of corridor, there are 51 of us. In each of the cages meant for two inmates there are at least twelve while each of the single cages hold between three and four detainees. The last two cages have been converted to toilets (and) the entire corridor is lit by two candles. Several of the detainees are completely naked and lying stretched out as best they can along the corridor...I sit down and examine the faces. Each face looks like a ghost, each person looks like a character from Michael Jackson's 'Thriller.' The only difference is that these people are real whereas Jackson's characters are the products of fiction.
>
> —Dr. Festus Iyayi, detained without trial in Nigeria in July 1988.

WHEN NIGERIA BECAME an independent nation in 1960, it built its new political system upon the twin principles of respect for human rights and majority rule through electoral democracy. The Independence constitution and later the 1963 Republican constitution both included a bill of rights in line with the Universal Declaration of Human Rights (1948), protecting life, dignity, liberty, fair hearing, privacy, freedom of thought, conscience, and religion, freedom of the press, freedom of peaceful assembly, freedom of movement and freedom from discrimination. The constitution also gave Nigerians the right to choose their own government leaders through free elections. These rights were the ultimate prizes that Nigerians won from the British colonialists who ruled the country until 1960.

Yet Nigeria plummeted from these high hopes for democracy and prosperity ignited by independence into despondence and helplessness in less than six years. Our democracy had been subverted; vote rigging, government intimidation of voters, arrests of political opponents, and the politicization of the judiciary became rampant. The politicians had betrayed the people and the nation was in crisis. The eyes of the world were turned on us. What had happened to Africa's great chance for a model democracy? What could be done? Which way Nigeria?

Nigerians were not to wonder for long. The military seized power in a bloody coup in January 1966 and democratic ideals were thrown overboard. Parliament was dissolved and the military assumed the executive and legislative powers; laws, decrees and edicts could now be made without the people's consent. Some provisions of the constitution were suspended while others were modified. Human rights and freedoms were trampled upon.

The military government enacted several decrees that were completely contradictory to accepted international standards of democratic practice. State Security (Detention of Persons) Decree No. 3 of February 1966 named twelve persons, mostly politicians, to be detained for six months. Nine similar decrees enabled the administration to detain forty-one other people without trial between February and July 1966. The Suppression of Disorder Decree No. 4 dealt with civil disturbances and established Nigeria's first military tribunal, composed of seven officers of the rank of Major and above. Another decree—the Armed Forces and Police (Special Powers) Decree No. 24—empowered the Inspector General of Police and the Chief of Staff of the Armed Forces to order the arrest and detention of "troublemakers." A common feature of most of these decrees was the suspension of the fundamental rights provisions of the constitution, thus preventing the courts from using the constitution as a defense against actions carried out under these decrees.

Assuming power in a July 1966 "counter-coup" and ruling for nine years (including the two-and-a-half year civil war), General Yakubu Gowon entrenched these provisions and added new ones. The Robbery and Firearms (Special Provisions) Decree No. 47 of 1970 established military tribunals to deal with armed robbery. Decisions of this tribunal were not subject to judicial appeal. The military governors of the states were the only "appellate" authorities empowered to confirm or annul decisions of the tribunals. A 1974 amendment, however, provided for direct appeals to the highest court of the land, the Supreme Court.

Although they seized power in August 1975 pledging to implement the transition to democracy that General Gowon had indefinitely postponed, Generals Murtala Muhammed and Olusegun Obasanjo did not differ dramatically in their treatment of human rights. Legislative and executive functions were still vested in the Supreme Military Council while arbitrary arrests and infringements of rights and freedoms continued. Indeed, the 1979 Public Security (Detention of Persons) Decree No. 1 provided for a renewable detention period of three months for acts deemed a threat to public security, and this decree was not challengeable in a court of law. Yet Obasanjo—who became head of state upon the assassination of Murtala Muhammed in February 1976—faithfully implemented the military's program for democratic transition, which culminated with the inauguration of Nigeria's Second Republic in October 1979.

The return to elected, civilian rule brought an end to the various military decrees that justified continuous and intolerable violations of freedom. The 1979 constitution fully restored the original bill of rights, and lawmaking power was once again vested in the people's legislature under constitutional restraints. Although human rights problems did occur under the new government, the courts provided a useful check and prevented many offenses. This period witnessed intense judicial activism and initiative in the protection of constitutional rights. For example, the courts were able to nullify the Ministry of Internal Affairs' decision to deport Alhaji Shugaba Darman, an opposition majority leader in the Borno State legislature, after the Ministry alleged that he was not Nigerian. This period was shortlived, however. Constitutional government —already disfigured by electoral fraud, corruption, and abuse of power—was overthrown by a military coup in December 1983. The new military government headed by Major-General Muhammadu Buhari suspended or modified important provisions of the bill of rights and the constitution. For example, law enforcement agents were no longer required to charge suspects with a specific crime within twenty-four hours of their arrest. The military enacted a familiar set of repressive decrees as well. The now infamous State Security (Detention of Persons) Decree No. 2 of 1984 authorized the Chief of Staff (the number two officer in the government), if he is "satisfied that any person is or recently has been concerned in acts prejudicial to State security or has contributed to the economic adversity of the nation, or in the preparation of instigation of such acts, and that by reason thereof it is necessary to exercise control over him, he may by order in writing direct that the person be detained..." for a period of three months. Decree No. 3 on "The Recovery of Public Property" reversed the time-honored legal principle of innocence until proven guilty. Decree No. 4, "Public Officers (Protection against False Accusation)," permitted the imprisonment of journalists charged with publishing articles that embarrassed the government or its officials, regardless of their truth. Two journalists, Tunde Thompson and Nduka Irabor of the *Guardian* newspapers, were convicted and sentenced to prison under this decree. The Miscellaneous Offenses Decree prescribed the death penalty for those convicted of a wide range of crimes such as drug trafficking and damage to certain public property. Violating another fundamental principle of natural justice, this decree was given retroactive effect and three previously detained Nigerians were executed for drug trafficking.

Again, none of these decrees could be challenged in a court of law for contravening any of the remaining fundamental human rights provisions in the ravaged 1979 constitution. Many workers were forced to quit their jobs and ordinary citizens, journalists and government critics were arrested and jailed indiscriminately, some under forged detention orders. A climate of repression set in that was unprecedented, even given Nigeria's previous experiences with military rule. People lived in fear and the atmosphere was tense.

In August 1985 General Buhari's government was overthrown by General Ibrahim Babangida. The new government promised respect for human rights and a return to civilian rule in 1990 (later extended to 1992). The Public Officers (Protection against False Publications) Decree No. 4 was repealed and the two journalists who had been convicted under the decree in 1984 were pardoned. The government released hundreds of detainees across the country while some other repressive decrees underwent amendment in response to public criticism.

Unfortunately, this shift in attitude proved to be only temporary. The Babangida administration soon lost patience with its critics. The State Security Detention Decree was amended to increase the maximum detention period from three months to six months and two additional government officials—the inspector general of Police and the minister of Internal Affairs—became authorized to issue detention orders. The National Association of Nigerian Students (the principal student organization in the country) was banned, *Newswatch* magazine was proscribed for six months, and journalists and other government critics were constantly being arrested and detained. It was in this atmosphere that the Civil Liberties Organization was born.

The civil liberties organization

The CLO was founded on 15 October 1987, by Olisa Agbakoba and myself. Olisa Agbakoba, then thirty-four, had already been a lawyer for nine years and had just set up his own law chambers in Lagos. Admitted to the Nigerian Bar in 1979, he obtained a Masters degree in Law in 1980 from the London School of Economics. He spent time as a Research Fellow at the prestigious Nigerian Institute of International Affairs before commencing full-time legal practice. Between 1981 and 1982, Agbakoba was involved in the Committee of Concerned Citizens, a group set up in 1981 to strengthen democratic consideration of the political and social issues affecting the country.

I graduated from the University of Nigeria, Nsukka, in 1984 and qualified as a lawyer in 1985. Ironically, it was during the repressive regime of Buhari that I spent my year in the government-sponsored National Youth Service Corps (a year of national service required of all college graduates in Nigeria) working for the Nigerian Legal Aid Council. During this time I became involved in prison affairs at the Ijebu-Ode prison in Ogun State. My duties at the Council included regular prison visits, during which I sought out people who had been awaiting trial in the hope of rendering them legal assistance. However, the Legal Aid program was restricted to three criminal offenses: murder, manslaughter, and common assault. People awaiting trial for armed robbery, petty theft, grievous assault, and other such crimes were not eligible for help. I was deeply touched by the plight of these detainees, and I was able to assist many of them before I left the Council in 1986, following the completion of my national service.

Agbakoba and I met for the first time in December 1986 through a mutual friend, and when he opened his new law practice in July 1987 I joined him as an associate partner. Three months later I walked into his office and told him of my experiences with the Legal Aid Council and of the inhuman conditions in which the inmates at Ijebu-Ode prison were held. I wanted to form an association to help these prisoners and to advance the cause of human rights in Nigeria. Agbakoba shared my concerns, and together we created the Civil Liberties Organization (CLO). We designated the law office as the operational base of our organization.

We were then faced with the daunting task of outlining the program and vision of the CLO. I took on the responsibility of drafting a constitution. We agreed that CLO membership should be open to anyone who was genuinely interested in promoting and protecting human rights in Nigeria in accordance with universal standards, such as those envisaged in the Universal Declaration of Human Rights. But where to find members? Agbakoba pointed out that we should try to recruit journalists, and the first person that came to mind was Abdul Oroh, a correspondent with the *Vanguard* newspaper in Lagos. We invited him to a meeting the next day, and he was immediately willing to help us. He listened to our plans and then began to encourage other journalists to join. We had put the ball in motion. During this early period, Agbakoba was chosen to act as president and I as National Secretary.

We decided that our first duty was to investigate conditions in the prisons. Fortuitously, Oroh had just written a story about a man named Joseph Odogu in Ikoyi prison who had been detained on suspicion of robbery for eight years without trial. This became our starting point. I visited him at the prison to decide on the feasibility of legal action on his behalf. Odogu was, naturally, excited to hear about this new group which was ready to fight for his release. He told me about the general conditions and his personal ordeal in the poorly maintained and overcrowded prison. During his eight-years' detention he had lost his business, his wife and children had left him, and his mother had died. He also told me about Kanwa Kyauta, his cellmate and a former lance-corporal in the Nigerian Army, who had been in prison for ten years without trial.

In November 1987 we filed a legal action seeking Odogu's release and published a "Mini Report on Human Conditions in Ikoyi Prison." We sent copies of the report to the prison authorities and the Federal Ministry of Justice, and it attracted some media attention. Then, shortly after the report was published, we filed another legal action on behalf of Kanwa Kyauta who had become half blind and mentally unstable as a result of his long detention in the dark, crowded, unventilated prison.

We were successful on both counts. Odogu was released from prison in April 1988 with a compensation of only N2,000 (about $250), while Kyauta was released in June 1988. In neither instance did the police or prosecuting authorities possess any evidence linking either of the former inmates to a crime. Soon after Kyauta regained his freedom we took action to try to officially reinstate him into the army, which had declared him AWOL while he was in prison. We were able to get him formally discharged and the Army agreed to pay him his cumulative back pay of N47,000. These two cases provided the impetus for several more legal actions filed by the CLO on behalf of thousands of prisoners who had been awaiting trial for one to ten years.

We held the first general meeting of the CLO on 23 January 1988 in Agbakoba's chambers at Apapa, Lagos. Twenty-seven people, primarily lawyers and journalists, attended. At this meeting we approved a working constitution for the CLO and elected a Board of Trustees composed of Olisa Agbakoba, Abdul Oroh and myself. The meeting also confirmed the positions of Agbakoba and myself as president and national secretary, respectively, and approved nominations for other offices that had been created by the constitution. These officials became our Board of Governors. The meeting adjourned with an agreement to attempt to recruit more members into our fold and to expand our activities throughout all of Nigeria's twenty-one states and into its institutions of higher learning.

All of our members paid admission dues of twenty naira (about three dollars) and an annual subscription fee of one hundred naira (about fifteen dollars), but this was not a substantial amount of money. Agbakoba (in particular) and I bore most of the financial expenses required to run the CLO's activities. At first we used this money primarily to file legal actions, conduct investigations, and carry out administrative tasks. Agbakoba's office facilities were at our disposal, so fortunately we did not need to pay staff and phone bills.

Our main activities at this point involved filing legal actions on behalf of long-term detainees held in various prisons and on daily monitoring of, and public commentary on, various human rights developments in Nigeria. Our next legal moves included a class action suit filed on 20 May 1988 on behalf of seventy inmates of Ikoyi prison who had been there from three to ten years. Thirty-five of these prisoners were subsequently released between June and September 1989, while the remaining thirty-five were put on trial within the same period. We initiated another class action suit on behalf of fifty-one detainees held at Kirikiri prison under the draconian

State Security (Detention of Persons) Decree No. 2. Twenty-five of them have since been released while the case affecting the rest is pending at the court of appeal.

Most of our first cases were initiated through information we received from individual prison staff members who, although delighted with our work, could not associate with us openly for fear of losing their jobs. Soon, however, the prisoners themselves became familiar with us and now eagerly supply information to us directly. Our response to the cases brought to our attention is usually determined by the extent of violations of rights in each instance and, of course, by the nature of the case.

In August 1988 we got involved in a most sensitive assignment —investigating the existence of a detention center allegedly maintained on Ita-Oko Island off the coast of Nigeria. It started with a letter we received from Nobel Laureate Professor Wole Soyinka. He passed on a complaint he had received from an inmate of the island, and asked us if we could look into the matter. We questioned various people, but no one appeared to be aware of this island. We extended our inquiries to the police and various arms of the state security structure but made little progress, as the few people who appeared to have heard of the island were not willing to talk. The mystery deepened and we became more curious. After about two weeks we had pieced together enough information to persuade us to take a trip to the island. Three CLO officials—Agbakoba, Ms. Amma Ogan (our publicity director and then editor of the *Sunday Guardian* newspapers), and I—set out on the journey.

We hired a boat at Epe shores on the Lagos coast and had a turbulent four-hour sail on the Atlantic Ocean before we landed at the quays of the detention island. Access to the island appeared almost impossible, as it was securely guarded by anti-riot policemen. Yet a stroke of luck got us through these precautions and we were able to interview Segun Adebajo, the inmate who had written the letter to Professor Soyinka.

Adebajo, a former teacher, had been picked up on suspicion of bank-draft forgery in Lagos in April 1987 and soon afterwards was flown to Ita-Oko. He told us of his harsh life of detention on the island, which was ridden with dangerous marine life, reptiles, and insects. Once an inmate who attempted to escape from the island was eaten alive by sharks and his bones swept ashore by the waves. The prisoners on the island were provided with raw food which they cooked on their own. They lived a boring, monotonous life —no books to read, no games or sports facilities, and no means of receiving information from the outside world. In 1984 there had been 500 inmates held on the island, but by the time of our visit in 1985 this had been reduced to 19. They were mostly common criminals, although we heard a rumor that two were Army officers.

We quickly returned to Lagos where Amma Ogan wrote an article about the island for the *Guardian* newspapers. The story was published on 18 September 1988 and elicited widespread public outrage. A stinging *Guardian* editorial drew an analogy between Ita-Oko and South Africa's notorious Robben Island.

We filed a legal action in the Lagos High Court asking for the release of Segun Adebajo and for a declaration that the use of the island as a prison was illegal. The court gave us leave to pursue the action. The federal government was very embarrassed by all of the publicity and controversy, and responded by immediately moving the inmates of the island into regular police cells. Segun Adebajo and the others were released on bail by the court early in October 1988.

Our attention then shifted back to Ikoyi prison in Lagos. Our investigations revealed that fifty-four inmates of the prison had died between January and June 1988, a period of only six months. We forwarded these details to the prison authorities, the Minister of Justice, and the press. Three of Nigeria's leading privately owned dailies, the *National Concord*, *The Punch*, and the *Nigerian Tribune*, all published editorial comments on the report, and we received an audience with the Minister of Justice to discuss the situation. At the end of our meeting the Minister promised to set up a panel to look into the matter, but he never did so.

We followed up on our investigation the next year and, in October of 1989, released a report on the conditions in Ikoyi prison. Little had changed—between January and September of 1989, 78 prisoners had died. Ikoyi prison, originally built for a maximum of 800 inmates, now holds 2,400. Sanitary conditions are appalling. The food is poor and scarce, and many prisoners awaiting trial must rely on external support from family and friends to survive. They are permitted to leave their cramped cells for only an hour each day, there are no resident doctors, and most inmates are not permitted any form of recreation. Considering these very typical Nigerian prison conditions, one wonders how any of the prisoners are able to survive at all. In June of 1989 we filed a suit against the Minister of Internal Affairs on behalf of 1,000 inmates of Ikoyi prison, seeking an order that "the Ikoyi prison be closed forthwith on grounds that the living conditions therein render the prison unfit for human habitation." The case is still pending in court.

On 10 December 1988, as a part of the activities marking the fortieth anniversary of the Universal Declaration of Human Rights, the CLO published a report on "Violations of Human Rights in Nigeria" which covered the use of banning and proscription orders, dissolution of labor union executive committees, deportation, suspensions, and harassment of journalists and dissenters. The founder of Amnesty International, Peter Benenson, officially released the report at the CLO offices. While introducing the report, Mr. Benenson stated that since the CLO could publish such a report in Nigeria, the human rights situation must not be that bad.

About six weeks later four CLO officials (Agbakoba, Emmanuel Erakpotobor, Mike Ozekhome, and myself) were arrested because of the contents of the report, which were alleged to be subversive and consequently to have the potential to disrupt President Babangida's transition program. Over the subsequent five days, the police, from the Central Investigation Bureau in Lagos, interrogated us, obtained statements from us, and took our photographs and fingerprints. They prepared formal charges of subversion against us and informed us that we were to be the first Nigerians arraigned before the Transition to Civil Rule military tribunal. However, the charges were dropped on the fifth day after we met with the inspector general of police, Muhammadu Gambo, who asked us to consider the problems of the police force and the government and to exercise restraint in our actions.

What I believe was a further attempt to deter the work of the CLO occurred in March 1989 when I was attacked near my home in Lagos by about fifteen armed bandits as I was on my way to the Lagos International Airport to board a flight for the United States. My assailants stabbed me several times in the head and stole my passport, tickets, and other travel documents. I was hospitalized, and my head was sewn up and plastered. I may have been lucky, however; events surrounding the incident indicate that the attackers probably intended to kill me. Strangely, the "bandits" left my baggage, but called my office the next morning to inform me that they had all the stolen documents in their possession. These documents were never recovered.

Such harassment and violence have never affected our determination and resolve. Our CLO activities were so numerous and had reached such a frantic pace by the first quarter of 1988 that we opened an independent headquarters (separate from Agbakoba's law chambers) in June. The new office, on the Lagos mainland, gave us more room to operate so that we could increase our members' ability to participate in CLO activities. Soon afterwards, we opened offices in Calabar and Enugu to service four eastern states, and later developed plans to open two more offices in Jos and Ijebu-Ode, to service northern and western states, respectively.

Funding, however, has always greatly limited us. The central CLO office remains inadequately equipped; we began with a little furniture and an electric typewriter. At first we could hire only two staff members, a typist/receptionist and a clerical assistant, but we have since been able to add three more part-time staff workers. I myself regularly spent eighty percent of my working hours voluntarily serving the organization. Because of financial constraints, some of our projects have yet to be executed while others are carried out on a very modest scale. Our financial support has come primarily from membership fees and donations, which have not gone far. We have had to survive on a shoestring, taxing our personal resources and time to insure the success of our organization.

Although the government is suspicious of us, it has been quietly responsive to some of our criticisms. The CLO's statement in July 1989 on behalf of the one thousand inmates of Ikoyi prison led to the creation of a prison monitoring panel that has been working (albeit slowly) to improve the prison system. Our legal actions on behalf of a journalist, Tony Ukpong, and a Liberian drug suspect, Betty Mason-Chidebe, who were both being detained under the State Security Detention Decree, led to their release by the government even before their cases were concluded in court. When we raised doubts in September 1989 about whether or not the Ita-Oko Detention Island had actually been closed, the government responded by opening up the facility for media inspection. And, in the heat of public demand for the abrogation of the State Security Detention Decree in September 1989, the police sought our help in determining the exact number of people detained under the obnoxious law.

Late in 1989 the CLO released its 1989 "Report on Human Rights in Nigeria," and in 1990 it published a special report on the Kirikiri maximum security prison. The "Report on Human Rights" documents again the government's many abuses of Decree Number Two and the horrific conditions in which detainees are kept. We chronicled, for instance, the imprisonment without charge of activist Chief Gani Fawehinmi for four months in a remote prison in the north. Chief Fawehinmi—who sought to prosecute two high-ranking state security officials for the murder of the crusading editor, Dele Giwa—told *Newswatch* afterwards: "They physically tortured me...there is no way air is going to penetrate this cell...the windows are so tiny...It was extremely hot and sweat was just dropping from my head as if there was rain...I was not allowed to read newspapers or anything at all." He was held in solitary confinement during the entire time and had no bed, mattress or blanket in his cell. The report also told of the many indiscriminate police killings, brutalities and arrests during the year. As Olisa Agbakoba bluntly stated in his introduction, "1989 has been a terrible year for human rights in Nigeria."

The CLO's report on the state of Kirikiri prison, released in March 1990, also revealed unimaginable yet hauntingly familiar conditions. Godwin Uwagbale, who was detained there without trial for two and a half years until we were able to secure his release in 1989, described the prison to us:

> The medical care...is appalling. It's true people die often as a result of improper medication, lack of food, and the congestion in the cells. For example, the southern block known as block one measures eight feet by eight feet with no less than sixteen people in one cell. You sleep for few hours at night; wake up for another person to take his turn, and you don't dare sleep in the daytime. Almost everyone on this block has skin diseases, cough, swollen stomachs with skeleton legs, hands, and chest, heads like robots. Quote me, it is worse than a war front or the apartheid South Africa or those people in Ethiopia.

Our investigations showed that the prison is holding almost 72 percent more inmates than it was designed for, allowing sleeping prisoners only one foot of space. The poorly ventilated cells are infested with bedbugs, lice, mosquitoes, and cockroaches, and disease is rampant. Only two Youth Corps doctors and two nurses are assigned to handle the 1,645 inmates at Kirikiri, and yet they also care for inmates in three other prisons, bringing the total number of prisoners that these four people are responsible for to almost 8,000. The government provides a paltry N3.50 each day to feed each prisoner. The inmates are not allowed reading material, radio, or television, and thus are completely ignorant of events in the outside world. Given these horrifying statistics, it is not surprising that an average of three people die each week in Kirikiri. Most of them are prisoners still awaiting trial.

In eerie contrast to this high death rate are the great number of prisoners on Kirikiri's death row who have been languishing in these squalid conditions for up to twenty years. One of them, Felix Ogunmola, has gone mad. The prisoners say that they are treated

118

as though they were already dead, making those who are actually executed the lucky ones. In response to this, the CLO made a special plea for international support to press for the release of these condemned men.

The report concludes that "the fundamental aim of [the prison] is the *dehumanization* of inmates...this makes it imperative for us to raise the question of the purpose of this penitentiary...to this end, we suggest the setting up of a Standing Committee on Nigerian Prisons." This committee would inspect the prisons, publish its findings, and advise the government on ways to make conditions more humane. This along with more immediate measures rectifying the most egregious prison injustices will improve the life of inmates— yet only a nationwide prison referendum can solve the fundamental problems.

The imperative of freedom

We have only begun our long, uphill battle to improve the human rights situation in Nigeria, but, on the whole, the CLO has been able to accomplish much in the brief period of its existence. To what do we owe our success?

The first reason lies in our strong commitment and dedication to the cause of freedom and human dignity. In spite of serious risks to our lives and livelihoods, we have remained unswayed. We have also been able to introduce a high level of professionalism into our work. Because human rights is a very sensitive topic in Nigeria, we felt that we could achieve significant results and draw attention to human rights abuses by using the legal process, which we know well. But, importantly, we make a great effort to avoid giving an impression of opposition to the government. Our criticisms are usually focused on particular issues and we suggest concrete ways in which the problems can be rectified. In addition, in a country like Nigeria with diverse peoples, religions, interests and affiliations, our success has also been enhanced by our ability to remain independent from all forms of political, ideological, religious, or sectoral affiliations.

The support we have received from the media has helped us significantly. Besides publicizing our activities, the media have served as an avenue for us to reach out to the Nigerian people and make them aware of their rights. Press coverage of our activity draws attention to particular problems and wrongs. But even more so, media reports on our court challenges to government abuses show the public that when the actions of the government are illegal, they have the right to resist. Media coverage of the CLO has included our court cases, our various human rights and prison reports, and our criticisms of specific government practices. The recent Kirikiri report was given extensive publicity, with newspapers shouting such headlines as "Living in a Hell Hole" and "Slammer of Horrors." Newspapers have manifested further support for us by publishing numerous editorials on our activities, and in September 1989 Nigeria's leading newsmagazine, *Newswatch*, featured the CLO as its cover story. The international news media have also spread information about our work. The British Broadcasting Corporation and the Voice of America have constantly reported our activities to the world, and in June 1989 the *New York Times* published an extensive report on our efforts to improve the human rights situation in Nigeria. We achieved further international recognition when I was honored with a "Human Rights Monitor Award" by the international group Human Rights Watch for my "outstanding contributions to the development of human rights in Nigeria."

Our contacts with various international human rights groups have been very useful to us. For four weeks in March and April 1989, Agbakoba, Amma Ogan, and I met with several human rights groups in the United States, including Amnesty International, the American Civil Liberties Union, the American Bar Association, Human Rights Watch/Africa Watch, the Lawyers Committee for Human Rights, the National Democratic Institute for International Affairs, and Defense for Children International. During this trip we toured some U.S. prisons and jails, which provided us with a standard for assessing Nigeria's prisons, widely considered to be inhuman. The CLO in turn has hosted visiting human rights activists and groups in Nigeria, such as a delegation from Amnesty International in September 1988 and Marcel Zwarmborne, the Deputy Director of the Netherlands Institute of Human Rights, in October 1989. These visits have been excellent opportunities for us to exchange ideas and opinions on human rights issues.

Looking back to 15 October 1987 when the CLO was founded, I must confess that I am amazed by the tremendous influence we have been able to exert on the human rights front in Nigeria. However, our success so far has not been aided by the benevolence or magnanimity of the Nigerian military government. All in all, it has been clear that the government does not appreciate our activities—they would prefer we exist as impotent testimony to an apparent tolerance for dissent. Indeed, on the fortieth anniversary of the Universal Declaration of Human Rights the Minister of External Affairs stated publicly that the CLO reflected the government's respect for human rights. Governments all over the world, and especially those in developing countries (no matter how dictatorial and repressive they may be) are very conscious of their public image. This situation provides an insurance of some sorts for us, yet experience has taught me to be prepared at all times for an arrest or an invitation to "chat" with security men.

We also had to deal with the initial suspicion that greeted us from many sides. Some people were skeptical about our motives, especially since there had been no effective human rights group in Nigeria beforehand. Several ulterior motives—including political ones—were ascribed to us. But we have been able to overcome these suspicions and skepticisms and have established the CLO as a very potent and legitimate force in the democratic struggle in Nigeria.

The constitutional rights program
In most developing countries where democracy has been subverted or imperiled by dictatorships, active and independent groups like the CLO are of great importance. In the absence of strong and organized opposition parties, such groups serve as watchdogs on government's actions and policies that affect the fundamental rights

and freedoms of the people. With the need to establish a multiplicity of Nigerian human rights groups in mind, in February 1990 I left the CLO and founded the Constitutional Rights Project.

The CRP is distinct from the CLO in that its focus will be an active campaign to promote the independence of the judiciary in Nigeria. It is a staff-run, non-membership organization with a supervising board of directors. It too focuses on class action suits and litigation, but has an added dimension: The CRP publishes a quarterly journal, the *Constitutional Rights Journal*, which seeks to promote and protect respect for human rights and the rule of law in Nigeria. This is the first human rights publication of its kind in Nigeria, providing detailed investigations and analyses of human rights problems, publishing articles by human rights experts, examining legislation and its human rights implications, and discussing the human rights experiences of other African countries. The CRP will also publish newsletters and reports as the need arises. The CRP complements the CLO and other Nigerian human rights groups and will work closely in association with them in order to achieve greater freedom and awareness in Nigerian society. It will not become involved in partisan politics of any kind in order to render unbiased service towards improving the human rights situation in our country.

Democracy, development and human rights

The developing world faces serious threats to democracy. Many human rights abuses occur and persist either because government officials and security agents do not know the legal extent of their powers or, in some cases, because people are ignorant of their rights and do not understand how they can respond to official abuses. Yet even when they are aware of their options, people living in acute poverty are usually too busy trying to survive and feed themselves to take the time, resources, and risks to fight violations of their rights.

Governments in developing countries use the excuse of "salvaging" the national economy to suppress the people's rights and freedoms because they perceive democracy as antithetical to economic development, and thus they subvert and marginalize those institutions of state which promote or protect freedom. They render the judiciary ineffective and spineless by making the tenures of judges insecure and denying the judiciary financial independence, while trade unions, mass organizations, students, journalists, academics, social critics, and other potential sources of "trouble" are silenced either through proscriptions, arrests or detentions. Needless to say, in these nations human rights organizations like the CLO and the CRP are especially crucial. They constitute the last line of defense of human liberty.

Human rights are no longer seen as an exclusively domestic issue, but increasingly as an issue of legitimate international concern. True development can only occur in an atmosphere of peace, freedom, and justice, and unless these values prevail in a country, other nations should be wary of giving its government their aid and support. The recent upheavals in Eastern Europe that brought down entrenched dictatorial regimes raise hope that the developing world, including Africa, can move from authoritarian to democratic forms of government. International efforts must be made to support independent democratic institutions in developing countries in order to hasten the pace of democratic reforms.

A look at some of Africa's dictatorships reveals that their leaders depend greatly on support from Western countries, whose main objective in supporting them has been to protect Western investments and to prevent the spread of Communist ideals. Perhaps the end of the "Cold War" will now expose these leaders for what they are— opportunistic, exploitative, and directionless rulers who must immediately be consigned to the dustbin of history in the pursuit of genuine freedom and democracy.

Promoting Democracy and Building Institutions in Thailand

Chai-Anan Samudavanija

SINCE THE BEGINNING of my career as a political scientist in Thailand almost two decades ago, I have pursued a parallel career as an advocate and activist on behalf of representative democracy and participatory political institutions. At one time or another I have served as a leader of student demonstrators, an advisor to prime ministers, a drafter of proposed laws and constitutions, a university professor, and—more recently—director of the Institute of Public Policy Studies, a prodemocratic "think tank." The single theme that links together all my various titles and job descriptions is, I believe, my role as a civic educator. To explain to my fellow citizens why they should want to make their country a democracy, and to show them how it can be done, have always been my goals.

The task has not been simple, not least because the ground has often given way under my feet. Recent Thai history is a story of sweeping transformations and dizzying political uncertainty. The late 1950s and 1960s (to begin with a useful benchmark) ushered in a series of rapid, far-reaching social and economic changes whose effects are still making themselves strongly felt. The economy expanded at a clip of around seven percent a year as urbanization and industrialization surged, especially in and around the capital of

Bangkok. Improved public health programs were fostering explosive population growth; for the first time ever in Thai history, new land for agriculture was running short and the countryside was becoming crowded. Income disparities, meanwhile, were widening in ways apparent to rich and poor alike. Moreover, Thais were coming into close contact with the modern West in the form of tourists, imported goods, and the thousands of U.S. soldiers stationed on Thai soil. In view of this tremendous ferment, it is hardly surprising that new groups were emerging in Thai society, or that hitherto muted demands for participation were mounting in volume and intensity.

Yet throughout the course of these eventful years, Thailand's political system remained sadly stagnant. Military rulers like Field Marshal Sarit Thanarat (prime minister, 1958-63), and his successor Field Marshal Thanom Kittikachorn (1963-73) maintained order through a combination of bribes, threats, and coercion. Potential opponents became targets of intimidation or suppression, intellectuals and businessmen were co-opted, and the media were subjected to state control. Patronage and outright corruption were widespread. Such an ossified political system could no longer meet existing needs, let alone those of the future.

Before 1973, the rate of political participation was very low. National elections were held intermittently and turnout was always relatively light. Such organized interest groups as did exist were mainly commercial and trade associations, all operating under close official supervision. Groups seeking to influence public policy in the interest of farmers and workers were almost nonexistent. At the same time, however, a multitude of subgroups based on intricate networks of patronage could be found clustered around Thailand's powerful state bureaucracy. These groups competed for control over limited budgets and such lucrative bureaucratic functions as the granting of public contracts, permits and licenses. Big business interests, meanwhile, formed tight alliances with bureaucratic politicians. Pervasive corruption ensured the thorough intermingling of personal and group interests.

A student-led uprising in October 1973 toppled Prime Minister

Thanom and led King Bhumibol Adulyadej, Thailand's constitutional monarch, to name Sanya Thammasak, one-time chief justice of the Supreme Court and rector of Thammasat University, as the new premier. Open politics and democratic experimentation had returned. The new democratic regime, however, suffered from an extremely low level of political institutionalization, while the "opening up" of politics soon resulted in an overload of fresh demands on the system.

The constitution drafting committee

Among the many necessities pressing on Thailand's political system in the wake of the student demonstrations and the military's fall from power, two stood out as most critical. The first was the need to restructure the old political and patronage relationships left behind by the ousted military rulers. Second, the constitution, the legislature, and the party system—the institutional guarantors of stable democracy—would have to be completely refurbished. These two problems, knotty in themselves, were also intricately intertwined. As the euphoria that immediately followed the uprising began to subside, the challenge they posed became manifest in all its true immensity.

I was twenty-nine then, an academic greenhorn who had come back from graduate school at the University of Wisconsin just in time to take part in the events that led to the student upheaval of October 1973. The uprising had barely ended, it seemed, before I found myself named to the eighteen-member committee that was to draft a new constitution. In my several meetings with Prime Minister Sanya at around this time, he was concerned over the past lack of democratization and recommended that the drafting and promulgation of the new constitution (which he had publicly promised would be finished in six months) be reinforced by an urgent drive to foster public awareness of and participation in the political process. The goal was to ensure that Thailand could effect a smooth transition from the authoritarianism of the past to a new era of freedom and democracy.

The prime minister specifically asked a group of active political scientists to help him with this great task; it was a noble—and formidable—challenge for us all. Among our constitution-drafting committee's first acts was the establishment of a secretariat and three operational subcommittees (devoted to research, legal drafting, and public participation, respectively). The aim was to acquire more knowledge about various types of electoral systems, referenda and local governmental structures, as well as to give the public opportunities to participate in preparing the new constitution. I became the spokesman for the whole committee while serving concurrently as deputy chairman of the subcommittee on public participation. My subcommittee's chairman was the elder statesman M.R. Kukrit Pramoj, the president of the National Assembly.

The Constitution Drafting Committee wasted little time, completing its efforts on 8 January 1974. The Research Subcommittee produced 120 studies and reports in three months, while the Legal Drafting Subcommittee worked on alternative language for various sections of the new constitution. As the deputy chairman of the Public Participation Subcommittee, I received full authority from the chairman to plan and implement its activities.

My involvement in this assignment taught me the value of participation through networking. My first move was to enlist the support not only of the academy, but of business and the media as well. Academics throughout the country formed a network that we used to organize discussion groups, seminars, exhibitions and freewheeling public debates in the style made famous by "speakers' corner" in London's Hyde Park. We invited a number of prominent journalists and broadcasters to serve on the subcommittee and take an active part in public meetings and discussions. Finally, I recruited a group of young, energetic artists from the world of private advertising to create easily understandable posters, pamphlets and slide programs expounding the essentials of democracy.

From late October 1973 to January 1974, I organized more than 120 seminars, panel discussions, and public meetings all over Thailand. While these were going on, small teams of students were travelling the country on behalf of our subcommittee compiling lists of people's demands, grievances and expectations. In many areas, the students' solicitousness toward the people's concerns roused the ire of local officials. We had become a threat to the entrenched bureaucratic system.

We had also become an even more direct threat to extremists of both left and right. Left-leaning students and the Communist Party of Thailand (CPT) saw us as "reformists" whose success at institution-alizing "bourgeois democracy" would deal a grievous setback to the revolutionary cause. The military and its ultra-conservative support-ers, on the other hand, suspected us of being stalking horses for communism. Our attempts to mobilize the masses, it was thought, were undertaken solely for the sake of subjecting them to Communist subversion.

Although arousing enmity was not our intention, sometimes we had to accept it as an inevitable consequence of our project. The task was a long-term one, and called for great patience. The Public Participation Subcommittee and its work were utterly without prece-dent in the history of Thailand. The hearings we held, the discussions we sponsored, and the information we disseminated were helping to produce something wholly new: the close involvement of num-erous ordinary citizens in a national political issue.

Our access to the mass media proved a great help. Public meetings and panel discussions were broadcast live on radio and television. After the Constitution Drafting Committee finished its proposal in January 1974, I went on national television with Prime Minister Sanya, the deputy prime minister (who served ex-officio as chairman of the committee), and M.R. Kukrit Pramoj to report to the people on important features of the proposed charter.

I also asked major radio broadcasters and newspaper columnists to invite the public to write the Drafting Committee with their views. From November 1973 to January 1974, we received about 2,500 letters, mostly from rural areas. When the draft constitution was completed and submitted to the National Assembly, the Drafting Committee chairman personally signed letters thanking every letter-writer and sent each of them a printed copy of the draft constitution. I kept these letters, later publishing some of them with my introductory remarks in a book entitled *Voice of the People*. Careful study of these letters revealed a serious problem. For all too many Thais, constitutionalism was only a word, an airy concept bereft of any substantive significance. Most correspondents expressed vague hopes that the new constitution would somehow improve their livelihood. Yet the letters also contained many signs of intense political distrust. A majority confessed to having mixed feelings about the constitution and democracy; bitter past experiences with politicians, bureaucrats, and other such "influential persons" had left them with a sense of alienation. Nonetheless, many expressed a desire to participate in the political process despite their frustrations.

The activities of the three subcommittees thus stood in strong contrast to the traditional pattern, according to which the political elite remained insulated from public opinion and popular demands. The response our subcommittees elicited showed clearly that there were strong, albeit latent, demands for political participation in Thai society; given the right opportunity, these demands could quickly become a potent force for democratization.

The draft constitution of 1974 was the most liberal political charter Thailand had ever seen. It generally reflected the views of the progressives who gained dramatically greater access to power following the events of October 1973. The document covered the entire gamut of institutional issues facing the political system, removing many of the institutional mechanisms that the armed forces and the bureaucracy had used to dominate politics for forty years. In a major innovation designed to effect separation of powers, for instance, it decreed that any military or civilian official elected to either house of the legislature had to resign from the executive branch.

The new charter formed a promising basis for the reconstruction of Thai political life. Many of its provisions, however, did not survive subsequent review by the new, indirectly elected National Assembly. It was evident that the more conservative elements in society had begun to reassert themselves after the aberration of October 1973.

Although I was among the 299 delegates elected to the National

Assembly, I was disqualified because I had not yet reached the minimum age of thirty-five required by the 1968 constitution then in effect. Undaunted, however, I resolved to continue the prodemocracy work I had begun with the Constitution Drafting Committee by establishing a Legislative Innovation Project. Using a grant from the Ford Foundation, I recruited twelve graduate students to work along with me as legislative staffers for the members of the National Assembly. We made it our mission to supply them with information necessary for the consideration of major bills.

At the same time, I was appointed to act as secretary to the Legislative Reform Committee, and my university seconded me to the Secretariat of the National Assembly. My job there was to establish legislative reference and research divisions for the Secretariat, which in 1974 had no such divisions and restricted itself to administrative duties connected with chamber business.

I persuaded about ten people from universities and other government departments to work with me. With the help of the prime minister, we managed to secure more than 100 new positions and a much larger budget for the Secretariat. During the latter half of 1974, a reorganization decree was proposed that officially established the new reference and research divisions. In November, however, our hopeful plans were dashed. The president of the Assembly, giving way under intense pressure from military foes of reform, dismissed me and my staff from the Secretariat. My year-and-a-half-long effort to create a viable support system for nascent democratic institutions was at an end.

In October 1976, a year after the new constitution was promulgated, the military staged the bloodiest coup d'etat in Thai history. Hundreds of students were killed; more than two thousand others fled to join the Communists. By that time I had become totally disillusioned with the whole political system, and left the country to take up a visiting appointment at Princeton University's Woodrow Wilson's School of Public and International Affairs. There I concentrated on scholarly work. My book, *Political Conflict in Thailand*, written with my good friend and Princeton colleague David Morell, dates from that period.

For the three years following the October 1976 coup, Thai society was severely polarized into left- and right-wing factions. Neither the government nor any other important organization showed any serious interest in democratic reform. The only ones to benefit from this polarization were the Communists. Liberal democrats, on the other hand, found their ranks thinned by defections from the center left, many of whose members either became radicalized and fled to join the Communist cadres in the countryside, or succumbed to paralyzing disillusionment and numbing cynicism about everything connected with the state.

Promoting democracy—The Institute of Public Policy Studies

In March 1980, a new government led by General Prem Tinsulanond came to power with the help of younger army officers. The Prem administration showed a genuine desire to heal the wounds inflicted by the 1976 coup. I myself was appointed an advisor to the prime minister. We took as one of our main tasks the re-establishment of democratic government. Using lessons learned from the 1970s, the military officers and the technocrats forged a more moderate constitution providing for a nonelected prime minister. From 1980 to 1988, the technocrats ruled the country, creating political stability and fostering unprecedented economic growth.

Ignoring pleas to stay on, I resigned my advisor's post in 1981. I left because I saw that what was being created under Prem was an entrenched technocratic polity rather than the democracy of my hopes. Government remained stable, to be sure, but only at the price of a conscious effort to depoliticize every important decision. By 1987, the government was coming under severe criticism for being too concerned with strengthening the private business sector at the expense of the vast majority of the people. There was no systematic effort even at administrative decentralization, let alone democratization. The House of Representatives, the only elected branch of government, was overshadowed by the appointed Senate and by the prime minister and his military allies.

After I resigned from the prime minister's advisory group, I decided to give democratic activism yet another try. In 1984, with funding from the Konrad Adenauer Foundation of West Germany, I founded the Institute of Public Policy Studies, a nongovernmental body dedicated to the civic education of the Thai people. The size and complexity of the task were immense; there could be no hope of accomplishing it without both a well-integrated package of programs and a nationwide network through which to disseminate them.

I dedicated myself to this task and have accomplished much since then. The Institute itself has a full-time staff of only six people; its director and program directors are part-time. Nonetheless, it has ties with all of Thailand's major universities and teachers' colleges; provincial secondary schools, councilors, mayors, and chambers of commerce; and nongovernmental organizations all over the country. The Institute also works closely with all the standing committees of the National Assembly, and cooperates with both the Assembly Secretariat and the Secretariat of the Cabinet in a number of joint activities.

In designing our civic education program, I took into account five important factors responsible for the low level of political literacy in Thailand. First, the dissemination of essential information on public policy issues has been dominated by government organizations. Second, cultivation of the interests, attitudes, and values that all citizens must have to become intelligent, effective, and responsible participants in the political system has always been controlled by the bureaucracy. Third, the frequent interruption and displacement of participant political institutions, like parties and elected legislatures, has complicated the task of democratic political socialization by robbing it of continuity and intensity. Fourth, the tenuous relationship between bureaucrats and politicians, and the anti-politics attitude of the elite have resulted in a lack of faith, concern, and commitment to democratic ideals and procedures on the part of the bureaucratic politicians. Fifth, the negative image of politicians the media presents to the public heightens public cynicism and apathy.

The Institute works to bring together public officials, parliamentarians, scholars, and the general public with the goal of fostering

133

and strengthening participatory institutions in Thai society. It serves this general goal by pursuing five objectives:

• To identify and to encourage and to support research on significant social and economic issues.

• To promote contact and cooperation among academics, elected officials, civil servants, the media, and other concerned groups and individuals, for the independent study of public policy issues affecting Thailand's economic development and popular participation in government.

• To organize training programs, conferences, workshops, and seminars for members of parliament and provincial and local representative bodies.

• To increase public knowledge about the general principles of democracy, and the legislative and administrative processes of Thailand's emerging democratic system.

• To foster the exchange of information, ideas, and experiences on economic development and democratization among scholars and decision-makers in all the countries of Southeast Asia. This includes the encouragement and support of exchanges with other Southeast Asian scholars, as well as with researchers from the Unites States, Canada, Western Europe, Australia and New Zealand.

The activities of the Institute aim to benefit members of parliament, academics, civil servants, businessmen, local government representatives, provincial chambers of commerce, and the broader citizenry, and key on the Institute's agenda now is the involvement of members of these groups from abroad in our program. The Institute is currently exploring ways to accommodate visiting scholars from Laos, Cambodia, Vietnam, Australia, New Zealand and the United States and to intertwine their research interests with those of the Institute and its target groups. Arrangements for scholarly exchange with several Australian and American universities specializing in southeast Asian studies are presently in the making.

The Institute defines its role as that of a mediator in the network of political education. It is strictly nonpartisan, and never attempts to interfere in any decision-making process. It aims only to provide relevant information and policy options to concerned parties at all levels of government and civil society. It seeks to marshal intellectual resources from various scholarly disciplines and parts of the public and private sectors in order to enrich reflection and inform debate about the vital questions of the day.

Encouraging political discussion

The Institute has continuously maintained five major programs since 1984. These are the *Parliamentary Newspaper*, the MPs' Dialogue program, publications, the "Public Policy through Radio" program, and seminars and workshops. A sixth, the Parliamentary Development Plan, was initiated in 1989.

Parliamentary newspaper

The *Parliamentary Newspaper* is a monthly publication with a circulation of over 20,000. It is distributed free to members of the National Assembly, members of the Social Science Association, teachers colleges, and major secondary schools all over the country. The paper gives equal coverage to government and opposition parties. It covers legislative activities and carries interviews with MPs; reports on parliamentary committees, parliamentary conferences, seminars, and workshops (especially those organized by the Institute); and features articles on the parliamentary systems, committee systems, and legal and constitutional systems of other democracies.

MPs Dialogue program

The Institute, with the cooperation of the Secretariat of the National Assembly, sponsors an MPs Dialogue program involving panel discussions and lectures at various provincial universities, colleges, and secondary schools. Institute policy requires that members of parliament who participate in the program must not speak at panels held in their home provinces or electoral constituencies. This is a very important measure, for it guarantees the Institute's strictly non-partisan stance. Initiated in 1987, this program has gained tremendous recognition and support from every political party. Prominent members of government and opposition parties alike have participated. In keeping with the plan of the Institute, the Public Relations Division of the Secretariat of the National Assembly has been trained to run this program, a task it will assume by 1992 at the latest.

Publications

The Institute's publications cover a broad range of topics, including rural development, public administration, national-level decision making, trade policy, the environment, and electoral issues. To date, the Institute has grouped its publications into three series: "Academic Documents," "Amendments of Laws for Development," and "Research and Information on Public Policy." Beginning in 1990, a new series dedicated to "Electoral Politics" appeared. The addition is timely, for election campaigning, election financing, and the general workings of the electoral system have become major constitutional as well as social and political issues.

Public policy through radio program

This program is run by Somsakdi Xuto, a university professor who served as a cabinet minister in 1980, and Mr. Amnart Sornimsart, a professional radio personality with mass appeal. This combination of a professional radio programmer and an academic who used to serve in government has made this program very popular. It seeks to provide expert political commentary in a widely accessible manner and has become very popular since it first went on the air in 1987. Members of Parliament, prominent public figures, and businessmen are invited to speak or be interviewed for a period of fifty minutes. The show airs nationwide every Saturday, and tapes and transcripts are made readily available.

Seminars and workshops

The committees of the Thai Parliament had no tradition of organizing hearings to seek opinions and information until the Institute initiated the first seminar on the issue of copyrights at the Parliament in 1987. In the past, although various parliamentary committees had tried to call civil servants to testify, most were reluctant to come and usually sent low-level officials instead. Since there is no such thing as a contempt of parliament provision, parliamentary committee meetings in Thailand were, until recently, closed-door deliberations on bills among MPs. The Institute started and encouraged seminars and workshops, initially held outside Parliament. Since 1987, however, the Institute has been able to organize its seminars and workshops in cooperation with various parliamentary committees. The seminars and conferences are attended by MPs, senators, academics, businessmen, concerned interest groups, and the media.

On 1 March 1990 the Institute organized a pre-cabinet meeting workshop attended by 180 people representing members of parliament, city councils, municipalities, chambers of commerce, university and teachers' colleges, farmers associations, and nongovernmental voluntary associations. After the workshop, the Institute recommended twelve people from the group to meet with the prime minister on 4 March after the cabinet session had ended to discuss their demands and opinions about the development of the Southern Region.

From 1990 on, at least half of our activities are to be carried out in various regional centers (North, Northeast, and South), a move in line with the 2 March 1989 meeting of the cabinet outside the capital city.

Parliamentary development plan

In early 1989 the Institute, through the good offices of the House Affairs Committee of the House of Representatives, initiated the first Parliamentary Development Plan. Unanimously accepted after lengthy parliamentary debate in mid-1989, the plan sets the framework for democratic institution-building and for the first time gives parliament a leading role to play in the promotion of Thai democracy. Such

137

a role had been traditionally played by the Ministry of Interior and the military. The plan calls for parliament and its secretariat to propagate democratic ideas in various ways, including the operation of a radio station and the conduct of research and development programs.

The Institute in the 1990s

The Institute will continue its present programs and will make necessary preparations to extend its activities as follows:

• In 1989 the Institute acted as a consultant to several parliamentary committees, including the House Affairs Committee, the Committee on Interior Administration, the Committee on Social Welfare and Labor, and the Committee on Science, Technology, and Energy. In 1990, we sought to consult with all of the major parliamentary standing committees.

• In 1989, we continued our research on development of the law, and in 1992 we will update the law development handbook.

• In 1989, the Institute began publication of "White Papers," allowing us to reduce the number of our "Documents Summarizing Research" and our other information on public policies. From 1990-1992, we will continue to emphasize the publication of "White Papers" both in Thai and in English.

• In 1989 the Institute began planning for the Representative Institutions Leadership Training Program in cooperation with the House Affairs Committee, the Human Resource Institute of Thammasat University, and the Sukhothai Thammathirat Open University. In 1990 the Institute launched its first training program, bringing together twenty-thirty members of representative institutions (parliament, municipalities, provincial councils, and provincial chambers of commerce) for an intensive three-month training program.

• The Institute is now endeavoring to expand its activities to the Southeast Asian region. In 1987-88, the Public Policy Studies Program began preparing for this new move by making video tapes in English, translating some of its publications into English, and in November 1988 producing its first work in English ("Agricultural Administration: Exogenous Factors Affecting Farmers' Income and Welfare"). A book, *The Road to Parliament*, has also been translated into English.

• In 1989 the Institute made contacts with other institutions in the region and began sending them our English publications so that in the 1990s, as the Institute implements its new programs, we can incorporate field trips to ASEAN countries as an important part of fulfilling the objectives of our projects and programs.

• In late 1989 the Institute initiated a plan to establish an Exhibition Hall of Democracy in Thailand. The Exhibition Hall will contain documents, films, slides, videotapes, movies and interactive exhibits concerning the history and function of constitutional government in Thailand.

The challenge of democracy

My experiences in seeking to strengthen parliamentary democracy have taught me several important lessons. The first of these is the importance of disinterestedness and nonpartisanship. Thailand is rife with competing factions and political parties; it is therefore essential for me to stress that I and my work will not benefit any particular party, but will be useful to the legislative-development process as a whole.

Similarly, it is vital to try to avoid unnecessary or premature involvement in any of the highly controversial issues before parliament, since such involvement can only impede the larger goal of strengthening the democratic process itself. However, sometimes such involvement can be successful in spite of the risks. For example, in May 1988 I almost put the program in jeopardy when I spearheaded the movement to petition the king concerning the actions of the incumbent prime minister, which I saw as intimidating political parties in the process of their preparation for the 1988 elections following the dissolution of Parliament. The then Prime Minister Prem rallied various groups of military commanders in a show of support, obliging party leaders to support his continued presence in office as a non-elected prime minister. My action could have had serious negative consequences, but fortunately popular pressure was soon generated as a result of the petition. The king sent it directly to Prem, forcing the general to reluctantly decline the offer to become prime minister once again. Hence from August 1988 we have had, for the first time since the institution of this constitutional regime in 1980, a prime minister who is an elected member of parliament.

Third, networking has been the key that has enabled me to achieve significant results on a shoestring budget and a skeleton staff. My own resources are slim, so I must seek as much support as possible from other organizations, both public and private.

Fourth, I have learned that I must firmly establish my own credentials as a liberal democrat in order to distinguish myself from the revolutionary socialists. This lesson was learned the hard way, at the cost of much misunderstanding from conservative groups to whom the distinction between reformers and revolutionaries has not always been clear.

Using these lessons, I gradually built up the "Public Policy Program" with assistance from a number of colleagues and students. I chose to call it a "Public Policy" Program because the program is conducted under the auspices of the Social Science Association of Thailand, and there is a law prohibiting associations to be involved in "political" activities. Since I go directly to parliamentary committees instead of to political parties, I could defend our activities as part and parcel of the legislative process itself.

After five years of patience and low-profile gestures, I accepted the offer of the chairman of the House of Representatives Affairs Committee to be the Committee's expert. I also accepted the prime minister's nomination to the Senate in April 1989.

My formal institutional linkages with both the elected House of representatives and the appointed Senate have been tremendous assets for me. I have been able to work "within the system" while maintaining very strong links outside it with academia and nongovernmental organizations. My efforts are also meeting with more understanding and appreciation as the military and the general public gain a clearer picture of the genuinely democratic forces operating independently in our society.

Despite this change of attitude, the Secretariat of the National Assembly is still a major obstacle to legislative development. The political conflict and instability that have predominated over the past decade have made National Assembly staffers indifferent to the role of the legislature. They have gradually developed a deep-rooted belief that their chief function is to provide efficient support, primarily in the form of clerical assistance, for chamber activities. Since the legislative process in Thailand has always been more a matter of symbol than substance, Assembly staffers often do not sense any need to do more. Parliamentary committees are moving towards greater roles in policy consideration, but very slowly. In the meantime, most individual members still rely on the bureaucracy for information. Such environmental factors have contributed to a legislative staff culture and set of attitudes that are status-quo oriented.

Many senior staffers, themselves former clerks, are attached to the old institutional culture of parliament and antagonistic toward the new Legislative Reference and Research Sections. The old guard sees legislative development not only as a threat to established routines, but to the established distribution of power as well. The newly established information and research branches, it is feared, will quickly overshadow the rest of the Secretariat.

These constraints have kept my efforts from being as fruitful as I had hoped they would be. Yet a combination of alertness, sensitivity, and flexibility have secured a degree of success for the Institute's undertakings. Certainly the Institute's position outside both the bureaucracy and the legislature has been a help. We maintain an appropriate distance from the Secretariat and continue to work through the committees. At the same time, however, our intention is not to displace the Secretariat but to train it to perform the kinds of sophisticated legislative services that the Institute has been performing over the past six years. We seek to institutionalize the Institute's program, but not the Institute itself. The Secretariat must remain, even while its institutional behavior must change.

Fifteen years have passed by very quickly since I began my efforts to help create a viable parliamentary democracy in Thailand. At first, my efforts were cut short by military coups which were rampant and violent. During the 1970s, active Communist political propaganda and armed insurgencies were also major obstacles to democratization. However, since 1980, parliamentary democracy has not been disrupted. Such continuity and the demise of the Communist party have made possible a revival and revitalization of participant political activities.

Representative democracy in Thailand has yet to be institutionalized. In a country where military and civilian bureaucracies have dominated politics for so long, there is widespread contempt for the elected legislature. Pressure and interest groups at all levels bypass participant institutions like parties and the National Assembly, articulating their demands through the executive branch instead. Parliament remains far from the center of politics.

Under these inauspicious circumstances, participatory institutions need constant financial and technical support. As parliamentary democracy develops and power is gradually transferred from military men and technocrats to elected politicians, it is important that the parliamentary Secretariat be well equipped and well staffed. In this information age, the parliament needs modern information technology. In the past, intellectuals have been all too ready to help military and bureaucratic elites legitimize their rule. If democracy is to succeed, intellectuals and technocrats must form active prodemocratic networks with nongovernmental voluntary organizations and the National Assembly.

The challenges facing the movement for democracy and freedom in Thailand are essentially problems of legitimacy. Legitimacy in the Thai case involves two levels of consensus. The first is inter-elite consensus concerning the rules of the game; the second is consensus between the elite and the masses. For the past five years, the Institute has been emphasizing consensus-building among elites. The challenge of the future will be to build consensus among the masses.

Political parties in Thailand are very weak and are essentially electoral parties rather than grass-roots organizations; they will need help if they are to broaden their appeal and create effective organizations. The Institute cannot assist parties directly, but it has begun several projects designed to educate rural opinion leaders, a must if wide-scale political mobilization is to occur.

In Western history, capitalism and liberal democracy have reinforced each other. In Thailand's case, however, economic development has left political development far behind. With rapid economic growth and industrialization, Thai civil society has undergone a highly complex transformation; what was until recently an agrarian society (albeit an advanced one) has now become a complex, urbanized society with a dynamic industrializing economy. Yet democracy has not been able to meet the challenge of creating and maintaining a national consensus under these conditions, and the monarchy has remained the sole authoritative source of political legitimacy.

The challenges facing democratization in Thailand are fortunately political and economic rather than religious, racial or ethnic as they are in many other countries. Thus we are hopeful that our efforts will not be in vain. Time is on our side, and if the democratic process is not interrupted by a coup, the political future of Thailand will be as bright as that of its economy. The approach of the twenty-first century finds Thailand gradually moving towards full membership in the new and larger community of liberal democratic nations that has begun to emerge as a result of the dramatic changes in Eastern Europe and elsewhere.

The Philippine Alternative Press and the Toppling of a Dictator

Felix B. Bautista

SEVERAL YEARS HAVE passed since those four days in February 1986, when the Filipino people stunned the world by deposing a firmly entrenched dictator in a bloodless revolution.

It was unique in the annals of revolutionary struggle. In countries across the globe, television audiences were forced to suspend their disbelief as they watched the Filipinos—men, women and children—linking arms and standing unmoving in front of advancing tanks. They could not understand how these Filipinos, scared to death though they were, with nothing more deadly than rosaries in their hands and prayers on their lips, could confront fully armed soldiers who had been ordered to shoot to kill. The viewers cheered when, in the end, the tanks turned around and the soldiers laid down their arms and joined the civilians. The dictator Marcos, abandoned by his cronies, quickly fled to ignominious exile in Hawaii.

The Filipinos installed Corazon C. Aquino as president. We remain solidly behind her as, inch by painful inch, she leads her people forward and rebuilds the devastation wrought by twenty years of rapacious misrule. We hope that the task of reconstruction will soon be completed so that these dreams of freedom and democracy, which refused to die through 400 years of Spanish colonial rule,

four decades of American governance, four years of Japanese occupation, and twenty years of oppression by Ferdinand Marcos, will
finally become a reality.

The legacy of the past

Filipino folklore holds that even the earliest Filipinos nurtured the
dream of freedom. Legend has it that during prehispanic times, a
group of ten datus (tribal chieftains), along with their families and
followers, fled Borneo and settled in what is now the Philippines
to escape tyranny and persecution.[1] One historian dramatized the
event, speaking for one of the datus:

> We, ten datus, have left the home of our ancestors in Borneo
> because we can no longer endure the misrule of Tuan Maka-
> tunaw. Our recent ruler exercises no self-restraint, regards not
> the rights of others, and has no respect for the law. Whatever
> he sees and wants, that he takes. Here we would settle, pur-
> chasing of the ancient owners of the soil the land whereon
> we shall make a new home, dwelling in harmony with our
> neighbors and living ourselves under the rule of law.[2]

This story's persistence in our racial memory suggests that the
early Filipinos harbored within them the seeds of democracy and
even then were laying the foundations for democratic structures. This
debunks the myth that democratic ideas were introduced into the
Philippines by America. As historian Encarnacion Alzona asserts, "Our
history disproves it. Our forebears fought Spain because they wanted human rights—freedom of speech, freedom of conscience, freedom of assembly, an untrammeled press, habeas corpus, and equality before the law—to be granted and guaranteed."[3]

The Filipinos, in fact, fought Spain fiercely from the very first
day that the Spaniards landed in our country. During the 400 years
they ruled, the Spaniards faced over 300 revolts by Filipino tribal
groups protesting unjust taxation, abuse of human rights, and cruel
and unusual punishment. The Filipino people paid a high price for
this intransigence. Our national hero, Dr. Jose P. Rizal, was executed

by a firing squad for writing two novels which fanned the flames of Filipino nationalism.

But when the Filipinos did defeat Spain during the Philippine revolution in 1898, we had no opportunity to savor our victory. For the Americans came and, after a bloody war which saw almost a million men, women and children killed, they took over the country.

While it is incorrect to say that the United States introduced democracy into the Philippines, it must be acknowledged in fairness to the Americans that it was they who instituted a political system. They set up a judicial system, organized a network of public schools that became one of Asia's first systems of universal education, and established a legislative branch of government, the first Philippine Assembly. The members of this body were chosen in the first general election in Philippine history.

Two political parties emerged, first (in 1900) the pro-American Federal Party (renamed the Progressive Party), and six years later (when the U.S. finally permitted a pro-independence party to form) the Nationalist Party. In the election of 1907, with control of the first Philippine Assembly at stake, the Nationalist Party won 72 percent of the seats, demonstrating anew the democratic spirit that burned in the hearts of Filipinos.

The Filipinos continued the fight for freedom—but with a difference. While all through the centuries of Spanish rule we chose to pit our puny spears against Spanish muskets and artillery, regardless of the cost, under the Americans we chose a more peaceful path. From 1907 until the early 1930s, the Philippine legislature sent mission after independence mission to Washington. Each one made a strong case for the cause of freedom. On 5 November 1935 Filipino persistence finally paid off. The Philippines, an American colony since the turn of the century, was granted Commonwealth status by the U.S. Congress. After a ten-year transition period ending in November 1945, the Philippines was to become fully independent, a truly sovereign nation. But World War II tragically intervened. Shortly after Pearl Harbor, the Japanese Imperial Forces conquered the Philippines; their occupation was to last four years.

The Filipinos mounted a fierce underground resistance movement, involving practically every able-bodied person. This brought cruel and savage repression by the Japanese, who inflicted an appalling number of Filipino casualties. "One million people died, out of a population of twenty million. This is more than the combined losses of the United States and Great Britain. It is proportionately twice as many as the casualties of France in World War I, which is the generally accepted yardstick for wholesale slaughter."[4]

Although World War II disrupted the independence schedule, on 4 July 1946 the Stars and Stripes came down, and the red, white, and blue of the Philippine flag waved alone for the first time since 1898, when the Philippine revolutionary forces hoisted it aloft after defeating Spain. This was a triumphant day for the Filipino people. But freedom is not a cure-all, and there were problems to attend to. First, there was the reconstruction. The war had devastated the country. Manila, it was said,was second only to Warsaw in the extent of the damage it suffered, and the economy was in ruins. But despite the niggardliness of American aid and the growing threat of insurgency posed by the Communist *Hukbalahaps*, the Philippines, under a succession of dedicated presidents—Roxas, Quirino, Magsaysay, Garcia and Macapagal—worked its way upward. By 1965, it was regarded as the most advanced and progressive country in Asia. With the possible exception of Japan, it was the country "most likely to succeed."

However, in the twenty years that followed, the Philippines lost its position of preeminence. Today, apart from Bangladesh, it is widely regarded as the basket case of Asia. What happened?

Much of the answer can be given in one word: Marcos.

The tragedy of Marcos

The tragedy of Ferdinand E. Marcos is that he could have gone down in history as the greatest Philippine president ever. Instead, he is now universally regarded with scorn and derision, portrayed, along with his wife Imelda, as a world-class thief who bled his country dry while lining his own pockets with ill-gotten wealth.

Marcos certainly had the credentials to do an excellent job of leading the Philippines. He had an enviable war record (or so the people thought when he was elected in 1965), he graduated valedictorian of his law class, and he topped the bar examinations. What made this latter feat especially remarkable was that he studied while he was confined in jail awaiting trial on charges of murdering his father's political opponent. Moreover, he defended his own case with such brilliance that the Philippine Supreme Court acquitted him.

Marcos had the preparation for the job. He had served two terms in the House of Representatives before winning a seat in the Senate and eventually becoming Senate president. He used this position as a springboard to the presidency of the Philippines.

Early in his second term as president, talk began to surface that he and his wife were corruptly enriching themselves. It was dismissed at first as idle gossip, but the rumors persisted. Marcos cavalierly shrugged them off with his soon-to-be classic retort, "Prove it!" As Manila's rambunctious press—at that time it was called "the freest press in the world"—continued to expose Marcos' wheeling and dealing, the country's students took to the streets. In almost daily demonstrations, the students denounced Marcos' misrule and called for his resignation. This spate of occasionally violent student protests had the support of the more radical segment of the student population, but it earned the antagonism of parents whose children's studies were constantly being interrupted. And because the demonstrations often culminated in vandalism, Manila's shopkeepers began boarding up their stores to avoid damage. Their businesses suffered.

So Marcos, with Machiavellian deviousness, used the demonstrations as an excuse to impose martial law on 21 September 1972. Many people welcomed the move, because they saw martial law as a solution to the unending protests. They accepted Marcos' explanation that the country needed a system of "constitutional authoritarianism" in order to neutralize the Communist threat and "build a New Society."

What the people did not realize at that time was that Marcos

THE DEMOCRATIC REVOLUTION

had resorted to martial law to keep himself in power. His second term would have been over at the end of 1973, and under the constitution he could not run for a third. But he had acquired a taste for power—as had Imelda—and what better way to hold onto it than by declaring martial law, cancelling the election, and imposing one-man rule?

In the process, he also abolished Congress and shut down all the media, print and broadcast, with the glib explanation that the country needed a new kind of democracy because the old kind, borrowed from America, had proven to be unsuitable.

Diosdado Macapagal, Marcos's predecessor, took vigorous exception to this:

> The claim that the American or Western type of democracy is not suited to the Philippines must be seen in its bare falsity and sophistry. It is argued that Marcos' martial rule is justified in the maintenance of a democracy suitable to the Philippines which is variously styled "people's democracy," "participatory democracy," "constitutional revolution," "constitutional authoritarianism," or some other label.
>
> It is instantly apparent that the favorite label, "constitutional authoritarianism," is a self-contradiction and a legal incongruity, for authoritarianism means and requires absolute obedience to authority, and therefore cannot be constitutional since the Constitution limits and does not countenance authority which is unqualified.[5]

Even the Catholic Bishops' Conference of the Philippines was initially taken in by Marcos's justification. In a speech before the bishops, Jaime Cardinal Sin, who would subsequently emerge as Marcos's most bitter and uncompromising critic and who was universally considered to be the architect of the People Power revolution that would send the Marcoses into exile, explained why he was supporting martial rule:

> The Church has shown that it can flourish under any type of government. In a presidential system such as the United

150

States, the Church thrives. In a monarchy such as Great Britain, it is alive and healthy. Even in a dictatorship, as in Poland, it flourishes. To the Church, it should not matter what form the government it works under tends to take. So long as she is free to spread the Good News, and so long as human rights are respected, the Church should remain above political systems.[6]

The church hierarchy adopted a policy called "critical collaboration," which meant that the church would collaborate with the government whenever, in the hierarchy's considered judgment, it was adopting measures designed to promote the public good. But it would be unequivocally critical whenever, in its considered judgment, these measures would work against the best interests of the people.

It soon became clear that the policy of critical collaboration would become increasingly critical and less and less collaborative. However, for a long while—from 21 September 1972 until 21 August 1983, the day that Senator Benigno Aquino, the Philippine opposition leader, was assassinated, the voice of the church (and more specifically, the voice of Cardinal Sin) was one of a very few that dared to protest Marcos's misrule.

This has puzzled students of Philippine history. Knowing our glorious tradition of resisting all forms of tyranny and despotism, they could not understand why we remained inert and passive for so long, why we stood by doing nothing while Marcos imposed one restrictive measure after another. This passivity prompted an American journalist to ask me, "What is wrong with you people? Why has the Philippines become a nation of fifty-four million cowards led by a bogus war hero with a chestful of fake medals?" The journalist's questions set me to thinking. But his questions merely triggered more questions.

What, indeed, caused the Filipinos to be so passive even when we were faced with concrete evidence that the democratic space we valued so much had shrunk to near nothingness? Was it cowardice? Was it our long-suffering nature and our high threshold for pain? Was it infinite patience that enabled us to bide our time without our pent-up hostility and anger exploding into the open? What made the Filipino of today so different from the ten legendary datus who opposed tyranny, so different from the nameless Filipino leaders who staged more than 300 revolts in a vain and fatal attempt to throw off the Spanish yoke, so different from the Filipino patriots who fought the Americans and the Japanese although they were slaughtered by the hundreds of thousands? At the time these questions were roiling in my mind (early in 1983, shortly before the Aquino assassination) there were no satisfactory answers. Today, after the bloodless revolution of February 1986, some answers can be ventured.

The Filipinos of yesterday took up the cudgels for freedom secure in the knowledge that they had the support of the masses. The masses, however, did not perceive Marcos as an enemy. In fact, many of them had voted for him, and many of them had received money from him during past elections. Some farmers in the provinces even saw Marcos as some sort of Lord Bountiful who had provided for them through a land reform program. It did not matter to the fisherman out at sea that the press had been muzzled. He couldn't afford to buy a paper anyway. To the tired mother working in a factory, Marcos' imposition of a curfew was welcome. At least she did not have to worry about her children staying out late.

Who were the people most discomfited by martial law? The members of the middle class—the journalist thrown out of work when Marcos shut down the media, the businessman paying through the nose to get an import license because corruption was so widespread, the teacher whose academic freedom had been taken away. These Filipinos chafed under the restrictions and constraints. We wanted a change, but the masses of people were not behind us. So what could we do? We knew enough history to realize that no revolution ever succeeded without popular support. We could not speak out in protest because the jails were overflowing with protestors. The laws against subversion were so stringent that a boy could be clapped behind bars if he were so indiscreet as to say that when he grew up he wanted to be president.

Besides, a revolution requires arms. At the start of martial law,

Marcos ordered us to surrender all our guns. Only the military had guns—and the Communists. The military could not be counted on as allies, for Marcos coddled them shamelessly. And no one was quite prepared to link up with the Communists.

On top of these factors, the message of the bishops constantly hummed in our ears: Avoid violence, choose the way of peace. The tone of this message never varied. Even in the wake of the snap elections of 7 February 1986, when Corazon Aquino was robbed of certain victory by unmitigated cheating and when the bishops declared that Marcos had no moral right to govern because of "the unparalleled fraudulence" of the election, the bishops hewed to the same line. In a strong statement, they said:

We are not going to effect the change we seek by doing nothing, by sheer apathy. If we did nothing, we would be party to our own destruction as a people. We would be jointly guilty with the perpetrators of the wrong we want righted.

Neither do we advocate a bloody, violent means of righting this wrong. If we did, we would be sanctioning the enormous sin of fratricidal strife. Killing to achieve justice is not within the purview of our Christian vision in the present context.

The way indicated to us now is the way of non-violent struggle for justice.

This means active resistance of evil by peaceful means—in the manner of Christ. And its one end for now is that the will of the people be done through various ways and means proper to the Gospel.[7]

What were those ways? One was pointed out by Corazon Aquino herself. In a rally attended by more than a million people, she advocated a policy of civil disobedience. She said that the people must immediately boycott products made by Marcos-owned firms, and indicated that non-payment of taxes, coupled with a refusal to obey all unjust laws, should be given serious consideration. Before these more drastic steps could be taken, however, we were overtaken by events. In February 1986, two of Marcos's closest associates, Defense

Minister Juan Ponce Enrile and Lieutenant General Fidel V. Ramos, vice chief of staff of the Armed Forces, broke with their erstwhile master. What followed was the Miracle of EDSA, the bloodless revolution that toppled the Marcos dictatorship. The people, brought to EDSA by Cardinal Sin's call to protect the puny band of rebels, stopped the advancing tanks sent to annihilate Enrile and Ramos.

There was something unique about that revolution. It was carried out by people who came exclusively from the middle class, the same people who joined the so-called "Yellow Revolution" waged earlier, when thousands upon thousands of businessmen, middle-level employees, college students, teachers, and other professional men and women, wearing yellow T-shirts and waving yellow banners, marched in the parliament of the streets demanding government reform. If there were any poor people on EDSA, the historic highway where the advancing tanks were stopped, they were a very small minority. The predominance of the middle class can be traced both to its enlightened self-interest and to the influence of the alternative press, that small band of publications that was not afraid to tell the truth about Marcos.

These were the people whom that American journalist disparaged as cowards. On those four fateful days when the Filipinos proved to the world how much we loved freedom, we regained more than our liberty. We won back our self-respect.

The Philippine press under martial law

21 September 1972, the day President Marcos imposed martial law, was a day of infamy in the history of the Philippine media. One of Marcos's first acts as dictator was to muzzle the press. Filipinos woke up early that morning and found no newspapers on their doorsteps. When they turned on their radios to find out why, there were no stations broadcasting. They then realized that the Philippine media had been silenced.

How did Marcos do it? First, he sent out teams of military men to all the newspaper plants and radio and television stations to shut them down. Then he sent other teams to the homes of scores of journalists. These journalists—publishers, editors and rank-and-file reporters—were hustled unceremoniously to detention centers where they languished for months.

One by one, some newspapers reopened, but this time under new owners. Not surprisingly, these owners were Marcos cronies or relatives. For instance, the *Daily Express* was controlled by Roberto Benedicto, Marcos's classmate in law school and ambassador to Japan; the *Times Journal* had Benjamin Romualdez, Marcos's brother-in-law, as its head; and the *Bulletin Today* was owned by General Hans Menzi, former aide-de-camp of the dictator. The *Manila Times* and the *Philippines Free Press*, the most popular and most critical publications, were never allowed to reopen. The former's publisher, Joaquin "Chino" Roces, and the latter's editor, Teodoro M. Locsin, were among the hundreds of so-called "dissidents" clapped into jail.

In the wake of the jailings came policies designed to make the rest of the journalists more amenable to working for the controlled press. As one writer put it, "the word in Manila was that many journalists switched from being 'developmental' to 'envelopmental' reporters, accepting the monthly stipends from ministries and other lucrative beats, which came in envelopes. Others were downright scared, remembering Primitivo Mijares, Marcos' information minister, who 'disappeared' after he defected."[8] David Howard Bain, in the *Columbia Journalism Review*, writes of a Marcos insider who told him about the "journalistic guidelines" of the Marcos government. He says: "At a Palace luncheon before the 1984 National Assembly elections, two dozen editors and senior staff writers of the *Bulletin*, the *Express*, the *Times Journal*, and a few others were invited by the First Lady to review campaign jingles. Most clapped along. At the close, [they] formed a line, each passing in turn into an anteroom where Imelda Marcos stood with a military aide, who handed her envelopes —'guidelines.' Inside were twenty thousand to fifty thousand pesos, depending on the [journalist's] importance. The whole world is corrupt, a few reasoned later. Why not take advantage of it?"[9]

For eight years, Filipinos could read only what Marcos wanted us to read. While there were no government men posted in newspaper offices to engage in pre-publication censorship, the editors were sufficiently intimidated—or generously "envelopmentalized"—to insure that nothing offensive to the powers-that-be was printed. They knew that retribution for any transgressions would come swiftly. If they were lucky, they would only be fined. If they were not so lucky, they would be jailed. And if their luck completely ran out, as it did for some twenty-five journalists from 1983 to 1985, they would be killed or simply disappear, never to be seen again.

But on 17 January 1981 the situation changed for the better— Marcos signed a proclamation ending over eight years of martial law. In many respects, it was just a cosmetic end to the repressive regime. Marcos retained the power to make laws by decree and all his previous decrees remained in force unless he specifically repealed them. Why did Marcos lift martial law? Pope John Paul II planned to visit the Philippines the following month. It would never do for the Pontiff to find out that the Philippines, the only Catholic country in Asia, "the beacon light of Christianity in the Far East," was being crushed under a man who called himself a Catholic. Now, if the Pope were to ask if the press was free, Marcos could answer that he had repealed the controls on the mass media. He could say with a straight face that anybody could begin his own newspaper without government permission.

As subsequent events revealed, the "lifting" of martial law was one of the biggest mistakes that Marcos could have made. For with the ban on new newspapers relaxed, it became possible for men and women with a passion for the truth to start their own publications. Thus the alternative press was born—tabloids and magazines, dailies and weeklies—so called because it provided alternative reading matter for citizens tired of a diet of lies. Most prominent of these alternative newspapers were *We Forum*, which began life as a magazine dedicated to monitoring campus activities, and *Mr. and Ms.*, a weekly on family life.

These two publications started testing the outer limits of press freedom, venturing, at first tentatively and later more boldly, into criticism of Marcos. At first Marcos thought it would be to his advantage to leave the publications alone, for he could use them to refute the charges, sporadically raised in the foreign press, that Philippine newspapers were controlled by the state. Besides, with their tiny circulation they hardly mattered.

In late 1982, however, when *We Forum* published a story charging that the Marcos collection of medals was fake, Marcos decided that enough was enough. He closed down the newspaper and arrested ten staff members. The charge was "subversion and conspiracy to overthrow the government through black propaganda,"[10] with a penalty of life imprisonment or death.

Immediately a universal howl of protest erupted, a protest so loud and insistent that Marcos, after a week, ordered the journalists released and placed under house arrest "in the spirit of the Christmas season." In a press statement, Gregorio Cendaña, Marcos' information minister, declared that the government would prove its case in an open and forthright manner without "delay and equivocation." He added that the case "would strengthen freedom of speech by confronting those who would subvert the Philippine press by using its mantle of prestige and credibility to conspire against the state."[11] Despite Cendaña's brave words, however, the case dragged on and on. By the time Marcos was sent packing four years later, it still had not been resolved.

One might have expected the *We Forum* case to cow the journalists working in the "crony press." But years of martial law repression, it became clear, had not snuffed out the libertarian tradition of the Philippine media. In 1982 and early in 1983, four female columnists for *Bulletin Today* were fired by General Menzi, presumably on Marcos' orders. All four had been extremely critical of Marcos and his wife. At about this time, eight other journalists—also all female—were "invited" by military intelligence agents to answer questions about their journalistic activities. The questioning was held under very cordial and civilized conditions, but there was no doubt in anyone's minds, especially those of the journalists, that the interrogations were designed to intimidate them.

The security agents issued the invitations under the authority of the National Security Code of 1978; its section on journalism described as offenses "uttering, publishing, distributing, circulating and spreading rumors, false news, information, and gossip, and causing the publication, distribution, circulation, or spreading of the same which cause or tend to cause panic, divisive effects among the people, discredit or distrust for the duly constituted authorities, undermine the stability of the government and the objectives of the New Society, endanger the public order, or cause damage to the interest of the State."[12] The penalty for these acts? Life imprisonment or death. The government also often filed libel cases as another means of repression. Mauro Avena, a reporter who was paid $40 for an article he wrote for *Panorama*, the Sunday magazine of *Bulletin Today*, was sued for $10 million.

After the assassination

The bullet that killed Benigno "Ninoy" Aquino at the Manila International Airport on 21 August 1983 has been described as the "shot heard round the world." Indeed, although that shot focused worldwide attention on the misdeeds of the Marcos government, and although it succeeded in opening the eyes of many American legislators to the folly of supporting the Marcos dictatorship, it did something infinitely more important for Filipinos, particularly middle class Filipinos. It woke us up from the lethargy of eleven years, it made us forget our fears, and with the encouragement of the church we mounted demonstrations.

If there was ever anything that could trigger intense soul-searching, it was the cavalier way that the controlled media treated the assassination and the subsequent funeral as a non-event. Over two million people turned out for Aquino's funeral. The procession lasted a full nine hours through driving rain and searing sun, but the people stayed. It was, in the opinion of foreign journalists, the biggest funeral in history, bigger even than that of Mahatma Gandhi.

Yet when Manila's residents picked up their papers the next morning, hardly a line had been written about it. *The Times Journal*, owned by Imelda Marcos' brother, immortalized itself with a classic headline.

Studiously ignoring the funeral, its banner story reported the death of a man hit by lightning. The Marcos TV station's newscast the following day showed Imelda Marcos looking at the lopped-off branch of a tree where the victim had been perched when the lightning bolt struck. Coffee-shop wags sarcastically commented, "Funerals are held every day, but how often is a man killed by lightning?"

In fact, the only radio station that covered the assassination, the wake, and the funeral was Radio Veritas, the Church-owned station. Despite repeated "requests" for it to tone down its broadcasts, it faithfully gave full coverage to the events. The people listened solely to Radio Veritas on those days. The virtual blackout on the Aquino story prompted a group of businessmen, at Cardinal Sin's urging, to resurrect an idea from the Bishops'-Businessmen's annual meeting in February 1983. We had passed a resolution to create a committee to study the feasibility of setting up a newspaper to report the news honestly, instead of the way it was laundered by the Marcos propagandists. The committee met a few times, but the members showed no real enthusiasm for the project. All of them agreed that such a newspaper was needed, but no one wanted to take the initiative for fear of jeopardizing his business.

We lost our fear when Aquino died. His murder forced our hitherto timid group to reexamine its priorities. We decided to establish a publication that "would dare to tell the truth." We appropriately named it *Veritas*, believing quite correctly that the name would immediately evoke the impression of Church sponsorship. We took the motto of the paper from the Gospel according to John—"The truth shall set you free." James R. Rush writes:

Among the most drastic consequences of the assassination of Benigno Aquino was the revival in the Philippines of a full-blooded independent press. First hastily produced pamphlets and tabloids, then newspapers and magazines, provided full and lively coverage of the funeral and subsequent rallies and demonstrations, articulating popular sentiments of grief and outrage and venting publicly long-suppressed political frustrations.

Faced with this display of dissidence, the Marcos government had not the presence of mind or the nerve to crack down harshly. As the President and his men gritted their teeth, an independent and highly critical press reemerged in the Philippines. It has since become a primary element in the unravelling of the New Society.

Among the more substantial of its publications is *Veritas*, a hardy weekly of news and commentary informally affiliated with the local Roman Catholic Church.[13]

The story of *Veritas*

I owe my readers an explanation for chronicling the role of the Philippine alternative press in the toppling of the Marcos dictatorship primarily through the eyes of *Veritas*. There are two reasons for this. First, I was the editor of *Veritas* and, consequently, was most familiar with its activities. Second, the Catholic church played a significant part in Marcos' ouster, and *Veritas* was widely perceived to be Cardinal Sin's publication.

But yet another reason is that the tumultuous series of events that culminated in the bloodless revolution was led—and almost exclusively participated in—by the middle class.

Quoting again from Rush:

For whom is *Veritas* written? Clearly not for the masses. *Veritas* quite consciously addresses a well-educated and influential minority, many of whom are also among the comfortable and affluent, and at least among the middle classes. The level of discourse in *Veritas* assumes a high degree of literacy, and much that is said in its weekly opinion columns would be only vaguely comprehensible to those not accustomed to writing and thought at the university level.

Veritas is by no means popular. It speaks to and from the upper echelons of Philippine society, the elite group, including the Church, which has traditionally provided political, social (and in its own eyes, moral) leadership. In this time of national crisis and excitement, it calls out to its own and says, We must do something![14]

Our decision to aim *Veritas* at the middle class was deliberate.

One reason was that because of the geographical configuration of the Philippines (an archipelago with over 7,000 islands), the only way for us to circulate *Veritas* nationwide was to distribute it by air. That jacked up its cost substantially, and only the middle class— the businessmen and the professionals—would be able to afford it. A man making two dollars a day could not shell out fifty cents for a paper.

Another reason was that, in the view of the *Veritas* board, the middle class needed to be jolted out of its apathy. For it was the middle class which chafed most under Marcos' misrule, the middle class which was most outraged by the way Marcos trampled on their rights. Again we turn to Rush:

To read *Veritas* is to hear the frustrated voices of Filipino citizens whose major act of citizenship is, all too often, to react to the awful truth, and to speculate frantically about it.

In reporting the news, *Veritas* concentrates on the major events that reflect badly upon the government. Statements of the President, actions and utterances of the First Lady, and the behavior of Marcos's ministers are subjected to the keenest skeptical scrutiny, and all the ambiguities, deceptions, and hidden agendas are held up to the light and exposed to ridicule, scolding, and righteous indignation.

But *Veritas* is considerably more than a single-minded harpy, its voice is not only an angry one. In the context of Filipino journalism, and of the journalism of opposition in particular, the voice of *Veritas* is also unusually literate, thoughtful, complex, and Christian. These qualities pervade the publication, but they are most obvious in its editorial writing.

In his lead editorials Felix Bautista reminds readers on almost a weekly basis of the "revolting ugliness of the repressive regime," reiterating the common grievances—dictatorial caprice, militarism, injustices, poverty, insecurity, and state violence— and restating the common demand that "our democracy (be) restored to us." Week by week, Bautista wraps this familiar litany around the latest scandal or issue, never straying far from the basic message—this government must go! He applauds the protesters, activists, and oppositionists and calls upon them to unify and to pursue their ends non-violently.... Knowing, however, that President Marcos holds most of the cards, and therefore all too aware that changes of substance must still come from him, Bautista directs most of his umbrage at Marcos personally, calling upon him to behave in accordance with the high principles and selflessness so characteristic of his rhetoric.[15]

Cardinal Sin, in a speech in New Delhi before the Congress of the International Union of the Catholic Press (UCIP) on 22 October 1986 described how *Veritas* contributed to the downfall of Marcos in more explicit terms:

Despite libel suits and contempt of court charges, despite almost continuous death threats by anonymous callers, despite the death of twenty-five journalists within a span of years, *Veritas* reporting continued to be fearless and scrupulously accurate. Its editorials were incisive and hard-hitting, and they were even more fearless.

It exposed, in a well-documented article, the fake war record of the dictator. It brought to light the travesty of justice that resulted in the acquittal of all the accused in the Aquino murder.

When the presidential elections were held last February, *Veritas*, with its customary courage and passion for truth, disclosed, in great detail and exhaustive pictorial coverage, the attempts of the dictatorship to manipulate the results and steal the election.[16]

What was *Veritas'* biggest contribution to the fight to restore democracy in the Philippines? In my opinion, it was our suggestion, made as early as November 1984, that the alternative to Marcos was Corazon C. Aquino, the assassinated senator's soft-spoken and unassuming widow. *Veritas* argued very forcefully that Cory Aquino was everything that Marcos was not, that she, better than anybody else, had the capacity to unite the people and to lead them out of the morass caused by Marcos' profligacy. Further, *Veritas* embarked on an unrelenting editorial campaign for the holding of snap elections. Marcos, we argued, had lost his credibility both domestically and abroad, and the only way he could rightfully claim to be the true leader of the Filipino people was for him to contest—and convincingly win—a presidential snap election.

The second most significant, and perhaps the most dangerous, contribution of *Veritas* was its publication of a thoroughly researched and authenticated expose on Marcos' fake medals. The research, done by Yale historian Alfred McCoy after he had stumbled upon the documents while working on a paper on the guerrilla movement in the Central Philippines, was an eye-opener. Instead of being a war hero who, as his biographer claimed, had single-handedly delayed the fall of Bataan by three months, Marcos was unmasked as a collaborator, a man who sold scrap iron to the Japanese.

McCoy gave his findings to Veritas. On 24 January 1986, just two weeks before the snap election, Veritas published the expose. The extras sold like proverbial hotcakes, and Marcos's fate was sealed. As David Bain explains, "After weeks of putting his opponent on the defensive, Ferdinand Marcos found himself in that position—and far more vulnerable to attack than the 'mere housewife' he had felt it 'embarrassing' to run against."[17]

The *Veritas* expose prodded Marcos into spending billions of pesos in a desperate effort to buy votes to insure his victory. But Cardinal Sin, with front-page coverage by *Veritas*, told the people: "An immoral contract is not binding. If a candidate has given you money, you are under no obligation to vote for that candidate. Accept the money, for you are poor, and it is the people's money anyway."[18] Marcos and his supporters cried bloody murder. "Cardinal Sin," they shouted in unison, "is engaging in partisan politics." In reply, the prelate said, "This is not a contest between two presidential candidates. It is a fight between the forces of good and the forces of evil. In such a fight, the Church cannot stay neutral."[19]

It is estimated that fully 85 percent of the voters chose Cory over Marcos. But the Marcos-controlled legislature, with a callous disregard for the truth, proclaimed Marcos the winner anyway. That was the last straw for the long-suffering Filipinos. Enrile and Ramos defected, and Cardinal Sin urged his flock to spill out into the streets and protect them from certain death. Through People Power and Prayer Power the bloodless revolution succeeded in unseating Marcos. Cory Aquino was sworn in as President on 25 February 1986.

A new beginning

The task of *Veritas* did not end with the revolution—the work of restoring democracy had just begun. But sadly, in the first few weeks after the revolution we realized that the days of *Veritas* were numbered. While we were fighting Marcos, while our staff members were placing their liberty and even their lives on the line with every issue, *Veritas* had something to offer that the crony press did not— the truth. Because the people were hungry for the truth, *Veritas* sold well. It subsisted primarily on street sales, as only the bravest companies placed ads in it for fear of reprisals by a vindictive government. With Cory in office, the media environment changed. Suddenly all the newspapers, including the crony ones, discovered that they too could tell the truth in the new atmosphere of freedom. So *Veritas* became no different from the rest—its primary selling edge was gone.

The first task that Cory Aquino had to tackle was dismantling the dictatorial apparatus that Marcos had put in place. To do this efficaciously, she was forced to borrow some of her predecessor's authoritarian powers. She nullified the Marcos constitution, abolished the rubber-stamp Marcos Congress, and drew up what she called a Freedom Constitution. She would rule under this constitution until such time as the Constitutional Commission which she had set up had designed a new and democratic constitution. Concomitantly, she revamped the entire judiciary from the Supreme Court down to the smallest municipal trial court, ridding it of deadwood and making it a responsible and co-equal branch of government.

When the constitution was ratified in February 1987, she immediately called for congressional elections. In May of that year, the members of the new Congress, twenty-four senators and 200 congressmen, were chosen by the people. The Congress met in session on 16 July 1987.

Democracy had returned. The three branches of government were in place and every Filipino could now—despite repeated coup threats and despite destabilization attempts by Marcos loyalists and by the insurgents—work towards strengthening that democracy.

And *Veritas*, for its part, could retire from the scene. The task which we began in November 1983, when our first issue was published, was over. When we started operations, freedom did not exist. Human rights were not respected, people were denied the right to assemble peacefully, and freedom of the press was a mockery and a travesty. Truth, in truth, had become a rare commodity. *Veritas* set out to change all that. Perhaps we were biting off more than we could chew, perhaps we were sending our staffers to imprisonment or worse. But we were willing to try.

On 2 December 1987, at the celebration for the release of my book on Cardinal Sin, President Aquino delivered a speech. "If I am president now," she said, "it is in large part due to *Veritas*." To the staff of *Veritas* who had risked everything for freedom, that said it all.

Notes

1. William Henry Scott, *Prehistoric Source Materials for the Study of Philippine History* (Quezon City: New Day Publishers, 1984), p. 103.

2. Encarnacion Alzona, "Ideals of the Filipinos," (Lecture delivered before the Biennial Convention of the National Federation of Women's Clubs of the Philippines, 2 April 1954).

3. Ibid.

4. Quentin Reynolds and Geoffrey Bocca, *Macapagal: The Incorruptible* (New York: David McKay, 1956), p. 11.

5. Diosdado Macapagal, *Democracy in the Philippines* (Quezon City: New Day, 1976), p. 3.

6. Jaime L. Cardinal Sin, "The Church Above Political Systems," (Speech deliv-

ered before the Catholic Bishops' Conference of the Philippines, Baguio City, Philippines, 29 January 1973).

7. Felix B. Bautista, *Cardinal Sin and the Miracle of Asia* (Manila: Vera-Reyes, 1987), pp. 176-177.

8. John A. Lent, "Freedom of the Press in the Philippines: A Post-Martial Law Account with Update Since Aquino Assassination," (Ph.D. Dissertation, Institute of Mass Communication, University of the Philippines, Diliman, Quezon City, 1984), p. 2.

9. David Howard Bain, "Letter from Manila," *Columbia Journalism Review* 25 (May/June 1986), p. 32.

10. Lent, "Freedom of the Press," p. 5.

11. Ibid.

12. Ibid., p. 8.

13. James R. Rush, "The Voice of Veritas in Philippine Politics, "Universities Field Staff International, Inc., Reports, Indianapolis, 27 (1985), p. 1.

14. Ibid., p. 2.

15. Ibid.

16. Jaime L. Cardinal Sin, "Communication, Culture, Religion: The Philippine Experience," (Speech delivered before the Union Catholique International de la Presse (UCIP) Congress, New Delhi, India, 22 October 1986), p. 5.

17. Bain, "Letter from Manila," p. 31.

18. Cited in Bautista, *Cardinal Sin*, p. 171.

19. Cited in Bautista, *Cardinal Sin*.

The Struggle for Free Expression in South Africa

Anthony Hazlitt Heard

FOR THIRTY-FIVE YEARS I have worked as a journalist in my native country, South Africa. They were years of statutory apartheid, violence, repression. The white minority held power and blacks fought for it. Nearly half my time as a working journalist was spent editing the country's oldest-established daily, *The Cape Times* (founded in 1876). As a liberal voice, it was increasingly caught between warring white and black nationalisms. I was reared in a professional tradition which supported free expression and opposed all forms of state censorship.The years saw a steady erosion in these values. Only from 1989 was there relief, after President F. W. de Klerk came to power. De Klerk brought with him the prospect of major improvement.

When I entered the profession in 1955, the right to publish, report and comment—which had been taken for granted for years by an established press catering mainly for white interests—was coming under increasing attack from government and from other quarters. As I write, with the 1990s holding out a real prospect of democratization in the country, it is an open question what will happen to the cause of free expression. Much will depend on the views and norms of black South African leaders who will, inevitably, replace the white rulers. Much will depend on the calibre of the journalists and thinkers who will fight for the public's right to know. Much will depend on whether the public cares. Almost everything, I believe, will depend on the establishment of a democratic culture before a change in government.

When I joined *The Cape Times*, my professional mentors were "old school" people wedded to the rudiments of good journalism. They saw the craft we pursued as a means, in simple, easy-to-understand language, to communicate news and ideas to the public, or at least that section of the public who could read. In that professional tradition, the maxim was: facts are sacred, comment free. The expression of opinion had to be clearly identified as such, and, though forcefully delivered, was discouraged among younger journalists. The prime function of the press was the reporting of facts, and conveying —accurately, fairly, fully—the views of others. There was little delving beneath the news to find out the whys and wherefores of events, nor much emphasis on the personalized comment which marks editorial and op-ed pages today. My predecessor at *The Cape Times* was specifically instructed in his letter of appointment in 1944 not to use "bylines," or names of writers, which restriction had happily eroded by the time I took over in 1971. But it well illustrates the old approach: provide news, untainted by personal opinion.

My newspaper, in common with most other established papers, lived by the dictum of *"audi alteram partem"* ("hear the other side"), and our newsroom would go to exhaustive lengths to get the "other side" of every story. This was a necessary practice—no, a ritual. The newspaper world was simple, and two-dimensional. The established groups' newspapers were divided between those, appearing in the Afrikaans language, which supported the government and those, in English, opposing the government. The ownership of the former was indistinguishable from the National party which ran the country; the ownership of the latter was traceable to the same monopoly source, the mining industry which ran the economy. The Boer War was fought, over and over again, between the loyal scribes employed by these interests, generating much power-ful rhetoric, but more heat than light. Yet there was an unspoken coalition between government and business: don't rock the boat too much. At all costs, do nothing that could risk losing white power to blacks. And blacks, who did most of the hard work in South Africa, had few media outlets. Those that did exist "for them" were generally owned by the large white interests. Radical news-papers were suppressed with fury. Communists, black nationalists and militant liberals were banned or jailed. That world was simple, and—for whites—comfortably free. It seemed it would go on forever.

These conditions changed, in fits and starts, as the South African political landscape altered. As early as the 1950s and 1960s, in my own reporting experience, events such as bus boycotts, a major Trea-son Trial, the Sharpeville police shootings, indicated major political turbulence ahead. And not only for the country but for the press. The orthodoxy of apartheid was being challenged by massed blacks and a few white militants. A new Nationalist government, elect-ed in 1948, had set about the systematic segregation, by law, of South Africans in every conceivable sphere—political rights, residen-tial areas, sexual relations, schools, beaches, transport, taxis, hos-pitals, cemeteries and so on. A conservative, Calvinistic way of life was imposed on all. Censorship of books, magazines, films and objects was prissy and politically strict. No serious revolt by news-paper was to be tolerated. This remarkable post-war attempt at social engineering by the dour advocates of apartheid put free expression, and therefore the press, under severe pressure. The English-language newspapers fought with varying degrees of enthusiasm against institutionalized apartheid—many of them having put up with a less formal color bar with ease for years. Their sustained criticism did not go far enough to command mass black support, yet drew extraordinarily strong fire from the government, which regularly took action against newspapers and journalists. Writers who in a more tolerant society would be "middle-of-the-road" found themselves castigated as revolutionaries.

Numerous measures were applied to curb free expression. These bore down heavily on newspapers. Scores of laws were passed which would infringe the U.S. First Amendment; intimidating commissions of inquiry were appointed; editors, managers and proprietors were warned from on high to "put their house in order;" journalists were detained, charged in court and generally harassed by the police and politicians. It was an exciting but hair-raising time. The world-class liberal *Rand Daily Mail* of Johannesburg went through unbelievable state persecution before being closed by its own timid owners in 1985, ostensibly for "financial reasons." The government had secretly funded a major competitor which helped bury the *Mail*. Life became hazardous for a profession that had once been comfortable and secure—and almost totally "white." Talented journalists left the country, voluntarily or under duress, or sought refuge in public relations, academe or inconsequential magazines. The period of National Party rule was disastrous for the cause of free expression...which means for democracy.

Things rumbled on from crisis to crisis until unrest hit South Africa, countrywide, in 1984. Then state repression, already severe, was intensified. The government employed a series of state-of-emergency measures to try to contain the unrest—repeating the harsh tactics employed after Sharpeville in 1960. Under President P.W. Botha, emergency powers restricted the right of the press to report and comment. The higher courts, initially helpful to the press, were in time rendered virtually powerless to bolster the cause of free expression. Every time they found a loophole in the emergency regulations, it was rapidly closed by government. Coverage of the unrest was reduced to a series of daily bulletins from Pretoria, like weather reports—and often as enlightening. The growing constraints on free expression were in direct relationship to the unfolding crisis in the country—which had already begun to worsen in the mid-Seventies with the Soweto revolt and the collapse of the Portuguese African empire, followed in 1980 by the fall of Ian Smith's white minority regime in Rhodesia (Zimbabwe).

Only when, through the almost divine intervention of a presidential stroke, Botha reluctantly handed power to the younger, more pragmatic F. W. de Klerk in 1989, did things ease up. De Klerk, though still resorting to extraordinary measures to contain major unrest in the country—and hamstrung by rightwing security forces whose repressive actions frequently exacerbated unrest—allowed the media to operate more freely, though still under considerable legal restraint. He was strongly, almost blindly, backed by the established newspapers in his moves to reform the country, as he systematically stole the clothes of the liberal opposition. His stunning legalization of the African National Congress and the South African Communist Party took him light years ahead, in political terms.

In the years leading up to De Klerk, it should be explained, the curbs on free expression went well beyond direct government controls on the media. There were many other factors and tendencies which denied the public the right to know—some of which could rightly be laid at the government's door, others not.

The institution of Parliament as a valuable check on the executive had suffered major setbacks. Parliament had previously run in dual harness with the press in curbing excess and exposing abuse, if only because of the conventions of question-time and free speech within its precincts. The fact that, since the Union of South Africa was established in 1910, only whites could sit in Parliament obviously limited this role. Yet Parliament did manage, particularly through the public-spirited efforts of MPs such as Margaret Ballinger and Helen Suzman, to play an important braking role on the executive. What MPs said in the House could be reported without fear of legal or state action.

Under Botha, a move ostensibly away from the "Westminster" constitutional model but in reality away from public accountability, placed many important matters in secret committees. Moreover, the functions of government were obsessively clothed in secrecy, and much power was given to security-related bodies dominated by Botha and his hand-picked minister of defence, Magnus Malan. Non-accountable presidential government was the result. The media were thus frustrated when it came to informing people of what was going on. Moreover, in the 1980s the liberal-inclined Progressive Federal

Party lost its position as Official Opposition in Parliament to the right-wing Conservative Party; and from then on the main onslaught on the government in Parliament was from a rightist and racist, not democratic, quarter. Parliament became an irrelevant debating shop between warring Afrikaners—with inconsequential chirping from white liberals, colored (mixed race) and Indian (ethnic Asian) minorities from the sidelines.

The state-run television service was another factor which operated against the public's right to know. People, denied TV until well into the 1970s, were the more gullible when it arrived. They would instinctly believe what they saw on the "box," compared with societies which—through lengthy exposure to this fleeting, often inadequate medium—develop a healthy skepticism. Arguably television, under tight government control, proved to be *the* major factor in influencing the body politic. The message of newspapers, more enlightened, was no match for the impact of TV. The fact that once-banned black nationalist groups could, according to opinion polls, maintain substantial support among the masses in spite of TV is to their considerable credit. They did it against the tide of government propaganda, manipulation and repression.

Noteworthy also was a significant move towards the journalism of background and analysis, under the pressure of TV. This followed a world trend, but in South Africa it robbed the press of its primary reporting function, leaving the public more reliant for their basic information on state-run TV and radio. And those services were biased in favor of government. Moreover, among the new generation of journalists—many of them black—the cause of "advocacy" or committed journalism was understandably popular. It involved indulging in subjective rather than "straight" reporting. This, too, was part of a world trend. In South Africa, many people implacably opposed to the system argued that it was impossible to be neutral; journalists must either support or write against apartheid. The effect of this, however laudable in making journalists choose sides against the evil of apartheid, was to neglect large areas of primary reporting. The prism through which the South

African public saw reality was thus limited. Reporting became too much a point of view.

The struggle against repression

In the atmosphere of the unrest of the 1980s, the role of what were termed "alternative newspapers" came powerfully to the fore. These publications drew their strength from churches, campuses, trade union and other interest groups. They were grassroots newspapers, generally more militant than the established press. Some achieved enviable reputations—such as in Johannesburg, the *Weekly Mail*, spiritual heir of the *Rand Daily Mail*; the gutsy liberal Afrikaans weekly, *Vrye Weekblad*; and the Catholic Church-backed *New Nation*; and in the Cape province, papers such as *South* and *Saamstaan* (the latter honored in 1988 by South African journalists for exceptional courage under government attack). The alternative newspapers tended to have their ears close to the ground and got the first breaks on events close to the communities they served. They often set the agenda for coverage by the larger, slower-moving and generally more conservative established papers. In this, the two—established and alternative press—formed a useful coalition against tyranny and abuse. Yet it was the alternative papers that felt the cutting edge of government wrath. Instead of simply ignoring their activities, the Botha government drew extra attention to them by virtually declaring war on them as a revolutionary force. Staff were detained, papers seized off the streets, warned or suspended. The government was, in effect, their public relations officer. They survived, though embattled, and frequently upstaged the journalistic efforts of the staid, established papers.

The established English-language papers were not a political cause, but part of business life. They placed a high premium on making profits for shareholders, and their owners were the cautious mining magnates who had to remain on reasonably good terms with government, for a whole range of good business reasons. Hence, liberal editors were on more than one occasion ousted, and over-adventurous journalism was discouraged...as I discovered in 1985 when, in addition to arrest and charge in court, I was given a rebuke from my own company for publishing an "illegal" interview with the banned Oliver Tambo, head of the African National Congress. There were fleeting moments when the mining interests pursued adventurous strategies with the ANC, e.g. by meeting with its leadership in Zambia in 1985 in defiance of the wishes of the government of P.W. Botha. But big business generally played a "low profile" role and sought minimum trouble with government. After De Klerk took over in 1989 it became easier for contacts to be made across the political divide—because he had taken the bull by the horns and legalized the ANC and the Communist party.

Generally, the business establishment did little to hold the line against government excess; it thus carried joint responsibility for the erosion of press freedom. Some business figures who were publicly strongly committed against the government, and champions of the liberal press, joined the brain-drain to foreign shores; others were quieted down by conservative boardroom colleagues. The relaxed way the business establishment of Johannesburg shrugged off the closure of the *Rand Daily Mail* in 1985 showed business in its true colors: by and large, no guardian of free expression. Where that guardianship is to come from is a big question for the future.

Meanwhile, editors were left to work out "their own salvation and damnation," in the words of a past editor of *The Cape Times*, Sir Maitland Park, referring to the more placid early twentieth century. An idea of the sort of problems encountered under Botha can be gained from this internal report (one of many) drawn up at *The Cape Times* which has not previously been published. Dated 10 November 1986 it said:

> Harassment of staff by detention, arrest or threatened prosecution has taken place intermittently since unrest began in September 1984 and has continued since the promulgation of the current state of emergency on June 12.
> Within a day or so of the declaration of the emergency in June, our reporter Andre Koopman failed to return from an assignment to cover a church service in Elsie's River [a

suburb near Cape Town]. It later transpired that Mr. Koopman had been detained along with the entire congregation. In terms of the regulations his detention could not be reported until it was raised in Parliament and his name was mentioned on the floor of the House at question time. When *The Cape Times* sought an urgent Supreme Court interdict to secure his release, Mr. Koopman was suddenly let out of detention—nine days after his arrest—and the application did not need to be pursued.

A member of our photographic staff, Obed Zilwa, was arrested by police while covering unrest at Crossroads [a famous squatter area near Cape Town] in May. He was taking pictures when he was arrested and placed in a police van. At the police station, Guguletu, Zilwa was questioned for an hour or so. His efforts to establish the charge against him were unsuccessful. Meanwhile, the news desk (city desk, in the USA) had been unable to establish his whereabouts. A report appeared in the following day's "Burger" newspaper suggesting that he was arrested in possession of petrol bombs which was without foundation in fact. Our news editor, Jane Arbous, eventually traced Zilwa to Guguletu police station and after calling there in person at midnight she was able to secure his release the following morning. When released, Zilwa was told there was no charge against him.

Our municipal reporter, Peter Dennehy, was arrested at *The Cape Times* office by Lieutenant Mostert of the Security Police on August 2 and, in spite of our protests, he was taken away. At his home in the suburbs security police then conducted a search which lasted for two hours. A book was confiscated. After intervention by our attorneys, Mr. Dennehy was released on his own recognizance. He subsequently appeared in court and was charged with possession of a banned book. At a subsequent appearance the charge was withdrawn.

This is pretty well the standard pattern which official intimidation and harassment of our staff has followed: staff are summarily arrested and even incarcerated, implying a serious offence, but eventually any charges are almost invariably dropped, sometimes after we have incurred considerable legal expense and much time of staff and senior executives has been expended.

A charge against photographer Alan Taylor was withdrawn a week or so after it had been pending for more than a year and he had made a number of appearances. Counsel had been briefed. Taylor was charged with taking a picture of a man under arrest by the military during unrest at the University of the Western Cape last year.

There are still threatened charges pending under the Police Act against reporters Tony Weaver, Clare Harper and Chris Bateman, arising out of their coverage of unrest-related incidents involving security force action. Police Act charges against reporter Malcolm Fried for his account of the killing of a suspected crayfish poacher have been withdrawn.

The successful actions brought in the Natal Supreme Court made life easier in some respects. At the same time, however, the Commissioner of Police issued new and rather more explicit orders dealing with the reporting of security force action.

Picking one's way through the minefield of security laws, even when the emergency was eased by De Klerk, required living with lawyers at one's side—preferably the type who could, decisively and at a moment's notice, advise on publication of news or political advertisements, or assist when staff were detained without trial or apparent cause. When the full-scale emergency was introduced in 1986, *The Cape Times* went to the trouble, and cost, of seeking the opinion of lawyers as to whether, in their view, we could have fallen foul of the vaguely drawn and wide emergency rules over a period of several weeks. Newspaper interests, both established and alternative, sought orders in court challenging the emergency, and (as indicated in the above memo) in some cases won. But the government moved quickly to close loopholes.

In the early 1990s, as new constitutional arrangements were being considered, there was an overwhelming need for the state's control of broadcasting and influence on the media to be ended. This dangerous and critical period of constitution-making was supremely the most important moment when a free press was needed. The public needed a guide to the future, independent of government and main political players. They needed independent information and commentary on the various constitutional options on offer. They needed writers who would debunk political myths, and bravely question all politicians' motives and objectives.

Strengthening the democratic media

In this situation, what, then, could or should be done to nurture free expression as a vital part of the democratic process in the unfolding South Africa? One crucial need is to strengthen the democratic forces that still exist in the media, and I have a few proposals.

Anything calculated to improve the environment of freedom is welcome. And that should preferably be in the private domain. Resources, clearly, are needed. A certain amount of money, and a great deal of effort, can be generated locally in South Africa in the cause of free expression as the exciting era of change dawns. But it is doubtful that the job of nurturing a democratic culture in the press can be effectively accomplished without international support. Locally, every effort should be employed to convince the powerful business and mining interests that, in a country that is three-quarters black, its future lies elsewhere than in bolstering a dead-end white power structure. De Klerk, surprisingly, seems to have gotten this message himself. The mining industry spends vast sums each year, quite rightly, on mine safety, research, new technology and other necessary work to ensure its future, but it has done little to support "alternative" causes, in the media or elsewhere. Its record in supplying the public with information is equally patchy. It must be made to appreciate that business requires an environment of freedom in which to operate successfully—and this includes freedom of information and ideas. Thought control from whatever quarter, whether in the now-collapsed East Bloc or elsewhere, is simply bad business.

After the era of sanctions, world business interests will return to South Africa. But to what? Will they know what is happening to their investments? They need the benefit of a free flow of information to be able to develop their markets and monitor their performance. The all-pervasive secrecy of the past must be changed into a new openness—led by the media—as South Africa re-enters the world. And the micro-chip, satellites and computers will do the rest to speed news to and from South Africa.

Helpful to these ends, I believe, would be the establishment of a new rallying point for free expression. It could take the shape of an independent trust called the Free Expression Foundation. Such a body could involve itself in a wide range of activities: for instance, the training of journalists, exchanges and grants for further study in South Africa or abroad, the purchase of press and broadcasting capacity so that those who wish to may more easily air their views, the encouragement and subsidization of worthy media causes, a legal fund for those falling foul of the law, conferences, seminars, a research effort to monitor the cause of free expression, the award of prizes for excellence, possibly the endowment of a chair at a respected university which would further the cause of free expression. Such a body should stand outside the control of government, big business or any particular interest group.

More specifically, a Free Expression Foundation could organize conferences and seminars on the theme of the free flow of the news, not unlike those run by the International Press Institute and the Nieman Foundation (or the Johannesburg *Star* at the time of its centenary in 1987). This could serve to put pressure on all concerned—journalists, management, proprietors and government—to re-think the need for a freer environment. A research staff attached to such a Foundation could monitor the performance of the print and electronic media, gather factual information, and issue regular commentaries that would be published locally and abroad. A system of "Pulitzer"-type prizes could be established to encourage journalistic initiative, delving for facts and faithfulness to the record. Such an award could go further than encouraging journalistic enterprise and excellence—it could cover the whole area of free expression in the broadest sense. It could be run in close cooperation with press freedom organizations abroad, and could therefore enjoy some international recognition.

On the broadcasting front, it will be a most complicated job to mesh the views of those who want to perpetuate the nationalization of the air waves with those who see the best avenue ahead in a proliferation of stations under privatization. The basic step that should be taken is the drafting of a new charter for the South African Broadcasting Corporation, so that it will serve the broad interests of all the people, and not just the sectional interests of one group as has happened under the Nationalist government. Accountability to the public at large, by whatever mechanism, is the important principle to establish. Press and broadcasting must be steered away from the smothering clutches of government, and of commercial monopolies.

Overall, there is a powerful need to underpin free expression at the southern end of Africa. A new breath of freedom there can help this potential powerhouse country to play an enlightened role in Africa and the world. If the country is finally to come to grips with its basic problems—and that seems more likely now—it must, sooner rather than later, replenish its resources of freedom. Whites had a measure of press freedom for years till it was lost as the grip of a determined government closed in. Blacks have never had freedom worth talking about—of expression or anything else. Whoever inherits control of the country in a future dispensation will be more likely to respect press freedom if it is an up-and-running tradition, and not something still to be won or rediscovered. Most of the key players in the unfolding South African drama have emphasized that they wish to uphold freedom of expression. A bill of rights and an independent judiciary figure prominently on most agendas. That is encouraging, even if it is only lip-service at present. But, once in power, a new government will be pressured to attend to other, material and more immediate-*sounding* causes than the public's right to know and impartial justice. In the clamor, it might not recognize these values for what they are: at least as important as housing, education, jobs. For this reason the foundations of freedom must be built now—and quickly.

Nigeria's Embattled Fourth Estate

Ray Ekpu

NIGERIA, A COUNTRY with a unique ability to bounce back from adversity, has never given up on the quest for democracy. When the country became independent from Britain on 1 October 1960, its new leaders were optimistic about the prospects for nurturing responsible nationhood in Nigeria through the democratic process, and adopted a parliamentary system of government patterned after the Westminster model. But within five years the bottom fell out of our democracy. The politicians reduced governance to a do-or-die affair, introducing thuggery, corruption, election rigging and violence into the political process. Democracy, as then practiced, turned into a nightmare. It was no surprise when, on 15 January 1966, soldiers overthrew the civilian government of Abubakar Tafawa Balewa in a violent coup d'etat that claimed the prime minister's life and the lives of several other prominent politicians.

Major-General Johnson Aguiyi-Ironsi, head of the Nigerian Army and an Ibo from eastern Nigeria, became the first military head of state. But Ironsi's administration was shortlived. On 29 July 1966 he was killed and his government overthrown in a counter-coup. Lieutenant-Colonel Yakubu Gowon, a young northern officer, took over the reins of government and tried to weld the country together despite the poisoned atmosphere occassioned by earlier ethnic recriminations. However, continued ethnic conflict and violence deteriorated into a secession by the east which now called itself the Republic of Biafra. War ensued and dragged on for thirty months. The "Biafrans" were defeated by the federal troops and the easterners returned to the Nigerian fold in January 1970. That year, Gowon announced that his government would hand over power to an elected civilian government in 1976. However, in 1974 he declared that this date was no longer realistic because the politicians, like the Bourbons, had "learnt nothing and forgotten nothing."

The public felt miffed by this about-face and openly charged the Gowon government with attempting to overstay its welcome and prolong military rule. A year later, on 29 July 1975, the military overthrew the Gowon government and promptly announced an agenda for the transition to civilian administration in 1979. On 13 February 1976 the head of state, Brigadier Murtala Muhammed, was assassinated in an attempted coup, but this did not deter the new government of Brigadier Olusegun Obasanjo from maintaining the plan to return the country to civilian rule.

The rapid creation of about fifty-five political associations clamoring to be registered as political parties exemplified the euphoria that greeted the government's lifting of the ban on political activity. This was an unprecedented event in our country's history. Five political parties were officially recognized to contest the 1979 general elections. The National Party of Nigeria (NPN) emerged victorious and on 1 October 1979 General Obasanjo passed the baton to an elected civilian government under Alhaji Shehu Shagari. His government, an American-style presidential system, survived only until 1983 when the military intervened in the face of massive government corruption, ethnic quarrels, election rigging, mismanagement of the economy, and violence. Once again Nigeria's democratic dream had floundered. On 31 December 1983 the soldiers, under Major-General Muhammadu Buhari, left their barracks for the state house. They arrested and detained hundreds of politicians and suspended the 1979 constitution. But, in an ironic conclusion, twenty months later that extremely repressive government was overthrown by another group of soldiers led by Major-General Ibrahim Babangida. To dispel doubts about his motives for taking power, Babangida announced at the earliest opportunity that his government intended to put in motion a realistic process to hand over power to an elected civilian government.

Babangida set up a Political Bureau to assess Nigerians' views on the sort of government that they would prefer (within the framework of a presidential system). In addition, a Constitutional Review Committee was charged with revising the 1979 constitution, a Constituent Assembly was set up to examine various areas of constitutional concern and make recommendations to the government, and the ban on political activities was eventually lifted. However, hoping to start with a clean slate this time, the government banned most past politicians and office-holders from participating in the politics of the new Nigeria, in light of their previous ignoble activities in the political arena and the public service.

In addition to the political structures embodied in the constitution, the government has attempted to foster an enduring democratic culture by launching an extensive effort at "mass mobilization" to educate the people on their political and social rights and responsibilities. This aims to improve the political education of the electorate so that the ugly flaws that wrecked the First and Second Republics do not recur. In order to ensure that millionaire contributers cannot hold political parties at ransom, the government is building offices and providing funds for the two new political parties it created in 1989, after it found to be inadequate all of the political parties that sought recognition to compete in the new mandatory two-party system.

Thus, Nigeria seeks to develop a new breed of politicians who are committed to serving the public rather than to feathering their own nests. However, old habits die hard. It will not be easy to get the politicians to shake off the corrupt political practices of the first two republics. But the press can contribute towards changing public attitudes and can assist in trying to ensure that democracy works this time around in Nigeria. The Nigerian press is a student of history.

Nigerians now have an unmistakable aversion towards military rule. In 1966 there was a sense of euphoria and jubilation after the corrupt politicians had been driven out of office by the soldiers. But five coups and six soldier-presidents later, the civilian population has become convinced that the only difference between military and civilian leaders is that one wears khaki and the other the flowing agbada gown of civilian traditional dress. In terms of corruption, mismanagement, and the throttling of human rights they are both alike—we are simply "exchanging a monkey for a baboon."

After all, soldiers have ruled Nigeria for twenty out of the thirty years that the country has been independent and yet they have not performed significantly better than civilians. Despite their lengthy experiences with it, Nigerians still see military rule as an aberration, tolerable at most for only a short time. A vigorous debate has been conducted on how to curb soldiers' greed for political power. Some analysts have even suggested that all Nigerians should be permitted by law to carry arms so that they will be in a position to resist any group of ambitious soldiers who may wish to forcibly take over a civilian government in the future. That, in a nutshell, is the mood of the nation. President Babangida himself has said that he hopes his present military government will be the last in Nigeria.

However, Nigerians have not demonstrated much enthusiasm for the current transition plans. Part of the reason is that disappointment with the politicians of the past has induced widespread cynicism and apathy. The other part is that because of our serious economic problems and the accompanying hardship most people are more concerned with the politics of the stomach. They are busy trying to eke out a living and looking forward to improvements in the badly battered economy. Currently, Nigeria is carrying a heavy foreign debt burden of $30 billion. In order to escape from the present economic wilderness the government has embarked upon a Structural Adjustment Program (SAP) that has severely devalued the naira and removed the petroleum subsidy, among other measures. This has inflicted untold pain upon the people, particularly those in the lower income brackets. The problem has been Nigeria's excessive dependence on the export of crude oil, which brings in about 95 percent of our foreign exchange earnings. When the demand and price of oil fell, Nigeria found itself in dire economic straits. But with a more prudent husbandry of the economy the impact of the world recession on Nigeria could have been greatly minimized since the late 1970s and early 1980s. This is one of many critical points the Nigerian press has made as it has exposed the corruption and mismanagment of one Nigerian government after another.

Newswatch—Battling repression

Newswatch magazine was born on 28 January 1985, at a time when the iron-fisted government of General Buhari was clamping down hard on the freedoms of speech and the press. Soon after Buhari's seizure of power, his government promulgated a law, known as Decree 4, which sought to punish even truthful statements if they proved embarrassing to the government or its officials. The regime pressed ahead with this obnoxious measure despite press opposition. To demonstrate its resolve, the Buhari government arrested two reporters for the *Guardian*, a privately owned Lagos newspaper, and gave each of them a year in jail for violating the decree. From then on, the battle lines were drawn. They were to remain in place even after the new military government of President Ibrahim Babangida withdrew the decree and announced its intention to guide the country back to civilian democratic rule.

It so happened that this period of political change came at a time when the four young editors who were to found *Newswatch* were looking for a new journalistic enterprise to pursue. The founders of the magazine were Dele Giwa, Dan Agbese, Yakubu Mohammed, and myself. Giwa, then thirty-eight, had a master's degree in Public Communication from Fordham University. In 1974 he began working at the *New York Times* as a news assistant, but soon progressed to the national, metropolitan and foreign desks as well as the United Nations bureau. As a courageous young man who believed in equality and justice, he was one of those who, along with other blacks, sued the *New York Times* for racial discrimination against minorities. He was awarded $2000 in damages and later promoted to reporter. Upon his return to Nigeria he worked as the features editor of the *Daily Times*, and in 1980 moved on to become the pioneering editor of the Sunday *Nigerian Concord*. In 1983, the fourth and final year of Nigeria's ill-fated Second Republic, he was arrested and spent two weeks in jail for publishing government documents. After several court battles, he won both damages for wrongful detention and a public apology from the police.

Dan Agbese, at forty-one the oldest of the four, studied at the University of Lagos and went on to earn a master's degree in Journalism from Columbia University. After graduation he worked at the *Nigerian Standard*, where he became editor in 1978. In 1982, he was made editor of the *New Nigerian*, a federal government paper where he had once been a reporter. In addition to these journalistic positions, Agbese had also held several important communications and information posts in the government of the state of Benue.

Yakubu Mohammed, thirty-five, studied Mass Communication at the University of Lagos and did additional studies in management in Glasgow. He was the managing editor of the *New Nigerian* before moving on to the Concord Group, where he became the editor of the *National Concord*.

I was thirty-seven at the time *Newswatch* was conceived, and was serving as chairman of the Concord Group's editorial board. I graduated in Mass Communication from the University of Lagos and then took an advanced journalism course at Indiana University. I was subsequently the editor of the *Nigerian Chronicle*, the *Sunday Times*, and the *Business Times*. These journalistic activities in the years before I joined Concord had twice earned me police detention; in 1983 I was arrested again and held for seventeen days until freed by court order.

Together, Giwa, Mohammed, and I headed the Concord Group's three major organs. As chairman of the Group's editorial board, it was my particular responsibility to oversee the opinion pages of all three English-language editions of the *Concord*. Our boss was Chief Moshood Abiola, the multimillionaire International Telephone and Telegraph (ITT) executive who owned the *Concord* newspapers. Chafing at Abiola's attempts to control editorial policy, all three of us resigned simultaneously on 17 July 1984. At about the same time, Agbese was coming under pressure from politicians who wanted him to subordinate the professional integrity of the *New Nigerian* to the interests of the government and the ruling party. Not surprisingly given these circumstances, he was glad to accept our invitation to join *Newswatch* as a cofounder.

Newswatch was thus the brainchild of a gang of disgruntled journalists who were far from satisfied with the existing state of things in the Nigerian press and who hoped that through their new, independent magazine they could contribute to the practice and growth of journalism in Nigeria. We were bound to one another by personal as well as professional ties, to be sure, but what proved decisive in bringing us together was the profound respect we had for one another's journalistic talents, and our confident belief that the following each of us had among newspaper readers would make *Newswatch* a publishing success.

The first hurdle to be overcome was money. While our enthusiasm and professional expertise were abundant, our financial resources were not. We refused to be daunted by the slenderness of our means, however, and began our enterprise by registering a publishing company called Newswatch Communications, Limited. The initial share capital was pegged at N500,000 (then equal to slightly more than $500,000). Each of us controlled 15 percent of the stock, and 5 percent was to be distributed among the staff. The remaining 35 percent was to be sold to investors. We eventually found four businessmen who jointly invested N850,000, enough to cover start-up costs. None of the four was allowed to own more than 10 percent of the stock. Moreover, they all agreed to refrain from participation in partisan politics while their association with the company lasted. We, the founders, also signed a pledge not to accept any government appointment, whether full-time or part-time, or to run for any political office as long as we remained with the company. All these arrangements were born out of our desire to ensure that *Newswatch* would be vigorously independent. They were ways of insulating the magazine from the corrosive influence of partisan politics and of creating a solid foundation for *Newswatch*'s credibility. Financial viability, we thought, could be best assured by a combination of journalistic excellence and prudent management.

When compared with our high aspirations, the physical circumstances in which we began our work must seem humble indeed. We built the partitions in our rented office space ourselves. Our newsroom had only two desks and four chairs to start with; the staff used these in shifts or simply worked on the floor. We had no typesetting or printing equipment of our own, so we contracted out both jobs. We used the typesetting facilities of the *New Nigerian* in Lagos, about ten miles from our offices near Ikeja.

Our printer was Academy Press, the best printing outfit in Nigeria at that time. The managers there were used to the leisurely pace of general commercial printing, however, and the idea of producing a weekly magazine filled them with terror. When we refused their pleas to convert *Newswatch* into a monthly, they insisted on setting a stiff deadline: all material had to be received ten days before the publication date. In our desperation we accepted this condition, although we feared that it would ruin us as a news magazine. Happily, our fears proved unfounded, for as the printers began to master the production process we began to shift the deadline in our favor. Now we send them our finished copy on the Friday preceding the Monday on which the magazine hits the stands.

Before going into actual production, we did a preview issue of *Newswatch* to test the reactions of readers and advertising agencies. Despite the preview issue's imperfections, the public reception was encouraging. The advertising agencies, unfortunately, were not. They warned us that the extreme volatility of the magazine business in Nigeria had made advertisers very cautious; we would probably have to wait a year after our debut to get any paid ads. They were right, of course: in Nigeria, most magazines are "born in the morning and dead by the afternoon." Yet this gloomy observation only redoubled our resolve to survive and prove the doomsayers wrong.

The first full-blown issue of *Newswatch* appeared on 28 January 1985. The cover story dealt with drug trafficking, and the press run was 30,000 copies of forty pages each. The magazine sold so well that week that we printed 35,000 copies of the next issue. Week after week, our readers gave us a vote of confidence. By April 1987, our weekly circulation had risen to 150,000 copies.

Much of the credit for the magazine's success must go to our rigorous standards of staff recruitment and editing. Senior editorial staffers are recruited by invitation only; junior staffers are screened through a process of interviews and written tests. There is no lack of candidates at either level. We seek to guarantee *Newswatch*'s quality by holding our writers and copy editors to uniformly high standards, and by reserving final control over all articles to ourselves as founding editors.

But perhaps the main reason why *Newswatch* enjoys such a high reputation among our fellow journalists and such great popularity among readers is its unabashed stress on investigation. We are pleased to note that our magazine has given Nigerian investigative journalism a shot in the arm. While such reporting is often costly and time-consuming, we think that it merits the effort.

The perils of investigative reporting

Of course, while a muckraking magazine may be loved by its readers, it is likely to arouse feelings of quite a different sort in those who become the objects of its scrutiny. For such a magazine, trouble is a constant companion, and *Newswatch* has had its share. We first got into hot water when our first-anniversary issue appeared on 27 January 1986. The cover story that week (the magazine was dated 3 February) dealt with Justice Samson Uwaifo's judicial panel, a body of jurists charged with the responsibility of investigating political corruption cases dating from the period of the Second Republic. Uwaifo's panel, after shockingly perfunctory deliberations, had cleared former President Shagari and his Vice President Alex Ekwueme of all wrongdoing and recommended their immediate release from detention. Against a background of public outrage at this travesty, we ran a detailed analysis of the proceedings, and I wrote a column calling the trials "a farce," and accusing Justice Uwaifo of "abject naïvety."

The following day, five of our staffers and I received a summons to appear before Uwaifo to answer "contempt of the tribunal" charges. We contacted a brilliant radical lawyer, Chief Gani Fawehinmi, who generously praised the magazine's efforts and offered to defend us free of charge. I refused to recant before Justice Uwaifo, who detained us all for a few hours and later fined me N20. I appealed my conviction.

Uwaifo's petty harassment was merely an annoyance; it pales in comparison to the tragic loss we suffered later that year on 19 October when our editor-in-chief Dele Giwa was murdered by a parcel bomb sent to his home. The package was delivered by two men in a car to Giwa's security guard. Its top bore the words: "From the office of the C-in-C," and it was addressed to "Chief Dele Giwa." "This must be from the president," said Giwa as he held it on his lap and tried to open it. The explosion dismembered his lower body; he died at the hospital a short while later. His death saddened and angered millions of Nigerians who never knew him except through his articles, and the funeral obsequies accorded him were those of a national hero.

Shortly before Giwa was killed, state security officials had "invited" him to see them for several "chats"—secret policemen's euphemisms for interrogation. In the course of these sessions they levelled an array of bizarre and obviously fabricated allegations against him, including charges that he was plotting to foment a socialist revolution. They also accused him of planning a story on Ebitu Ukiwe, a deputy of President Babangida whom the chief executive had dismissed some weeks earlier. The police claim to this day that they have not identified Giwa's killers. Unfazed by this ominous official indifference to political murder, Gani Fawehinmi (who was himself jailed by the government in 1989) has waged a dauntless battle to prosecute two high-ranking state security officials, A.K. Togun and Halilu Akilu, for the killing.

Just as we were trying to recover from the awful shock of Giwa's death, another booby trap went off. On Sunday 5 April 1987 our printers delivered 150,000 copies of the magazine for sale the following day. The cover story that week was a detailed exclusive on the as yet unreleased report of the Political Bureau, a body set up by President Babangida to chart the course for Nigeria's return to civilian rule. The article's title was "Third Republic: A New Political Agenda," and it contained extracts from the report itself. This, we knew, was a banner issue, one of our best ever. We could hardly wait for it to come out.

A magazine under siege

Unbeknownst to us, however, some people in high government circles had gotten wind of the story we were planning to run, and had resolved to silence us. As Yakubu Mohammed and I sat in the office shortly after 11:00 P.M. on that Sunday night collating documents for the next day's board of directors meeting, the sudden wail of a siren announced the arrival of a dozen heavily armed antiriot policemen at our gates. After peremptorily ordering our security guards to admit them, the officers promptly sealed off the premises, declaring that no one would be allowed to enter or leave. This proved to be not precisely the case, however, as both parties to the confrontation were soon reinforced—we by our co-editor Dan Agbese, and the police by thirty-seven of their colleagues, all fully armed and chanting war songs. It was well into the wee hours of Monday morning before we were at last allowed to leave. The police stayed.

By that afternoon, the *Newswatch* offices resembled a war zone. Our staffers were in shock; they had not come to work expecting to find the occupying troops of an unfriendly power camped out in our newsroom. I spoke to them, recommending that we temporarily transfer operations to my home. After regrouping there, we decided that we would not let our anxiety about the police siege keep us from forging ahead with the next issue. A reporter was therefore dispatched to interview the president's chief press secretary, Duro Onabule, for the upcoming cover story, a piece to be entitled "Under Siege: Police Invade *Newswatch*." At the close of the interview, Onabule looked at our writer and asked, "By the way, where are you going to publish this report?" The import of this remark became clear later that day, when the government announced that publication of *Newswatch* would be suspended for six months. Accompanying this announcement was a statement citing *Newswatch*'s publication of extracts from the Political Bureau's report, "ahead of governmental consideration and decision," as grounds for the ban.

The official decree of proscription, appropriately backdated, came down four days later. The government froze all the accounts of Newswatch Communications, Limited. Agbese, Mohammed and I were all detained for a day, our offices and homes were searched twice, and our photographs and fingerprints were taken by state security officials. We were threatened with prosecution under the Official Secrets Act.

News of these events sent shockwaves across the country and abroad. Organizations such as the Commonwealth Journalists' Association, the New York-based Committee to Protect Journalists, and the Washington, D.C.-based World Press Freedom Committee, as well as numerous prominent individuals, appealed to President Babangida to end the ban. Yet while the government dropped the charges against Agbese, Mohammed, and me, it refused to budge on the proscription of *Newswatch* magazine itself. As May had rolled around without any sign of softening in the regime's position, we registered—under the names of some of our lesser-known staffers—a new company called Ultimate Publications, Limited. Before the month was out, Ultimate Publications was publishing a new human-interest magazine called *Quality*. (This journal happily lived up to its name, and we are still putting it out today.) Finally, on 26 August 1987 the government lifted the ban, which had been due to end in forty days.

The murder of Dele Giwa and the muzzling of *Newswatch* graphically illustrate the dangers that hedge about the practice of journalism in developing countries, especially those governed by military dictators. No method of reprisal seems too severe to use against a press that dares to adopt an independent and critical stance. The arbitrary treatment meted out to *Newswatch* is a case in point. The magazine was "convicted"—without benefit of anything even resembling due process—of an "offense" which did not even exist at the time it was supposedly committed. The decree of proscription was promulgated after the ban was announced and then backdated—a flagrant example of *ex post facto* legislation.

The ban also raised anew the oft-debated question of what constitutes an official secret. Can any piece of paper become a secret document simply because officialdom says it is one? Does the Official Secrets Act apply to private persons who have never taken any oath of secrecy? Is every "official secret" something that would harm the public good if exposed, or is it not possible that misconduct or malfeasance—things detrimental to the public good that must be exposed to be corrected—can also be shrouded with the veil of official secrecy and hidden away in government vaults?

The government's willingness to subject *Newswatch* to this ordeal evinces a profoundly disturbing contempt for the rule of law. Arbitrary, ad hoc decrees are the antithesis of equal laws, equally applied. In journalism, as in all areas of human endeavor that may be touched by the law, there must be reasonably clear boundaries between what is permitted and what is not. Otherwise, as we noted in an editorial shortly after *Newswatch* resumed publication, "the practice of journalism will at least be akin to jogging in the jungle and at worst to walking blindfolded through a minefield. The danger there is that you may never know when you have crossed the line of death, when your toe has touched the detonator. Where in place of clarity there is fogginess, in place of law there is whim, then journalism enters the realm of occultism."

Journalism is an endeavor in service of the public good; journalists must be just as dedicated to that good as they are to high professional standards. This is the principle that has guided *Newswatch* all along, and which accounts for our rigorous recruitment policy, our peculiar ownership arrangements, and our nonpartisan posture. Without them, we could never have achieved the expertise and independence that we must have if we are to render optimal public service.

Our concern for the public good underlies our stress on investigative journalism. Our willingness to undertake investigations is anchored in our belief that the people's right to know must be upheld, that the government must be held accountable to those whose taxes pay for it. We strive to defend stoutly the rights and freedoms of the people, as enshrined in the Nigerian constitution, because we believe that liberty is an inalienable human right, and that a threat to it anywhere is a threat to it everywhere.

Respect for human rights is one of the great pillars of civilization. Sadly, many governments in Africa and other parts of the developing world honor such rights more in the breach than in the observance. We think this is intolerable, and hope that our magazine's record of unwavering support for human rights may serve as an example and an encouragement to friends of liberty and justice, not only in Nigeria, but throughout Africa and even the world.

A culture of censorship

Although our ideals and aspirations remain high, our situation continues to be difficult. The journalist's lot is a hard one in many developing countries, where the obstacles to a free, accurate, and responsible flow of information are formidable indeed. The reasons are not far to seek. Most of the governments in Africa are either military dictatorships or one-party regimes, and most of the remainder are scarcely more democratic. Such circumstances invariably breed a culture of censorship that inhibits both the free flow of information and its concomitant, the free clash of ideas. Some governments use oppressive laws to trammel the press, while others resort to extralegal measures such as threats, harassment, arbitrary detention, and even outright brutality. Either way, the lesson should be clear: where the government is not truly democratic, the press cannot be truly free. The media in developing countries are often owned or controlled by the government, officials of which are usually on hand to remind any editor who would strike an independent note that "he who pays the piper, calls the tune." In Nigeria, for instance, the state owns most of the newspapers and all of the radio and television stations. It is thus largely left to a handful of private newspapers and magazines to offer fair reportage on events. But even these organs are hampered by laws like the Official Secrets Act and the Defamation Act, as well as by harassment from state security agents. Sometimes other, more subtle measures such as the withdrawal or withholding of government advertising or increases in the tariff on paper and printing materials are employed to bring troublesome publications to heel.

The low levels of both literacy and disposable income that prevail throughout much of the developing world are further banes to journalism, for they combine to place severe limits on readership. In lands where many either cannot read or must regard newspapers and magazines as unaffordable luxuries, considerations of journalistic objectivity and independence often have to take second place to the struggle to avoid drowning in a sea of red ink.

Other difficulties—especially the problem of maintaining clear distinctions between reportage and editorializing—stem from the poor training of journalists themselves. In some Nigerian publications, for example, there is no clear separation of news from views. The time-honored maxim that "news is sacred and comment is free" has generally been ignored. Journalism is more than mere superficial recording of what is said and done, of course, and we at *Newswatch* seek to provide our readers with in-depth coverage and explanation of events. Yet we also believe that it is best to lay the relevant facts and figures before our readers in a comprehensive manner that will enable them to arrive at their own informed conclusions, and we strive to avoid using our news columns to propagate our own opinions. Hence all the opinion pieces in *Newswatch* are labelled as such. Columns by the editors and guest columnists speak for their authors only; they do not represent the position of the magazine. On just three occasions in its more than four years of existence has *Newswatch* published editorials: one on 9 September 1985, when the Buhari government was overthrown; one on 6 January 1986, after a failed coup attempt against President Babangida; and one on 14 September 1987, when the magazine hit the streets again after its proscription.

In the murky political atmosphere that prevails in most developing countries, publishing a magazine is like flying through a fogbank—steel nerves and lightning reflexes are a must. The effort to remain independent and critical despite pressure from the government and other sources can be a perilous enterprise indeed, as witness the experience of a reporter in my country named Minere Amakiri. A few years ago, Amakiri wrote an accurate story for his paper, the *Nigerian Observer*, about a plan by teachers in the Rivers State to go out on strike because their salaries had not been paid. Amakiri was detained on the orders of the state's military governor. The reporter's head was shaved with a broken bottle, and he received two dozen strokes of a cane across his bare back. The governor's grouse was not because the story was false, but because the embarrassing story was published on his birthday! Although Amakiri later successfully sued for damages, his case reveals the lengths to which those in power will go to intimidate and muzzle the press.

In 1982, when I was editor of the *Sunday Times*, the ruling NPN began pressing me to toe its line. When I resisted, I found myself reassigned to the *Business Times*, a smaller paper owned by the same publishing company. I spent three weeks there, working in a windowless office next to the toilet, before a renewed attempt to pressure me provoked my resignation.

On 23 January 1983 the *Sunday Concord* ran a story of mine on the rising number of suspicious fires in government buildings. Corrupt officials, it seems, were committing arson to destroy records that might reveal their crimes. In the course of the article I warned that the Nigerian External Telecommunications building might be the next target, as there was a case of massive fraud in the organization. That building went up in flames the very next day, and two people died in the blaze. Three days later I was arrested and charged with murder. My detention lasted for seventeen days until the Lagos High Court quashed the "murder by pen" indictment that the government had lodged against me.

It would be gratifying to report that in Nigeria today outrages like these are a thing of the past, but that is not the case. The Babangida government—despite its professed commitment to human rights—continues to use Decree 2 (a writ first enacted by the highly repressive Buhari regime), which permits the detention of anyone deemed a threat to state security for up to six months without a trial. Several journalists have been jailed under this decree—some for longer than six months, as the term is renewable.

Government harassment of journalists takes many forms in Africa, as the famous Willowgate scandal in Zimbabwe demonstrates. The Willowgate Motor Industries is owned by a government conglomerate, and government officials used to order cars and trucks for friends and family, or to sell at high profits. Geoff Nyarota, editor of *The Chronicle*, heard about this and carried out a painstaking investigation. His story forced the Mugabe government to order a judicial inquiry resulting in the firing of many government officials. But soon afterwards, Nyarota was "promoted" to a public relations post as a result of government pressure on his newspaper company—investigative journalism was kicked in the shin.

In Ghana in 1986 the government withdrew the license of the *Catholic Standard* newspaper for writing "in a manner that clearly jeopardizes national interest." A few days later, the corpse of a priest, mistaken for the paper's proprietor, was found in the sea. Other newspapers, cowed by this clear warning, began to toe the government line, while the surviving government-owned papers such as the *People's Daily Graphic* spew nothing but propaganda.

In Sierra Leone, the hitherto independent private press has come under considerable pressure from the government. In 1983, eight independent newspapers were shut down by the then-President Siaka Stevens' All People's Congress while a committee was created to license the journalists and introduce other measures to keep the press in the government's pocket.

In most other African countries such as Kenya, Ethiopia, Zaire, and Liberia, the story is basically the same, and of course in South Africa banning anti-apartheid newspapers has been standard practice. The press is also under assault elsewhere in the developing world, as incidents from Chile and Turkey illustrate. In 1987 a Chilean court found Juan Pablo Cardenas, editor-in-chief of the weekly newsmagazine *Analisis*, guilty of insulting President-General Augusto Pinochet in print and sentenced him to eighteen months of "night prison" in Santiago.

Being a "responsible editor" in Turkey often means going to jail as well. In February 1989, Fatima Yazici, the editor of *Toward 2000*, was imprisoned. Her crime? Insulting President Kenan Evren by writing about two apartments he had bought for his daughters at rock-bottom prices. She was sentenced to twenty-eight months in jail.

Dictatorship versus a free press

In countries where just maintaining editorial independence and offering occasional critical commentary can prove hazardous to one's health, the risks involved in the practice of investigative journalism are terrible indeed. The nondemocratic governments that rule such countries naturally fear a free and vigorous press, and have created all-pervasive climates of threat, intimidation and unaccountability in order to stifle it. If repressive laws fail to deter the conscientious journalist, methods of an even more nakedly vicious sort may be tried. Sometimes the authorities will stop at nothing to prevent a dogged investigator from prying open this or that can of worms. The assassination of Dele Giwa, which was surely meant as a warning to other journalists who might have been made bold by his example, brought these dangers into sharp and terrible focus.

More prosaic obstacles also await journalistic investigators. Many Third World editors, finding themselves strapped for money, staff, and resources, are reluctant to underwrite long-term investigative projects and usually opt for the "quick fix" over the "fishing expedition." In addition, there is the general lack of accountability in developing countries. This culture of indifference is found at every level of government, and is exemplified as much by haphazard and shoddy recordkeeping as by official hostility to inquiries and complaints. The barriers thus placed in the way of in-depth reporting are considerable.

Yet there is no cause for despair; energetic leadership on the part of editors can do much to overcome these hurdles. We at *Newswatch*, for instance, have made a systematic effort to improve the competence of our staff through training seminars, subsidized travel, and the creation of a research library. We review the performance of each of our staffers twice every year; rewards are provided for those whose work is exemplary. Our goal is to foster a spirit of healthy competition which translates into a better magazine and thus boosts readership, sales, and advertising.

Experience shows that our commitment to excellence has been a wise one. Although the general economic downturn that struck Nigeria after the drop in world oil prices has affected *Newswatch* as it has every other enterprise, demand for the magazine has remained high enough to keep us in sound financial condition. Our healthy balance sheet is one fruit of our efforts to find and nurture able journalists who will give readers real news and analysis rather than the slapdash reporting and recycled propaganda found in much of the Nigerian press. The World Press Review recognized our efforts in 1987 when they named me the International Editor of the Year. In their citation, *Newswatch* and myself were commended for "courage, enterprise, and leadership on the international level in advancing press freedom and responsibility and defending human rights and furthering journalistic excellence."

The level of press freedom that prevails in any society is directly proportional to the level of other forms of freedom that are available there. A truly democratic society invariably offers abundant freedom to all its citizens, including journalists. But journalists must also place themselves squarely in the front rank of those who strive to uphold and preserve democratic ideals and practices. Over the last few years the Nigerian press has, much to its credit, been trying to do just this.

In most countries of the developing world, the road to democracy is blocked by rulers who seek only to maintain themselves in positions of power and privilege. They seek to stifle the emergence of a democratic political culture, and try to weaken or destroy such democratic institutions as do exist. Their resistance to democracy is a major cause of instability in these lands, as is the vaulting ambition of military officers who, having tasted political power, come to prefer the halls of government to the barracks.

The prevailing patterns of media ownership in the Third World represent another dimension of the problem. All too often the government pulls all the strings, and the functionaries who run the state-owned newspapers, magazines, and broadcasting outlets must either behave like pliant puppets or lose their places to others who will. When the mildest penalties for disobedience are instant dismissal and official disgrace, it is easy to see why many editors and media officials adopt an attitude of "my master, right or wrong" in response to pressure from on high. All that stands against the state's media juggernaut is the privately owned press, but it often lacks the necessary size, skill and prestige—or is too eager to play ball in order to survive in the harsh economic environment of Third World publishing.

If democracy prevails in the developing world, both the people and the press will surely benefit from the expanded frontiers of freedom that will result. But neither democracy nor freedom of the press can survive unless both the people and the press stand up against dictatorship and resist all assaults on democratic institutions. For as Edmund Burke once said, "The only thing necessary for the triumph of evil is that good men do nothing."

Thirty Years of Turbulent Journalism in the Sudan: A Personal Experience

Bona Malwal

IN THE CONTEXT of African tradition, no man who thinks of himself as whole, complete, and with something notable to offer to his society would sit down to write or talk about himself, unless it was in the form of praise-songs for his family, clan, and tribe. For this reason I was rather ambivalent about whether to write in detail about my personal experiences as a journalist of independent mind in the Sudan over the past thirty years. However, after much thought, I concluded that such a personal account would not be purely biographical, but would expose innumerable forces and problems I have confronted in pursuit of a free press, and therefore I owed it to posterity to put something down on paper. My media experiences are a part of the greater Sudan experience since independence and help illustrate that Sudan is not merely a developing country but one of the developing world's most polarized and divided.

Since beginning work in the independent media in the Sudan in March 1965, the main difficulty I have faced has been the head-on clash of values between myself and those who have ruled Sudan during that time. From very early childhood, my Dinka tribal upbringing emphasized the importance of telling the truth at all times, even at the risk of one's life. My father was a Dinka tribal chief and hence his family, especially the male children (from whom a future chief was expected to come), were required by custom to be of forthright character and an example to others. Being the eldest son, the onus to be truthful perhaps fell heavier upon me than upon my younger brothers. My tribal values were to clash continually and irreversibly with the Sudanese government and its representatives, who largely saw the truth as being the "truth" that they themselves created and circulated in the official media. Anyone who dared to contradict the government's "truth" would be branded as a traitor and an enemy of the state.

At the end of 1960, I won a scholarship to study journalism at Indiana University in the United States. The scholarship was one of many given to the Sudanese government by the U.S. Agency for International Development. The only proviso to the scholarship was that I commit myself to work for the Sudanese government for at least four years upon completing my studies in America.

Due to the nature of Sudan at the time, my acceptance of the scholarship was not without problems. By 1960, Sudan was engulfed in a civil war between the North and South that had begun in August 1955, some four months before Sudan gained its independence on 1 January 1956. I was already in a sense a by-product of that war. Sudan was then ruled by its first military dictatorship, which had come to power in November 1958. This military regime was quickly noted not only for its generally repressive policies, but for its attempts to forcibly convert the people of Southern Sudan into Muslims and Arabs. Painfully for me, many Southern Sudanese who did not know me believed I could have been awarded a scholarship to study abroad only if I had wholeheartedly endorsed the government's repressive policies in the South, betraying my own people. For a considerable time then, I had to live with this cloud hanging over me, until I could prove my critics wrong.

Upon my return to Sudan from the U.S., in compliance with my previous contractual commitment, I was employed as an official of the Ministry of Information's government-run English language newspaper, the *Sudan Daily*. For the next seven months I was a loyal but extremely unhappy employee of the government. By early 1964 the civil war had taken a turn for the worse, with indiscriminate killings of Southerners by the government's forces. Educated Southerners—whom the government generally suspected of masterminding the rebellion—increasingly became targets of the government's intention to extinguish any independent identity or character from the South, and to kill whole groups of potential opposition and leadership in the South. It rapidly became apparent to me that the only worthy young educated Southerner was the one who left Sudan to join the ranks of the Southern Sudanese Liberation Movement abroad, and thus continue the South's struggle in exile.

I had become an active member of a Southern Sudanese underground movement working inside the country by the time the increasingly repressive regime of General Abboud was finally overthrown in October 1964. A general strike had been organized nationwide, supported by sustained demonstrations in Khartoum and other major towns. When the army refused to fire on the demonstrators the regime collapsed.

At the outset of the general strike, I was one of the first people to bring the strike's official literature into the Ministry of Information, informing all the officials that the strike had started there and then. I walked out of the ministry as a striker to be followed by many others. My immediate supervisor marked me down as the ringleader of the strike in the ministry, and in the early hours of the nationwide protest when the regime was struggling to hold its own, I was tried in absentia by a summary disciplinary court in the ministry, found guilty and dismissed. However, as the downfall of the regime became apparent over the next few days, my "trial" and dismissal papers were torn up and I was reinstated in my job.

Following the overthrow of the Abboud regime, the internal underground movement of Southern Sudan was converted into a legitimate mass political movement called the Southern Front and I was elected as the Front's first secretary-general. Among the Front's more immediate objectives was the creation of its own media outlet to counteract the unfavorable coverage it received in the northern press and the state-controlled media. As the only member trained specifically in journalism and with experience in the field, I was the natural choice of the movement to establish a newspaper.

My subsequent resignation from the Ministry of Information was not a smooth affair at all. The powers-that-be at the Ministry were concerned over the establishment of the Front's newspaper, *The Vigilant*, and were also disturbed by my political activities as secretary-general of the Southern Front. They therefore tried to obstruct my resignation from the Ministry to prevent me from taking up these positions effectively. They claimed that the terms of the original journalism scholarship in America had contractually bound me to work for the ministry for four years, and that the resignation could only be accepted if I were to repay the full cost of my scholarship, a sum quoted in tens of thousands of American dollars. My insistence upon the resignation would mean being taken to court. However, I saw a clear political advantage in being taken to court by the government over this matter, and so I informed my superiors that I was leaving the ministry regardless and would eagerly await their next move. It took the ministry several months to decide to avoid any political showcase in court, and to release me from my contract by accepting my resignation.

Five years on *The Vigilant*

The Vigilant came into being during one of the most turbulent periods in Sudan's post-independence history. Within three months of Abboud's overthrow, by December 1964, the Southern Front had emerged as a major popular movement commanding vast support across the South, despite a campaign of intimidation, coercion and murder against its members by the powers in Northern Sudan. By March 1965, the Southern Front could boast a number of policy successes. Most importantly, the Front had succeeded in prompting the transitional government of Prime Minister Sir El Khatim El Khalita (in which the Southern Front held all four of the posts reserved for the South) to hold a Round Table peace conference in Khartoum to negotiate an end to the civil war in the South. The Round Table

Conference was convened amid preparations for a general election to be held in May. The Northern Sudanese political parties had been insistent that the elections be held in April or May 1965. This hurrying through of the political agenda before the Round Table Conference had met was unacceptable to the Southern Front, which organized a complete boycott of the elections in the South, having first insisted that Southern representatives to a parliament in Khartoum could not be elected until the conference had worked out a permanent solution to the situation in the South.

It was in this highly charged and exciting political atmosphere of early 1965 that *The Vigilant* was born. Well aware of the dangers and challenges that I was up against as the editor of this fledgling newspaper, speaking out in the name of the Southern Sudanese, I neither underestimated the task ahead nor took fright at it.

The Vigilant's first edition was published on 15 March 1965, a few days after the Round Table Conference had convened. The most immediate impact of the paper was to present an alternative view of the conference proceedings over those first four or five days. Up until then the only reports on the conference had been in the Arabic press, advancing a purely Northern perspective. As I was one of the Southern Front's delegates to the conference, I was in an ideal position to report the inside story of the conference, from the Southern perspective. All the later problems faced by *The Vigilant*, as well as all of its prestige, stemmed from this time when the paper set out to "pull no punches" in its coverage of the Sudanese political scene.

This period also saw the beginnings of my personal problems with the Sudanese government and its security apparatus. As editor, I took full responsibility for everything that appeared in the newspaper. The government never wasted an opportunity to prosecute me for anything in the paper that was considered offensive. By the time that Nimeiri's military coup overthrew the civilian government in May 1969, I had at least nineteen court cases pending against me in the various major cities and even in some small towns. Almost anywhere there was a news event that *The Vigilant* reported, there was a case against me in court. Not too surprisingly, these encounters with the government were to be repeated again and again over subsequent years, particularly because some of my adversaries from those early days, such as Sadiq El Mahdi, were to keep on reappearing in power.

Most of the cases against *The Vigilant* were concerned with our reports of atrocities against civilians in the South by government forces, which continued to pursue a military solution to the civil war in spite of the Round Table Conference. Following the May 1965 elections, a new civilian government had officially embarked on a campaign for military victory over the South, and the armed forces began an unprecedented reign of terror in the South, even more brutal than the forced assimilation campaigns of General Abboud. Educated Southerners—who had been encouraged to return to the South to administer their own people during the transitional period—again became a particular target of military action. On the nights of 8 and 9 July alone, in Juba, more than 1400 Southern civilians were massacred by the army. On 11 July, seventy-six senior Southern officials were slaughtered while attending a wedding reception in Wau. These incidents were followed by countless others, wherever educated Southerners were to be found. Reporting these atrocities in *The Vigilant* was the basis of all the court cases brought against me and the paper.

Between July 1965 and February 1966—the first and only time a case against *The Vigilant* actually went to trial—hardly a week passed without the current edition of the paper being seized, distribution prevented, and myself arrested. These were the days when even a Southern Sudanese still relied on the independence and fairness of the Sudanese judicial system. My lawyer, Abel Alier, a respected and distinguished former judge, had to appear almost on a weekly basis before the magistrates, arranging bail for me and flying to places around the country where *The Vigilant* or I myself was being prosecuted. The government objected to the overall tone of *The Vigilant*'s reports, charging it with sedition and the spreading of hatred against the state. In particular, certain words such as "genocide," "inhumanity," "barbarity" and "racism" were objected to, especially as they appeared more and more frequently in the detailed accounts of the atrocities in the South.

The one case that did proceed to trial concerned *The Vigilant*'s reporting of the 11 July 1965 massacre of Southern officials. With a packed courtroom each day due to intense Southern interest in the political and factual aspects of the case, the trial was guaranteed celebrity from the start. Witnesses for the defense included not only survivors of the atrocities in the South who were able to reveal bullet wound scars as part of their evidence, but also some senior government officials who were called on to testify whether or not people killed in massacres had been the government's own employees.

The trial ended with my acquittal on all the major charges. In his oral decision, the judge stated that the government had utterly failed to demonstrate inaccurate reporting or the preaching of hatred against the state, and that the defense had conclusively proven that a massacre of senior officials had taken place in Wau. However, as if to console the government for its legal defeat, I was found guilty on the lesser charge of having published a "letter to the Editor" from a University of Khartoum law student, in which the Anya Nya guerillas were described as a "national liberation movement." This term was deemed objectionable because it presupposed, in the eyes of the court, that Northern Sudan was acting as a colonial authority over the South. I was fined the token sum of twenty Sudanese pounds, which at that time was less than eight U.S. dollars.

There was no question in anyone's mind about the legal and moral victory we won in this court case. Not only were the paper and I free from further prosecution in the cases still pending, but the court ordered the government to release *The Vigilant*'s license and allow publication to resume immediately. In fact, the seriousness of the charges in the case meant that the verdict had to be confirmed by the Court of Appeal, which ruled that the government had been guilty of the callous disregard for the protection of the lives of innocent citizens in the South. In his report, Justice Abdel Majid Imam wrote, "Any citizen who points out the fault of the government, as the editor of *The Vigilant* did in this case, should not only be presumed innocent in the court of law but should indeed be granted the protection of the law against such a government."

With such a major indictment against it from the law courts, the government altered its tactics in its bid to prevent *The Vigilant* from reporting on events in the South. Taking the paper to court was now out of the question, so new means of harassment, with the intention of forcing the paper to close down, were utilized. Private businesses were threatened and prohibited from placing advertisements on *The Vigilant*'s pages. People were informed that *The Vigilant* was financially supporting the rebellion in the South. The paper was routinely denied licenses to import newsprint. The government's printing press, which was an independently run commercial concern, was instructed to end its contract to print *The Vigilant*, and government seizures of the copies straight off the press continued unabated, preventing distribution. I was also arrested on a regular basis. The government had given itself the power to detain a suspect for seventy-two hours without charge, which could be extended to seven days upon application to a court, and it made generous use of this power in its battles with *The Vigilant*. Conditions during these short periods of detention were usually appalling. I remember one such period when I was detained in a room full of human urine and had to stand up for the whole night.

The government's harassment was also physical in nature, especially in the South, where the armed forces had license to do as they wished despite the pretense of democracy in Khartoum. I recall a threat made against me in my absence by the commandant of police in Wau, which arose from his anger at an article I had written in *The Vigilant*. While accompanying a Southern cabinet minister on a tour of my native province of Bahr El Ghazal, we came across the bodies of four young Dinka men lying beside the road between Wau and Kuajok. Their throats had been slashed with knives and the bodies had been dead for merely an hour. The minister was told the identity of the army unit responsible for the murders. That unit had continued on toward Kuajok and so I expected that upon our arrival the minister would take some action against the people responsible. Nothing of the sort happened.

Upon my return to Khartoum I wrote a signed article questioning the right of anyone to remain a cabinet minister if he could not take action on such an obvious crime. Then, describing the scene of the murder in detail, I accused the soldiers involved of being so cowardly as to attempt to conceal the army's involvement by using knives instead of bullets. Denouncing the article as more contemptuous and offensive than the crime it reported, the local police commandant swore to his friends that if I ever came back to that province he would see to it that I never returned to Khartoum. The reference to "no return" was taken by my friends to mean that I would be killed, but I returned to the province several times a year in spite of the threats to my life. I never really felt alarmed by the physical threats except on one or two occasions when particular army officers attempted direct threats.

Reporting upon the war in the South, which continued until 1972, was difficult as a rule, even for the Arabic newspapers that were, by and large, sympathetic to the government's cause. It was made even more difficult by the government's attempts to completely close off the South from the rest of the world so as to avoid any damaging or embarrassing reports of what was actually taking place. For *The Vigilant,* the obstacles placed the lives of our reporters at risk. In order to get information out of the South, a complex clandestine smuggling network was devised. This also involved an equally complex arrangement for identifying informants and checking their reliability and the authenticity of their reports. It was important that the paper never be duped by false information.

Even in situations where *The Vigilant* sent in its own reporters to the South, there was never any guarantee for their physical safety nor that their reports or notes would not be seized by officials. In a number of cases, particularly those of the Juba and Wau massacres of 8 and 11 July 1965, our reporters were accosted by security officials and all their papers were seized. Yet detailed reports still appeared on *The Vigilant*'s front page the day after, with the names and addresses of the massacre victims. In each case, *The Vigilant*'s reporter had given a copy of the intended report to an ordinary Northern Sudanese passenger with instructions to deliver it to me personally at the newspaper, and this simple but efficient method worked every time.

Certainly, I was not immune to the problems faced by the reporters. On the occasions when I visited the South and had crucial information to report in the paper, I had to be equally devious to ensure that the information would arrive back in Khartoum and eventually be published without being seized off the press. It became clear that after I made a trip to the South, the police would closely watch *The Vigilant* for three or four days afterward hoping to destroy any major article that might report fresh atrocities. I would always delay writing and publishing the reports until the police observations had relaxed. Once I took the slow, four-day steamer journey so as to delude the authorities into believing that I had nothing of importance or urgency to report upon in the South. In fact I had spent the journey writing a series of reports on what I had seen and learned, although they could never be publicly referred to as a "series" because of the likelihood of the next day's edition being seized before the second article could appear, no matter how innocent the content of the story might have been.

Atrocities in the South were not merely committed against the educated Southerners. Uneducated villagers, like the four youths on the road to Kuajok, were often accused of harboring guerrillas and summarily executed. *The Vigilant* reported all such murders. Tribal chiefs were also a natural target of government violence because their position as leaders left them open to the accusation that they must be aware of the movements of guerrillas in their areas. If they failed to "cooperate" with government officials in such matters, they were likely to be executed. The most notable massacre was that of twenty-four Dinka chiefs at Bor in Upper Nile province. The chiefs had been arrested and detained in Bor town in 1966, when then prime minister, Sadiq El Mahdi, paid a visit. He was taken to see the grave of a Northern Sudanese army officer killed by guerrillas a few days earlier. The prime minister openly wept at the graveside and uttered words of vengeance before departing. That very same night the twenty-four chiefs were removed from custody and shot.

News of this atrocity reached Khartoum a few days later, whereupon *The Vigilant* gave the story prominent coverage and accused the prime minister of inciting the army to kill the twenty-four chiefs as revenge. The prime minister was enraged by the accusation and personally ordered that *The Vigilant* be closed down by the police and that I report to him at his office the next day. He informed me then that my activities at *The Vigilant* were no longer a question of freedom of the press but of state security and that he had decided to close down *The Vigilant*. He proceeded to warn me that he had had enough of me and that if I persisted in my activities I would be tried for treason. I vowed to go to court again in order to get the paper's license to publish released and told him that if and whenever I had a chance to report upon our meeting and the threats made to my person, I would do so, be it on *The Vigilant's* pages or elsewhere.

As I left the meeting, I met members of the executive committee of the Sudanese Union of Journalists who also had an appointment that morning with the prime minister to discuss the order to close down *The Vigilant*. As I was a member of the committee they asked me to join them in the meeting. Cutting short the Union's speaker, Prime Minister El Mahdi repeated what he had said to me earlier, that *The Vigilant* was being closed down for obstructing the discharge of security in a war situation in the South. The committee unanimously replied that if the Prime Minister had a case then it must go through the courts and that if he persisted with the immediate closure then all the newspapers in Khartoum would close down in solidarity with *The Vigilant*.

As the argument heated up, Minister of the Interior Abdalla Abdel Rahman Nugdalla strode into the room, having just returned from Bor, where he had been sent by the prime minister to determine the facts in the case. Sadiq El Mahdi's disposition visibly lightened as he believed his trump card was about to be played. He informed the gathering that the minister would no doubt confirm "what I have just told you about the lies of *The Vigilant*." However, to the surprise of everyone in the room, and to the utter amazement of Sadiq El Mahdi, the minister (whom I knew to be a truthful and honorable man) informed the prime minister that everything *The Vigilant* had printed about the killings of the tribal chiefs was accurate, and thus there was no way the newspaper could be suspended or closed down.

Despite our many victories and precautions, government harassment took its toll. For seven months between July 1965 and February 1966 *The Vigilant*'s license was suspended. An application for the paper to be allowed to publish while our court case was pending, on the grounds of financial and professional obligations to its staff and printers, was refused. This period of suspension was the hardest blow to *The Vigilant*, politically, financially, and otherwise. It was true that the wage bill was light because there were a minimal number of employees on the paper and most of the reporters and writers were Southern Front volunteers whom I had been training, but still suspension was felt severely by an infant newspaper. The recompense for all of this was, of course, the enormous moral victory over the government when the court case was eventually concluded and the professional respect that victory brought upon the paper.

The public, and the readers of *The Vigilant* in particular, were happy to see the newspaper return to the kiosks and stands in February 1966. Everyone, though, was surprised to discover that we had privately kept a small *Vigilant* daily throughout the period of suspension. From February 1966, each issue of the paper contained not only the current news stories but also a column relating what *The Vigilant* would have said about some event six months previously. In this way we hoped to bring the readers up to date on what they might have missed during the past seven months. It was also a political statement to the powers-that-be that *The Vigilant* had not been defeated or overcome by the crackdown. The government was both surprised at *The Vigilant's* vigilance over these previous months and disturbed that detailed stories of atrocities were now being published again. This was partly due to the change in policy of the government with regards to the South. By February 1966 the government was seriously concerned over the poor image all the wanton killings had been giving to the state, both internally and internationally. It was clear that the policy objectives in the South were being rethought if not immediately altered, and so the government would have preferred a re-emergent *Vigilant* to stick to reporting events as they now happened and not look back to the recent past. Public officials were offended by *The Vigilant's* new approach but were unsure how to react considering the paper's recent success in court. The campaign to starve the paper of funds continued apace. For example, I was prosecuted for receiving a private donation to the paper of $6,000 from an American friend. However, the court found everything above board and so the case was dropped.

Due to the financial strains upon *The Vigilant* during its suspension, when it first reappeared it was able to publish only as a weekly. This conversion from a daily to a weekly required specific permission from the licensing authority, which decided to interrogate us as to why we wanted to become a weekly. Why did we want to publish a paper when we could not afford it? How long was temporary going to be? Our reaction to these stalling tactics was to threaten to take the authorities to court if necessary, in order to obtain the relevant license. Eventually a license to publish a weekly on a temporary basis was issued to *The Vigilant*.

The Vigilant never did recover financially and it remained a "temporary" weekly right up until the last issue before the May 1969 military coup. Even as a weekly paper, *The Vigilant* was in a precarious financial state and was able to continue only with the help of a friend, Ustaz Beshir Mohamed Said, the owner and publisher of the noted Arabic daily, *Al Ayyam*. Ustaz Beshir was among the few Northern Sudanese who recognized the moral value in *The Vigilant* continuing to publish in a country where the voice of the South was not publicly available. In spite of all the government pressure to prevent Northerners from financially supporting *The Vigilant*, or maybe even because of it, he generously assisted us by reducing our printing costs and paying me a monthly salary in exchange for my help on the editorial column of his English-language daily newspaper, the *Morning News*. Much of my day was now spent at *Al Ayyam*'s offices where I had been given an office from which to produce both the *Morning News'* editorial column and the weekly *Vigilant*.

A normal working day for me began at 6:30 A.M. and usually continued on past midnight, almost non-stop. I would eat whatever was easily available at work. A friend who knew my schedule and believed that its hectic pace was due to the vigor of my youth was surprised to discover in the late 1980s, when I was working on the *Sudan Times* daily, that I had a nearly identical schedule and remarked to me: "Do you think you will stay twenty-five years old all your life?"

Respite for both *The Vigilant* and myself from the years of government harassment and persecution did not come until after I was elected to parliament from my Southern constituency in 1968. The government and its allies did their best to defeat me, intimidating my campaign workers and the voters. The need once more to answer legal cases against *The Vigilant* all over the country prevented me from making any serious personal appearances in the constituency during the campaign. While the Northern parties had several cars apiece, my student campaigners hitchhiked their way around the constituency, sometimes walking long distances to keep the campaign alive. Intimidated and instructed by the provincial authorities to help defeat me, the Dinka chiefs in the constituency skillfully balanced a public impression of non-approval with their private support for my election.

I was able to visit the constituency only twice during these three months, once to sign nomination papers and once on the day before the election. In the last weeks of the campaign one of my opponents circulated a rumor that I had been imprisoned in Khartoum for ten years and that even if I was elected I would not be able to take up the position in parliament. My election workers became concerned and decided that in order to overcome the confusion in people's minds I would need to appear in the constituency before the election.

My reappearance was a drama in itself. I arrived at the first polling station the day before it was due to open, travelling with a required army escort. Ostensibly for our protection, this enabled the army to watch me and prevent any anti-army or anti-government speeches. As a result, it had become a tame campaign by standards elsewhere in the world.

My main concern was to show the people I was there in the constituency and not in a Khartoum jail. This would not be an easy task while I was confined to the army escort convoy. We decided to arrange a traditional Dinka tribal dance that night so that I could slip away from the convoy and address that gathering. It would be a risk, but a risk worth taking.

The Dinka youth left the convoy to begin to beat the tribal war drums, and the tribe gathered quickly thereafter, believing the drums signaled an impending enemy attack. I stole away from the military escort and, in an area lit up by grass-bundle candles, declared to the huge crowd that I was obviously not in prison and that anyone who wanted to vote for me should do so the next day. Then I immediately returned to the convoy.

The only people to be surprised when the votes were counted ten days later were the senior government officials in the provincial capital of Wau who had believed the stories of my lack of support among the electorate. A Southern Sudanese leader who met the Governor a few hours later told me that the Governor described my election victory as "the worst thing that has happened in Bar El Ghazal." The people of Bar El Ghazal had put themselves at some risk by electing me and six other Southern Front leaders to parliament, as there was no way of telling what the authorities would do by way of "punishment." The least I could do was to try to demonstrate to the people that someone was doing something on their behalf. I returned to Khartoum and informed the Umma Party prime minister, Mohammed Ahmed Mahjoub, that the governor, the army commander, and the police commandant in Wau must be transferred immediately if he did not want the ten Southern Front MPs to resign from his government coalition. The significance of these ten seats was such that he acceded to my demands.

Simultaneously with the entrance into parliament of many Southern Front candidates in 1968, *The Vigilant* won overnight acceptance as a national newspaper of note. Businesses began to place regular advertisements. Not a single edition of the paper was seized off the press and denied circulation. Not a single court case was brought against me or the paper in that eleven-month period. From time to time I was summoned by the prime minister and the minister of the interior to hear their complaints and objections to certain reports in the paper, but nothing ever came of these discussions.

The Vigilant ceased to publish when Colonel Ja'afar Nimeiri seized power in a military coup in May 1969. All the newspapers were immediately suspended, but only *The Vigilant* was denied the right to reappear when the other newspapers resurfaced one week later. Nimeiri reasoned that *The Vigilant* was unlikely to cooperate with his government's policy of news management, and thus to allow the paper to function and then have to ban it would merely complicate the search for peace in the South. For twenty-three years *The Vigilant* has remained out of print, even though since 1986 I have held a license to publish it.

Sudanow magazine

The difficulties involved in running a newspaper in the undemocratic developing world are not confined only to the private media. There are just as many difficulties in running a state-controlled institution. Dictators in the developing world are rarely satisfied by the personality cult created around them and certainly will not accept any public criticism of government institutions. Such an attitude completely contradicts traditional Dinka values, which allow even the lowliest villager to criticize his chief in public without fear of repercussions. When my tribal background is added to my training as an investigative journalist, it is not so difficult to see why between 1972 and 1978 I found it hard to act as a mere "minister of propaganda" in General Nimeiri's cabinet. Not only did the lack of a free press stifle any opportunity for criticism, but also the introduction of a single-party political system that controlled the print media compounded my difficulties as minister of Culture and Information. My best bet would have been to avoid participation in Nimeiri's government. Indeed, I had always promised myself that I would never become a minister or a member of a Sudanese government while war raged in the South. However, with the signing of the Addis Ababa Accord in 1972 the war had been brought to an end. My small personal role in the negotiations leading up to that peace encouraged others to push me forward for government position, so when I was asked to go into the central government it was difficult to say no.

At my first session with General Nimeiri after having accepted a position in his cabinet, we discussed what I thought he should know about me before I took the oath of office. I told him I liked to speak my mind on issues, and given that in this new single-party system any free and frank talking would have to come from within, I reserved my right to do just that in the newspapers. Apparently unaware of how far I could go in this matter, Nimeiri readily agreed and told me that the problem would not be in controlling or preventing criticism but in finding people who would be critical. I was not in the least deceived by the dictator's smooth talking, knowing that it was merely designed to get me into the cabinet. After all, the same man had prevented the publication of *The Vigilant* in 1969. Yet I decided to discharge my duties as if I had really secured Nimeiri's tacit approval for everything I would do.

Nimeiri may have thought that by bringing me into his cabinet he could coopt me and temper my views. He may even have thought that I would be cowed by the position. Certainly, I was not cowed by the experience, but in the early years after 1972 my views were indeed tempered, mainly due to the positive policies adopted in the South immediately following the signing of the peace accord. The national government appeared to be generously supporting the reconstruction and development of the South. As the chief public relations officer of the government I felt comfortable with the promotion of its objectives and policies. There were indications that the Sudan was on its way to achieving real national unity and for a time I was happy to be a part of this mission.

In light of what I saw around me, I tried to open up a free, critical debate on public issues, encouraging members of the public to come forward and express opinions about aspects of government policy and its implementation. Naturally, I began with my own job and for two weeks there were public debates on the radio and television. With hindsight it is not too difficult to see the reasons for the failure of these debates. At the time, however, my idealism prevented me from predicting that serious-minded members of the public would not come forward to express critical opinions for the simple reason that they suspected it was an elaborate trap to help the government identify its opponents.

This attitude on the part of the public drew my attention to another human behavioral phenomenon. As people withdraw support from a regime, that act in itself can push a nondemocratic regime into becoming more repressive. I watched Nimeiri change from an openminded man into an unapproachable dictator. This character change was caused partially by his ministers and advisors gradually shying away from confronting him on any issue, until it reached a point where he could not be advised or corrected. In 1972 Nimeiri seemed to tolerate critical views from myself and others, not only in cabinet meetings but even in public. Five years later he had become almost completely intolerant of criticism. It has been said that Nimeiri bottled up his anger with people like me who continued to speak our minds and that my eventual imprisonment for a year between 1983 and 1984 without charge or trial came about as a result of that anger exploding. I have always argued that he was able to become so much more repressive only because the number of critics like myself had become so small and the others had become so afraid of him that he felt he could get away with anything without fear of risking a larger public outcry.

My idea of establishing *Sudanow Magazine* in January 1976 was more straightforward and well-intentioned than many realized. First, I wanted to publish a magazine that could write about what the government was doing independently and critically. I did not intend to create yet another propaganda tool for the government. There were too many institutions doing a poor job of that already. I wanted to establish a magazine that could speak the truth with accurate and courageous news coverage, whether it be pro- or anti-government. I also wanted to create a forum for differing views. I envisaged many long-term benefits for the government from such a magazine. Second, I intended to create a magazine with which the world community could relate without imagining that they were being forcefed government propaganda, a publication that could speak out for Sudan as a whole instead of solely for its government. Third, I imagined the magazine becoming a training ground for aspiring young journalists from the Ministry of Culture and Information. There was a good collection of bright, intelligent university graduates who joined the ministry during my time in office. I wanted to make sure that those young people who wanted to become professional media people had both the benefit of and access to my experience in this field. *Sudanow Magazine* and the Institute for Media Training, which I also established while minister, were two such ways of promoting the training of media personnel. I regarded this as being one of the most important of the long-term benefits for the Sudan in this much-neglected area of the media.

The *Sudan Times*

When compared with the hand-to-mouth existence of *The Vigilant* in the late sixties, the *Sudan Times* English-language daily was an exercise in professionalism and business stability. Publishing between July 1986 and June 1989, we had our own modest but independent printing plant as well as state-of-the-art typesetting equipment, and we rented independent offices.

The *Sudan Times* was established in 1986 to deal with the same issues that *The Vigilant* had dealt with, but from a different perspective. This newspaper was intended to be an independent, nonpartisan national newspaper. It was owned jointly by me and my Northern Sudanese friend Mahjoub Mohamed Salih, formerly editor of *Al Ayyam* newspaper and arguably one of the most distinguished and experienced Sudanese journalists. We were joined later by Ahmed Mahjoub, another Northern Sudanese friend, who brought with him his wide-ranging administrative and business experience.

When establishing the *Sudan Times* we agreed that the financial and administrative side of the paper would not pose much of a problem and we all expected to make money from the venture if it was successful. However, our main concern was to establish a paper of repute in editorial policy and content. The question of editorial policy was quickly resolved by all three of us agreeing that I would become editor and in that capacity would establish and follow the policy I thought best. However, the *Sudan Times* was to prove no less a headache for me than *The Vigilant* had been, when it soon became apparent that we would come up against some of my political adversaries from the 1960s. The newly elected civilian government that took shape in 1986 was dominated by the same political parties and personalities that had ruled between 1965 and 1969.

In 1986, as in 1965, Sudan was in a state of civil war—the Sudan People's Liberation Army had been waging war against the government's forces since early 1983. The people had only recently overthrown Nimeiri's military dictatorship and the transitional government had just handed over power to a civilian government following the partial elections of April 1986. Sadiq El Mahdi became prime minister of an Umma party and DUP coalition government in much the same way that he had in 1965. His attitude towards the raging civil war and towards what divided the Sudanese was to prove no more democratic and accommodating in 1986 than it had been twenty years earlier. He looked to himself as a leader who knew what was best for the country and set about achieving it in his own way, regardless of what others might have thought. He neither recognized the need to be guided by public opinion nor accepted the notion that the media were an important reflection of that opinion. These attitudes brought him and the *Sudan Times* into direct conflict. At the newspaper, we sought to highlight the failure of the government's policies as well as the negative effects they were having upon both the country at large and the fledgling democracy. In turn, Sadiq El Mahdi sought to repress the *Sudan Times* through repeated attempts to enact a press law that would have given him sweeping powers to ban newspapers. On two occasions he was denied such powers by parliament and so had to resort to other repressive measures.

The prime minister's increasing paranoia was perhaps best illustrated by an unprecedented outburst that he made on nationwide television in which he labelled me as public enemy number one. Acting upon some inaccurate information supplied to him by the Sudanese embassy in Washington, Sadiq El Mahdi accused me, in his television statement, of having testified against the Sudan to a U.S. congressional committee. This charge was simply untrue. In 1987 I had merely watched the proceedings of the Refugees and Hunger Committee as an interested member of the public, as this particular hearing concerned war and famine in the Sudan and Ethiopia. I was neither invited to the hearings nor asked to make a statement to the committee while I was there. Therefore, I was utterly surprised to witness the prime minister's outburst on television, which created the impression that I had secretly gone to the United States to plot against the country. It emphasized the prime minister's approach to public issues through deception and duplicity.

Unlike *The Vigilant*, the pressures put upon the *Sudan Times* in its brief four-year existence rarely involved court cases. It was the financial pressures put upon the newspaper that were most effective. The government refused to allow its advertisements to be placed in the paper and import licenses for newsprint were denied continually. Therefore we were forced to rely upon black market supplies, with their inflated prices. The newsprint situation became so acute that the original eight-page paper was reduced to four pages and circulation fell considerably. Individuals were also encouraged to bring libel cases against me personally as well as against the newspaper, and physical threats were made.

The *Sudan Times*, though, was not afraid of bringing its own pressures to bear upon the government. For instance, the paper's policy was to emphasize the good work of some of the little people in the government, the civil servants and the junior ministers. At the same time, I would dutifully and politely attend the prime minister's press conferences as well as the meetings of the media leaders that he called, and would report on these events as factually as I could. However, in the four years of the *Sudan Times'* existence, I never once asked Sadiq El Mahdi a question at these gatherings. He never had a single personal interview published in the paper while most other political party leaders, including members of his own coalition government as well as the opposition, had lengthy and periodic personal interviews published. I learned later from his friends that he had felt insulted by our approach because there was nothing he liked more than to be in the limelight. The *Sudan Times* was a very sought after forum. He was probably even more distressed when he came to learn, not only from the *Sudan Times*, but also from the Sudanese public, that he was perceived as unreliable and someone whose words carried very little weight.

Although the *Sudan Times* avoided any prosecution between 1986 and 1989, it became apparent that the government was beginning to think that some of the opinions expressed in the newspaper were partially responsible for the government's policy failures. By 1989 the prime minister and his government had had enough of me and decided to have me arrested. In June 1989 it was rumored that a warrant for my arrest had been issued by which I would have been taken into custody upon arrival from abroad at Khartoum airport. I was away in West Germany at the time attending the Federal Republic's Foreign Affairs Committee's special session on the situation in Sudan. The pretext for my arrest was to be what I had said in that committee hearing. In the hearing, just as I had routinely been doing in the pages of the *Sudan Times*, I accused the government of carrying out a policy of genocide in Southern Sudan through the wanton massacre of the civilian population by the armed forces, the use of food and famine as a weapon of war, and the continuing practice of slavery among the government-sponsored tribal militias of Southern Kordofan and Southern Darfar. My planned arrest was only thwarted by the Islamic Fundamentalist military coup d'etat on 30 June 1989, three days before I was due to return to Sudan from West Germany. The new regime quickly banned all newspapers, the *Sudan Times* included. I have remained in exile from Sudan ever since, not feeling the need to honor such a regime with my personal presence.

Resistance in exile—The *Sudan Democratic Gazette*

Over the years Sudan has had many difficult and unsettling political experiences, but nothing can quite compare with the trauma the Sudanese have suffered since the Islamic Fundamentalist takeover. On 30 June 1990 there were few celebrations, outside of Lieutenant General Omar Hassan El Beshir's personal circle and his fifteen-man Revolution Command Council, to mark the end of the darkest year for the people of Sudan.

Since 30 June 1989 the regime in Khartoum has engaged in systematic repression and violation of human rights at a level unheard of in Sudan's previous history. Public calls for a return to democracy and a respect for civil liberties were met with harsh and bloody measures. Strikers were sentenced to death, traders executed for engaging in commercial activities, and political prisoners tortured to death as the prisons overflowed with thousands of detainees. In only one year the junta has managed to execute or murder in prison four or five times the number of people executed in the previous thirty-four years since independence. It is impossible to know the exact number of people killed because they are snatched from their homes under cover of darkness, never to be heard from again. Many different security apparatuses have been created by the regime, and with the increased number of detention centers in the unlikeliest

223

of places, it is difficult to know who is being held where. Any person professing to be an Islamic Fundamentalist is granted the powers of a security officer authorized to arrest anyone he may suspect of being an opponent of the regime.

Not only does the regime commit wanton atrocities, it does so in a crude and vicious manner. The execution of twenty-eight army officers in April 1990 was carried out during the Islamic holy month of Ramadan in spite of Islam's proscription on executions and warmaking during this religious period of daytime fasting. The officers were murdered a mere twenty-four hours before the festival marking the end of Ramadan, converting a usually joyous occasion into one of mourning. The officers were bulldozed into a mass grave, some reportedly while still alive.

The Islamic Fundamentalist regime continues to prevent any free expression in the country, and attempting to publicly organize opposition to the regime is now a capital offense. El Beshir has stated that the regime will not tolerate any form of democratic institution. In light of this, I decided to publish a newsletter called the *Sudan Democratic Gazette* from my current location in England. Its first issue was released in June of 1990. It is a modest effort to provide Sudanese democracy with a voice, thus helping to create international awareness of the plight of the Sudanese people under the military junta and encouraging the international community to reconsider its diplomatic and economic relations with the Khartoum regime. The regime may be determined to cling to power, but it does not have the resources to do so without outside assistance. When that international recognition and help is no longer forthcoming, the nightmare of Islamic Fundamentalist rule can be brought more quickly to an end.

The *Sudan Democratic Gazette* concerns itself with analyzing the facts behind current events unfolding in the Sudan and publishes information that has not yet reached the pages of the international press. The *Gazette* does not advocate the political views of any particular group in Sudan—rather, it advocates the principles of democracy in general and of human rights issues in particular. To the extent that I share these views with members of the Sudanese democratic alliance, I hope the pages of this newsletter will act as a beacon in defense of the ideals of democratic pluralism in the Sudan.

Looking back upon nearly thirty years in journalism I have no regrets. None of my experiences, even the frequent imprisonment, dissuades me from doing exactly the same thing all over again in defense of the democratic values I cherish. I am certain that there are plenty of people whose paths have crossed mine over the years who have had serious disagreements with me, yet I hope that none of them could say that I have not acted frankly, truthfully, and fearing and favoring none. That I believe is the way of a free press.

Colombia and the Drug War: Journalists Under Siege

María Jimena Duzán

ON 26 FEBRUARY 1990 six armed men entered a restaurant in Cimitarra, Colombia, and wiped out the leaders of a nascent peasant union movement. Also killed in the shooting that day was a journalist named Silvia Duzán who was working on a documentary about the activities of the union leaders.

Silvia had hoped to describe an effort that to many Colombians seemed an impossible task. The union workers were attempting to find a peace formula for the Middle Magdalena Valley, a region of our country that has become a virtual no-man's land. It was first conquered by leftist guerrillas and, more recently, by an alliance of wealthy landowners, drug bosses, and the paramilitary groups that they control.

All that I have left of my sister Silvia is the last remembered echo of her warm laughter, the sole remaining wisp of her life, which seems to follow me, reverberating. She and the peasant leaders were killed by the forces they were trying to observe and negotiate with. They were but a few of the thousands of victims who have fallen in a twisted struggle that pits the Colombian establishment against the drug bosses and their allies.

Today Colombians confront much more than a group of drug

dealers intent on pursuing criminal profits. The cocaine business has exacerbated social and political conflicts to the point where ministers of state and peasants alike are threatened with death, and politicians, judges, priests, journalists, farmers and even shoppers in downtown Bogotá must face the prospect of a sudden bomb blasting apart their lives.

It was against this backdrop of explosions, assassinations and massacres that Colombians went to the polls on 27 May 1990 and elected a president who vowed to keep fighting the drug dealers. President César Gaviria was one of the survivors of the most bloody and painful political campaigns ever in my country, a campaign in which the most prominent candidates were killed. In the end, as a colleague put it, "Colombians voted for the dead." A lull has followed Gaviria's ascension to the presidency, but proclamations of victory for the democratic process could be quickly belied by a single attack.

There have been many massacres and many fallen innocents, yet not so many that we Colombians have become inured to the horrors. We have, however, become far too skilled in the business of dying. We make bitter jokes about it as a survival mechanism. "The only thing that has become democratic lately in Colombia has been the violence itself," a friend said to me not long after his mother was killed, one of the 120 people in the December 1989 terrorist bombing of an Avianca Airlines jet in Bogotá.

Ours is a bloody reality. While the world looks on stupefied, through its distant television sets, a massive criminal network surrounds us. This network, which only begins in the Andean countries, operates in the multibillion-dollar daily bank transactions of Europe and the United States, where cocaine profits are laundered and legitimized; on the streets of major U.S., and, increasingly, European cities where a street dealer may sell a kilogram a week and snort some of the profits himself; in the warehouses of international chemical firms, which produce more ether and acetone than legitimate business can consume, then ship it off through front companies by plane, boat, truck and canoe to the clandestine laboratories that need those materials to produce cocaine. This is the atmosphere under which Colombian journalists must work—one of coercion, terror, and, all too often, death.

Targeting the press

It was 7:00 P.M. on 16 December 1986 in northern Bogotá. As had been his custom for fifteen years, Guillermo Cano Isaza, publisher and editor-in-chief of *El Espectador*, took a final look around the newsroom and checked the latest reports before heading home. Nothing new had happened as far as he could tell. President Virgilio Barco Vargas had just decided to confront the Supreme Court with the highly sensitive question of Colombia's extradition treaty with the United States. As always, the nation was divided. Cano supported the treaty, under which major drug dealers could be dispatched for trial in the United States.

The atmosphere of those days was amazingly different from the present world of Colombian journalism. Several of us at *El Espectador* had written stories about drug trafficking, and, to be sure, tension permeated the city room. But on the surface, everything seemed calm. Of course, we had been warned. Three years earlier, a bomb had exploded at my house. Minutes later, my phone rang. A voice said, "The bomb was set by 'MAS: Death to Kidnappers' [a paramilitary group organized by the drug dealers]. The next one will kill you!" Three years later, the target was our publisher. Moments after he left the building, assassins gunned down Guillermo Cano. His "crime" had been to break the most significant story of the year about the drug bosses. For that he had to die.

Acting on a vague recollection, Cano had earlier set us to searching the files for a particular photograph of Pablo Escobar, now one of the most notorious drug dealers of Medellín. But in the early 1980s he was serving in Congress, elected as an alternate member in 1982. The picture, taken in 1976, revealed that the then-unknown Escobar had been arrested on suspicion of murder and cocaine trafficking, but had then been freed for lack of evidence.

We wrote a story describing the circumstances of that arrest and the courts reopened the Escobar case in 1984, thanks to the persistence of Justice Minister Rodrigo Lara Bonilla. The ensuing scandal led to Escobar's departure from Congress and his flight into the underground. But in what is considered to be the first political assassination by the cocaine dealers, the justice minister was murdered soon afterwards.

Cano was one of the first of the forty-two journalists who have fallen so far in a protracted battle for the future of Colombia. In targeting members of the media, the narcos have added a dimension missing from previous wars waged by organized crime. The Sicilian Mafia, for example, struck back at Italian judges, prosecutors, and members of the security forces. But journalists? Hardly ever.

The growing casualty list has resulted in an erosion of the active freedom of expression which, through good times and bad, has existed in Colombia. That freedom, in turn, is but one of society's casualties. By the time Cano was killed, MAS had been after me for three years, ever since I had begun preparing a series of articles about it. MAS, "founded" in 1981, was the first paramilitary group sponsored by drug bosses Escobar (now in hiding), Carlos Lehder (serving life plus 135 years in an American prison), and Jorge Luis Ochoa (who recently turned himself in to Colombian authorities after newly elected President César Gaviria promised not to extradite drug traffickers who submitted themselves to the Colombian law).

Their frequent threats led Cano to remark, "Now, there's even more reason for us to publish our stories." So we did, and for a year I had bodyguards wherever I went. Nevertheless, no matter how often I changed houses and places to sleep, the threatening letters never failed to find me. The most critical moment came when I decided to forego my bodyguards. It seemed ridiculous to me to have to go out in the streets looking for news with a security detail in tow. Cano always laughed about our predicament. He once told me, "I think that the day they want to kill someone, they'll do it with or without bodyguards." The day he was killed he had no bodyguards.

The drug dealers' campaign of violence against *El Espectador* and the Colombian press did not end with Cano's death. Months later the victim was our correspondent in the jungle city of Leticia, who was investigating the methods by which the narcos smuggle coca paste into Colombia from Brazil and Peru along the Amazon jungle border. Then, in March 1989, our lawyer was killed, just weeks after a judge ruled that Pablo Escobar was the "intellectual author" of the Cano assassination. On 2 September more than 200 pounds of dynamite exploded outside our Bogotá headquarters, destroying a good part of the building. No one was killed—the bomb was set to go off at 6:30 on a Saturday morning—but the blast injured about eighty people, most of them waiting at a bus stop nearby.

The following month, October 1989, our distribution and circulation managers in Medellín were shot down. Moments before these killings, the narcos phoned: "We give you three days to withdraw *El Espectador* from the streets of Medellín." The caller claimed to represent "The Extraditables," a reference to the narcos' campaign to block their extradition to the United States. The threat worked for almost a year. Knowing the dangers, we resumed circulation in Medellín in August 1990, determined to demonstrate that we had been wounded but not defeated.

Perhaps most exposed are the radio broadcasters of Medellín. Accustomed to producing popular-opinion programs, these people often seem to be toying with suicide. The latest of our broadcast colleagues to die, Roberto Surasty, always talked about the drug bosses in the most direct of terms. His death was practically announced ahead of time; assassins finally killed him one day as he was leaving work.

One well-known television reporter, Jorge Enrique Pulido, was cut down on the street after producing a special program on one of the key figures of the Medellín cartel, Nacho Abello. Abello had just been extradited to the United States in what was considered an important blow to the power of the drug bosses.

The latest move against journalists came in September 1990 when eight journalists disappeared, only to resurface apparently in the power of the narcos who were attempting to press the government to accept their demands for dialogue. Subsequently five of them were released; one (Diana Turbay, the daughter of a former president) was killed (apparently by the drug dealers) when the police tried to rescue her, and two were still held in early 1991 as human shields to press the government to accept the drug dealers' demands for a kind of amnesty.

If the point of the drug dealers' violence against journalists has been to muzzle freedom of expression, it has largely failed. Yet while we have not been silenced, we have, inevitably, fallen into the worst kind of censorship—self-censorship. It cannot be seen, but it hovers over us so that it seems as if we are working at knife point. Turning someone into a target prevents that person from thinking freely and rationally, which is the bare minimum needed in order to carry out proper journalism. Often worse than the official censorship of military dictatorships, self-censorship gnaws at the psyche, preying on fear and weakness. The boundaries of freedom are delineated by the shadowy power of the drug dealers.

Not even during that year of threats did I feel the way I feel today when I sit down to write my column or a report about the drug dealers. It is as if, with each word, I am fighting this imposed self-censorship that spreads over me like a hideous wave. Always prominent is the realization that writing can translate into death, not only for myself but for everyone else at the newspaper. That is the responsibility I feel. That is the real battle of Colombian journalists: to exorcise that fear and fulfill our obligation to report on what is happening in our country.

Our war of words

Jose Gonzalo Rodriguez Gacha, one of the most violent of the Medellín drug bosses, clearly expressed the narcos' attitude toward the press in August 1989. "If they don't bother with us, we won't bother with them," he told a Colombian journalist. "It's the intense types that are going to have problems." (Rodriguez Gacha was killed in a shootout with Colombian authorities the following December). Indeed, many journalists simply have fled. They wander aimlessly in

Europe, experiencing something we have begun to call narco-exile; in effect it is they, not the narcos, who have been extradited.

But it is not only journalists. Every judge who signs an arrest warrant against a drug boss is in effect signing his own death certificate and must escape the country. More than forty-five have been killed. Ours is an exile without precedent. We cannot take to the streets to protest, as Chileans or Argentineans used to do in Paris. On the contrary, the less visible we are, the more secure. There are even those who have gone to the extreme of altering their appearance—just like Pablo Escobar—to avoid detection.

So now, many of the remaining Colombian journalists have adopted radical security measures: wearing bulletproof vests, travelling with bodyguards, varying their routes between home and work, developing their own counterintelligence channels, and learning how to use firearms. We have been taught how to defend ourselves from the eventuality of an attack. Little by little, we start to acquire the habits of our pursuers, our would-be killers. The paradox is sad and telling.

Today, *El Espectador* seems more like a bunker than a newspaper office. Soldiers are stationed on the roof. Every hour, German shepherds make their rounds to check for explosives. In the newsroom, security agents are so numerous that sometimes they are mistaken for reporters. This is the atmosphere in which we work, always putting back together that which the last explosion blew apart. Often my North American colleagues ask us what it is that keeps us on the job. There is no concrete answer, at least not one that would sound rational to the U.S. press, accustomed as it is to neutrality.

Ours is a journalism that has never enjoyed the luxury of being neutral. For us, journalism has always been a vehicle for sending messages and fomenting revolutions. Simón Bolívar, the liberator of much of South America from Spanish domination, carried a printing press with him, which, he said, had to be used like a weapon.

It is not for lack of fear that we persevere in our work: the person who says that she is not afraid of death is lying. Nevertheless, risk and danger have always accompanied reporting in Colombia. We are a country that carries the weight of a violent history, and one where journalism has always played a leading role, especially in times of major political change. To the narcos, we are more than reporters. They fear us as much as we fear them.

This, then, has been the story of news reporting not only in Colombia but in the whole of Latin America. At times, we have had to take a stand for or against dictatorship, as in the case of Argentina and Chile in the 1970s. Today in Colombia, we have had to take a stand against drug trafficking. Colombians, especially journalists, who deal with these themes know that at such times our democracy itself is at stake in the form of our freedom of expression and our right to dissent.

We would like to survive to enjoy this democracy. We have seen enough victims to understand that the best way to contribute to the redemption of our country is simply to stay alive to question the anti-drug policies that have been shown to be ineffective. Dead, we would hardly be able to do that.

But the power of the drug traffickers will be difficult to overcome. This narcotics serpent has entwined itself throughout the economics and politics of Colombia and defies the forces of democracy to defeat it. The drug bosses are wealthy and influential businessmen, bank owners and farmers; they generate employment for thousands. Like the Italian Mafia, their endeavors straddle legal and illegal operations. They obtained, for example, the official franchise for the development of the state-controlled emerald-mining conglomerate. They have faithfully fulfilled an obligation that lulled the bureaucracy into complacence. As their operations grew, they paid high taxes to the government and good salaries to their workers. In the last five years, the drug bosses have bought so much land that it is no exaggeration to say that Colombia has undergone a cocaine-agrarian reform. Today the drug dealers own about 2.5 million acres of agricultural land. The irony is that despite the violence of their methods, their presence has saved the farm regions from an economic recession. According to Colombian economist

Salomon Kalmanovitz, about $3.5 billion enters the Colombian economy every year as a direct result of the cocaine business, representing 7 percent of the Gross Domestic Product. Today, the drug mafia owns radio networks, television stations, hotels and drugstore chains. In addition, the drug bosses own a majority of the nation's soccer teams, a sport with significant symbolic importance.

But perhaps the most dramatic effect of the penetration of the drug business can be seen in the decomposition and uncertainty that it has provoked on all social levels. For the nation's large middle class, including politicians, judges, soldiers, journalists and police, drug money has inundated economic life with a flood of corruption, wiping out any semblance of a code of ethics or a value system. Months before his death, Gonzalo Rodriguez Gacha laughed when he spoke of his relationship with the army: "While the government gives them medals, we just give them a little money." This is a terrorized political class that has delivered itself to the designs and money of the drug dealers. Those who stand up to the bosses and challenge them have fallen victim, brave politicians like Luis Carlos Galán, Carlos Pizarro and Bernardo Jaramillo.

Without a doubt, one of the sources of the nation's misery is also its greatest social problem—the plight of the subsistence poor. This class is avoided and forgotten, uncharted in the projections of government planning offices. These are the neglected residents of the nation's slum barrios, squatters who barely survive and who perpetuate their own endless cycle of tragedy. They live in the urban areas where the refugees of the violence of the 1940s and 1950s fled— 200,000 people died in the factional violence of those years. In these impoverished slums, the drug dealers have found the raw material for their projects of murder and terrorism in the form of tender flesh and blood, boys called *sicarios* who are transformed into assassins before they are fifteen years old.

In their netherworld, the hero to emulate is Pablo Escobar, who emerged from those same slums to become a bandit billionaire. His ascension through the underworld has made him the world's most wanted drug dealer and murderer, but for these teenage killers he represents not only a symbol of survival but a great benefactor who provides for their welfare on a scale that the Colombian government cannot rival.

To these marginalized people, the democratic banners festooned with pictures of Luis Carlos Galán say little. Nor do they care about the future of a republic which, when all is said and done, has no real impact on their lives. "The drug-paramilitary alliance is the only outlet in which these people can feel that they have achieved something," said Victor Gaviria, a young filmmaker whose work has investigated the sociological background of the child assassins.

If Colombia cannot somehow manage to incorporate this anomic nation-within-a-nation whose citizens murder in the morning to put bread on the table in the evening, if Colombia does not somehow manage to rebuild its justice system and reopen its stagnant political system, then the capture and extradition of individual drug bosses will mean very little indeed. We need true social reform, so that democracy—and not murder with impunity—will be universal.

We need not only a stronger governmental response to domestic social and economic problems, but a more coherent and appropriate international policy as well. The reliance on a military solution, promoted by Washington and furthered by Bogotá, has not worked. The narcotrafficking business has continued to reap enormous profits and has expanded into Europe, while Colombian society continues to pay the awful price.

Yet it would be wrong to say that Colombia is in its death throes. The amount of blood that has been spilled is testimony to the bravery of those who have chosen to resist the imposition of a corrupt system. Despite the threat of death, they fight for the survival of their country. If a peasant leader falls, if a political leader is slain, another stands up to take on the fight; and if the narcos kill him in turn, yet another will take his place. This dynamism persists, and gives our country vitality against all odds.

In the United States, the violence produced by the drug trade is not something that threatens basic democratic institutions. This is not so in my country. So perhaps only when things get much worse in the United States, when the violence spreads from the margins and ghettos of society into the mainstream, will North Americans understand why in Colombia they are killing judges, politicians, and journalists.

Contributors

María Rosa S. de Martini is president of *Conciencia*, a nonpartisan Argentine women's organization, which she helped found in 1982, to provide civic education and promote citizen participation in the democratic process. In 1985 she also helped found the Program of Civic Action (Programa de Accion Civica). Earlier, in 1976, she had helped found the Cooperative for Social Action (COAS), in which she served as first vice-president. Currently she is also a member of the Board of the International Institute for Women Political Leaders. In addition to her work in Argentina, she has participated in numerous international meetings in recent years on civic education, democratization, and the involvement of women in politics. Since 1985, she and her colleagues in Conciencia have helped create similar organizations in Brazil, Uruguay, Peru, Colombia and Ecuador, establishing a Latin American network with sixteen countries.

Henrietta (Dette) Pascual is the chairperson of KABATID (National Women's Movement for the Nurturance of Democracy), a nonprofit, nonpartisan public educational movement of women in the Philippines, dedicated to enhancing people's understanding of the responsibilities of citizenship. She was the founding executive director and is now a member of the Board of Trustees of the Evelio B. Javier Foundation, which trains municipal leaders in democratic governance. Previously she was Executive Director for External Affairs of NAMFREL (National Movement for Free Elections), and was during 1985-86 NAMFREL U.S. Liaison Officer and U.S. Correspondent for *Veritas*. A specialist in human resource development, she has lectured widely and conducted training, leadership, motivation, and teambuilding programs in a variety of industries, government agencies, and education institutions. A member of the Board of Directors of the Philippine Institute of Applied Behavioral Science, she has an M.A. in Educational Psychology from Ateneo de Manila.

Monica Jimenez de Barros is a prominent Chilean social activist who has dedicated her professional life to the recovery and institutionalization of democratic values smothered during fifteen years of military rule. She began her career as a social worker after receiving a master's degree from The Catholic University of America. For more than a decade, she was head of the Justice and Peace Committee of the National Episcopate, and for five years she was a member of the Pontifical Committee on Justice. In March 1988, she and thirteen other concerned citizens founded the Committee for Free Elections (CEL), which sought to register voters and educate them about their political rights. It organized the Crusade for Citizen Participation, which played a critical role in mobilizing Chilean voters for the December 1988 plebiscite in which General Pinochet's bid to extend his dictatorship was defeated. In 1989, she founded a new grassroots organization, Participa, to foster discussion of political issues and promote civic participation at all levels of Chilean politics. She also continues to serve as a full-time professor at The Catholic University and as member of its superior council.

Xavier Zavala Cuadra is director of Libro Libre, a nonprofit publishing program and democratic intellectual center for Central America, based in Costa Rica. Libro Libre publishes books on Central American history and current events as well as classical democratic texts. It was created to influence the political culture of Central America, defending and promoting the ideas, beliefs, values, and institutions that make democracy possible. Mr. Zavala is also the editor of *Revista del Pensamiento Centroamericano*, a distinguished intellectual journal that focuses on the contemporary political problems of the region. He is also a member of the Board of Directors of the Nicaraguan Permanent Commission on Human Rights, a private and independent organization that has been promoting and defending human rights in Nicaragua for many years.

Clement Nwankwo, one of Nigeria's most influential human rights activists, was a cofounder of the Civil Liberties Organization (CLO), a nonprofit group dedicated to the investigation and correction of human rights violations and abuses in Nigeria. After graduating from the University of Nigeria, Nsukka in 1984 and qualifying as a lawyer in 1985, Nwankwo spent a year working at Ijebu-Ode prison as a volunteer legal advisor. His experiences with prisoners and the inhuman conditions in which they lived inspired him to join forces with a fellow lawyer, Olisa Agbakoba, to form the CLO. Since its creation in 1987, the CLO has used the powerful combination of legal action and the press to expose flagrant human rights abuses, especially in the Nigerian prison system. In January 1989 Nwankwo was arrested by state security agents in retaliation for the CLO publication, "Violations of Human Rights in Nigeria"; two months later an attempt was made on his life. Recently he founded the Constitutional Rights Project (CRP) to promote the rule of law and respect for human rights in Nigeria through legal actions and assistance to human rights victims. The CRP also publishes the quarterly *Constitutional Rights Journal*.

Chai-Anan Samudavanija is director of the Institute of Public Policy Studies in Bangkok, a Royal Scholar at Chulalongkorn University, and a member of Thailand's Senate. One of Thailand's most honored and accomplished political scientists, he has written numerous books and articles in both Thai and English on the politics and history of Thailand. He was a leading member of the 1974 Constitutional Drafting Committee, secretary of the Thai Legislative Reform Committee (1973-74), and adviser to the prime minister (1980-81). In 1984 he founded the Institute of Public Policy Studies, a nongovernmental body dedicated to the civic education of the Thai people. In 1986 he was honored as the nation's leading researcher in political science by the Thai National Research Council, and subsequently was a visiting fellow at Princeton University's Woodrow Wilson School of Public and International Affairs.

Felix B. Bautista is an adviser to President Corazon Aquino of the Philippines. Prior to that he served as Public Information Director for the Senate of the Philippines. Mr. Bautista's experience as a journalist and editor spans four decades. He has been news editor of *Philippines Herald* (1949-51), senior editor, *Agence France Presse* (1951-56), editor-in-chief, *Evening News* (1960-65), and editor-in-chief of the Catholic newsmagazine *Veritas* (1983-86). From 1956 to 1970 he was head of the Department of Journalism, University of Santo Tomas in Manila, and from 1974 to 1987 he served as a special assistant to Jaime Cardinal Sin. Widely honored for his achievements, he received in 1985 and 1986 Press Freedom awards from the Catholic Mass Media Awards, the Manila Rotary Club and the International Union of Catholic Journalists. In addition to thousands of feature articles, editorials and speeches, he is the author of four books, the latest of which is *Cardinal Sin and the Miracle of EDSA*.

Anthony Hazlitt Heard was from 1971 to 1987 editor of the *Cape Times* of Cape Town, during which time he became the longest-serving editor of a major South African newspaper and won wide recognition for his achievements. In 1985 he was awarded the Golden Pen of Freedom by the International Federation of Newspaper Publishers for his published interview with the banned leader of the African National Congress, Oliver Tambo. In 1986 he received the Pringle Medal from the Southern African Society of Journalists. Prior to becoming editor he worked, from 1955, as junior reporter, parliamentary reporter, political correspondent, and assistant editor of the *Cape Times*. Since 1987 he has been a Nieman Fellow at Harvard University and a Visiting Fulbright International Fellow at the University of Arkansas. His personal account of the crisis in South Africa, *The Cape of Storms*, was published in October 1990 by the University of Arkansas Press. Currently he is an internationally syndicated freelance columnist based in Cape Town.

Ray Ekpu is currently editor-in-chief of *Newswatch*, a pathbreaking Nigerian weekly magazine of news and investigative reporting. Before joining in the founding of *Newswatch*, he was the chairman of the editorial board of the Concord Group of newspapers; he also edited the *Nigerian Chronicle* and the *Sunday Times*, one of Africa's best-selling weeklies. Mr. Ekpu holds a degree in communications from the University of Lagos, and has pursued advanced study in journalism at Indiana University. In 1987 the *World Press Review* named him International Editor of the Year, citing him for "courage, enterprise, and leadership on the international level in advancing press freedom and responsibility and defending human rights and furthering journalistic excellence."

Bona Malwal is editor-in-chief of the *Sudan Times*, an English-language daily newspaper of Khartoum that was banned when the military assumed power in July 1989. He is the author of two books: *People and Power* and *Sudan: A Second Challenge to Nationhood*. A former member of Parliament and minister of information and culture in the central government, he has also served in the southern regional government as minister of industry and minister of finance. Mr. Malwal was jailed for a year by the military dictatorship of General Jaafar Mohamed Nimeiri, and was also threatened with arrest under the civilian government of Prime Minister Sadiq El Mahdi. He is now publishing the monthly *Sudan Democratic Gazette* from exile in England, where he is carrying on the struggle to return Sudan to civilian democratic rule.

María Jimena Duzán is a columnist for the Colombian newspaper, *El Espectador*, with which she has worked for fourteen years. For the past ten years, she has played a leading role in the efforts of Colombian journalism to expose and denounce the drug traffickers and their violence. As a member of the investigative reporting team of *El Espectador* during the 1980s, she was the first to discover the alliance between narco-traffickers, federal military officers, and major landowners. Such efforts brought both her and her newspaper many threats. In September 1989 *El Espectador* suffered a massive terrorist bombing and in December of that year María Jimena was forced to flee Colombia after narco-terrorists attempted to kidnap her. Since then she has mainly been writing from abroad. Among the many honors she has been awarded for her courage and effectiveness in the practice of journalism were two prizes in 1990 from the International Women's Association and the Milwaukee Press Club. In 1989 she was honored in Paris by French President Mitterand on International Women's Day—one week after the assassination of her sister, Silvia, also a journalist. She also received the Simon Bolívar Prize for the best interviews published in 1986. From 1983-85 she was editor of the International Section of *El Espectador*. She is now writing a book about narco-trafficking in Colombia and her personal experience as a journalist.

Index

Committee for Free Elections (CEL), 76
Committee of Concerned Citizens (Nigeria), 110
Committee to Protect Journalists, 24-25, 192
Commonwealth Journalists' Association, 192
Communism, 12, 129, 169, 148-53
  See also Marxism-Leninism
Communist Party of Thailand (CPT), 129, 142
Concepcion, Jr., José, 54, 55
Conciencia, 10, 14, 17, 18, 29, 30-48
  Educational Programs Committee, 41, 49-52
  Principles of, 30
  Promotion Committee, 45
  Publications of, 34, 47
  Role of volunteers, 43
  School's Project, 35-36
  Seminar on Constitutional Reform, 39-40
  Symposium on Civic Education, 37-39, 41
Congress of the International Union of Catholic Press (UCIP), 162
Conservative Party (S. Africa), 172
Constituent Assembly (Nigeria), 183
Constitutional Review Committee (Nigeria), 183
Constitutional Rights Journal (Nigeria), 122
Constitutional Rights Project (Nigeria), 121-22, 123
Constitution Drafting Committee (Thailand), 127-32, 137
  Legal Drafting Subcommittee, 128

Legislative Reform Committee, 131
Public Participation Subcommittee, 128, 129
Research Subcommittee, 128
Corruption, 19, 57, 73-75, 90-93, 106-9, 123, 126, 148-58, 181-82, 184-85, 196, 202-3, 206, 214-15, 221, 223-24
Costa Rica, 13, 44, 49, 51, 52, 77, 89, 90, 92, 93, 99, 100
Crusade for Citizen Participation (Chile), 13, 18, 73, 75-86, 88
  Leadership training, 79
  Objectives of, 78
  Publications of, 81
  Structure of, 78-83
  Volunteerism, 79-81, 83
Cruz, Isagani, 5
Cuba, 12
Culver, John, 61

The *Daily Express* (Philippines), 155
Darman, Alhaji Shugaba, 107
de Barros, Monica Jimenez, 13, 14, 18, 75-77
Defamation Act (Nigeria), 195
Defense for Children International, 120
de Ghersi, Esther Silva, 29
de Klerk, F. W., 167, 171, 174, 176, 177
de Martini, Maria Rosa, 10, 14, 29-31
Democracy,
  Components of, 6-15
  Role of Women, 30, 33-34, 44-45, 46, 59-60, 63, 87
  See also Women's Movement for the Nurturance of Democracy

Roces, Joaquin "Chino", 155
Romualdez, Benjamin, 155
Round Table Conference (Sudan),
  205, 206
Roxas, Manuel, 148
Rush, James R., 159-60, 161-62

Saamstan (S. Africa), 173
Said, Ustaz Beshir Mohamed,
  213
Salih, Mahjoub Mohamed, 220
Salonga, Jovito, 62
Samudavanija, Chai-Anan, 14, 125,
  127-33, 139-41
Sandanistas, 13, 89, 93, 94, 99
San José, 77
Santiago, Miriam, 61
Santo Domingo, 45
Sarte, Elfren, 70
Schmitter, Philippe C., 12, 15
Shagari, Alhaji Shehu, 182, 189
Sharpeville police shootings (S.
  Africa), 169, 170
Sierra Leone, 197
Sin, Cardinal Jaime, 150-51, 154,
  159, 162, 163, 165
Sison, Sony, 60
Smith, Ian, 170
Sornimsart, Amnart, 136
South (S. Africa), 173
South Africa, 13, 14, 19, 22, 167-79,
  198
  Nationalist government in (1948),
  169
South African Broadcasting Corpo-
  ration, 179
South African Communist Party,
  171, 174
Southeast Asia, 134

Southern Front (Sudan), 203-4, 205,
  212, 216
Southern Sudanese Liberation
  Movement, 203
Soviet Union, 12, 90, 102
Soweto revolt, 170
Soyinka, Wole, 113
Spain, 147
Star (South Africa), 178
Stepan, Alfred, 7
Stevens, Siaka, 197
Structural Adjustment Program
  (SAP) (Nigeria), 184
Sudan, 13, 201-25
  Civil war (1955), 202-3
  Civil war (1986), 220
  Coup d'etat, 205, 213, 223
  General strike (1964), 203
  Independence (1956), 202
  Islamic fundamentalist regime
  in, 223-24
  Military coup d'etat (1969), 205
  Military coup d'etat (1989), 223
  Military rule in, 202
Sudan Daily, 202
Sudan Democratic Gazette, 223-24
Sudanese Union of Journalism, 211
Sudanow Magazine, 216-19
  Objectives of, 219
Sudan People's Liberation Army, 220
Sudan Times, 214, 219-23
Sunday Concord (Nigeria), 196
Sunday Guardian (Nigeria), 113, 114
Sunday Times (Nigeria), 186, 196
Surasty, Roberto, 231
Suzman, Helen, 171

Tambo, Oliver, 174
Taylor, Alan, 176

253

Thailand, 14, 125-43
  Bureaucracy in, 130, 141
  Communists in, 129, 131, 132, 142
  Constitution of 127-31
  Coup d'etat (1976), 131, 132, 142
  Economic Development, 125, 132, 143,
  Military rule in, 126, 130, 140
  Political Parties, 139, 143
  Student uprising (October 1973), 126
Thammasat, Sanya, 127, 129
Thanarat, Marshal Sarit, 126
Thompson, Tunde, 108
Times Journal (Philippines), 155, 158-59
Tinsulanond, Prem, 132, 140
Togun, A. K., 191
Tolentino, G. Noel, 65
Totalitarian rule, 11-14
Toward 2000 (Turkey), 198
Treason Trial (South Africa), 169
Turbay, Diana, 232
Turkey, 198

Ukiwe, Ebitu, 190
Ultimate Publications, Limited (Nigeria), 192
United States, 5, 23, 24, 77, 91, 92, 99, 134, 147, 148, 150, 202, 204, 221, 228, 229, 231, 236-37
Universal Declaration of Human Rights (1948), 105, 110, 115, 121
Upkong, Tony, 117
Uruguay, 44, 49, 50, 51, 52
U.S. Information Service, 23
Uwagbale, Godwin, 118

Uwaifo, Samson, 189-90

Vanguard (Nigeria), 111
Vargas, Virgilio Barco, 229
Veritas (Philippines), 13, 159-65
Vietnam, 12, 134
Vigilant (Sudan), 204-16, 217, 219, 220, 221
Voice of America, 120
Vrye Weekblad (S. Africa), 173

Weaver, Tony, 176
Weekly Mail (S. Africa), 173
We Forum (Philippines), 156, 157
Western Europe, 134
West Germany, 222, 223
Willowgate Scandal (Nigeria), 197
Wolfowitz, Paul, 71
Women's Movement for the Nuturance of Democracy (KABATID), 4, 10, 18, 54, 59-66, 70
World Press Freedom Committee, 192
World Press Review, 199

Xuto, Somsakdi, 136

Yazici, Fatima, 198

Zaire, 198
Zambia, 174
Zambia Congress of Trades Union, 14
Zavala, Xavier Cuadra, 13, 14, 23, 98-103
Zilwa, Obed, 175
Zimbabwe, 170, 197
Zwarmborne, Marcel, 121